PRISONER OF THE RISING SUN

Ens. William A. Berry, October 1941. From author's collection.

PRISONER OF
THE RISING SUN

WILLIAM A. BERRY

with James Edwin Alexander

University of Oklahoma Press : Norman and London

This book is published with the generous assistance of the Wallace C. Thompson Endowment Fund, University of Oklahoma Foundation.

Library of Congress Cataloging-in-Publication Data

Berry William A. (William Aylor), 1915–
    Prisoner of the rising sun / William A. Berry with James Edwin Alexander.
      p.   cm.
    ISBN 0-8061-2509-8 (alk. paper)
    1. Berry, William A. (William Aylor), 1915– . 2. World War, 1939–1945—Prisoners and prisons, Japanese. 3. World War, 1939–1945—Personal narratives, American. 4. World War, 1939–1945—Campaigns—Philippines. 5. Prisoners of war— Japan—Biography. 6. Prisoners of war—United States—Biography. I. Alexander, James Edwin, 1930– . II. Title.
D805.J3B38 1993
940.54'7252'092—dc20
[B]   92-50713
                                            CIP

The paper in this book meets the guidelines for permanence and durability of the Committee on Production Guidelines for Book Longevity of the Council on Library Resources, Inc. ∞

1 2 3 4 5 6 7 8 9 10

To the memory of

Harriett Virginia Berry
my mother

AND

Thomas Nelson Berry
my father

Occupy yourself with thinking about the possibility of escape and study the chances.

THE BLUEJACKET'S MANUAL

CONTENTS

ILLUSTRATIONS

MAPS

PREFACE

THE motivation for writing this narrative came to me while I was gathering information on my two grandfathers, both of whom fought in the American Civil War. It occurred to me that I know very little about their combat experiences because neither one thought to leave any records for future generations. For example, the extent of my knowledge about my mother's father, Samuel Jackson Patton, is merely that he was in the Union cavalry, but I know nothing about under whom he served or what part he played.

My father's father, William Edward Berry, was the eldest son in a large Kentucky family. He enlisted as a private in the Union army, Kentucky Infantry, in November 1861, and went through the Civil War as a foot soldier, ending up with the rank of sergeant. He established a record of participation in some of the major battles, but I know nothing about them. When he mustered out after the war, he came home to a hostile environment. Kentucky had been divided about half and half in favor of and against the Union, but all his neighbors had been alienated against his family, and he was made to feel unwelcome. The result was that he migrated to Oklahoma with his uncles, first occupying an Indian lease approved by the federal government, then reentering the territory in the famous run of 1889.

In thinking about my two grandfathers — wondering what they did during the war, what happened to them day by day, who their friends and acquaintances were, what battles they fought in — I got to thinking about my own children. I did not want them to be in the same condition I found myself in — not knowing the experiences of their father in the war. Incidentally, my own father, Thomas Nelson Berry, born in 1872, was considered to be too old for the First World War. My father did make the Cherokee Run of 1893 as a young man, however, and thus carved his own niche in history. Father stayed on the land long enough to "prove it up," but when at the end of four years he tried to register his claim he found that someone had already registered on it first. Nevertheless, he became successful as a farmer on land he purchased, and he went on to achieve success as a banker and an oil operator. Father was in his midforties when I was born, and his age and health were such that I never got to know him as well as I would have liked to.

A second motivation for starting this narrative came from Bob Russell, whom I write about in this book. Bob wrote of his experiences in a handwritten manuscript, which he left as a legacy to his children. He sent me a copy. And there was yet another: Tom Harrison wrote of his experiences on Bataan, the Death March, and the Hell Ship. I never met Tom during the war, but I have since become acquainted with him through his brother, Dick Harrison, a good friend. The examples of these two men caused me to think that if they could write about their experiences, so could I. Accordingly, I undertook the task without any strong inclination toward ever seeing it published.

Having now retired and with sufficient time for the task, I began dictating my experiences during my annual stay in California in the winter of 1990–91 with the thought that these events might some day be of interest to my family and friends. To the best of my memory, this narrative represents what happened to me during World War II. The reader needs to be cautioned that these events are recorded from my memory, nearly fifty years after the fact. Yes, there are occasional lapses in memory, and yes, many things are left out. But shaping the experiences of thirty-three months into a coherent narrative requires that some events be emphasized and others passed over lightly..

The reader may note that I speak of my mother quite a few times, particularly in relation to the photograph I carried of her.

How I happened to have it in my pocket when I escaped from prison camp, I'll never know. But it saved my life, and for that reason it merits discussion.

This book is not meant to carry a vendetta against my senior officers for the ill treatment I received as a recaptured prisoner of war, treatment resulting from their orders to reveal my true identity. Even though it was clearly known to the POWs of the time that the Japanese treated escape as a capital offense, many prisoners nevertheless made the attempt and were summarily executed for their efforts. It was the success of our escape and the legends that built up around it that caused the Japanese to publish new rules organizing prisoners into "blood groups" of ten men each; if one man escaped, all ten would be executed. I do not have proof of any instance where the Japanese ever carried out this harsh retribution on the remaining individuals; nevertheless, the prisoners had every reason to believe they would. So many rumors of such executions circulated throughout the camps that people believed them to be true, and that belief created a negative attitude and feeling of resentment among other POWs toward those of us who sought to escape.

If there is any blame to be placed, or any criticism to be made by me, it is aimed toward the American officials who provided the code of conduct for POWs. We were told that we should try to escape, think about escaping, and escape at any opportunity. In retrospect it seems to me that such a code took insufficient regard of the actual circumstances involved and the consequences it imposed on POWs.

I would like to take this opportunity to express my appreciation to various people who provided help and encouragement. The number-one person I wish to mention is Dr. James E. Alexander. After my having dictated my thoughts during the winter in California, my secretary, Linda Harris, took it upon herself to transcribe the cassettes during her spare time. When Dr. Alexander told me he would be interested in reading my story, I handed him the transcription. The next day he came back to me and said, "I think you have a publishable project. May I see what I can do with it?" I told him that I would be pleased for him to. He took it from there and has worked very hard, adding to and taking from, telescoping certain events to make them more concise, and researching various historical facts.

In its original form, the manuscript was filled with redundancy, inasmuch as I would typically dictate from fifteen minutes to an hour at a time, then return the tapes to Oklahoma City for Linda Harris to transcribe. Sometimes an event that I mentioned on one tape would be repeated on another. Dr. Alexander is the one who eliminated the repetition and made all the parts fit together. I don't think anyone else could have done the job that he has done, and I truly appreciate his carrying it forward. Nevertheless, it remains my story of the events that happened to me.

Again, I want to express appreciation to Linda Harris for her interest in this project, for the hundreds of hours of her own time she spent transcribing the original version of the manuscript, and for her unflagging enthusiasm and support.

Also, my personal thanks go out to Dr. Paul and Yvonne Ashton, who critiqued the manuscript and supplied several of the photographs; to Don T. Schloat, who made a new drawing for this publication, and to my son, Nick Berry, for supplying the cover painting.

In reflecting on this story, I cannot help looking back on our recent past and thinking of the Persian Gulf War. How great it was for our men and women in the army, navy, air force, and marines to take a difficult, hazardous situation such as war in the Persian Gulf and make it look almost easy. And in contrast, my mind went back to Bataan and Corregidor, and I thought of how the boys on Bataan coined the lament, "We are the bastards of Corregidor and Bataan, no mama, no papa, no Uncle Sam."

WILLIAM A. BERRY

Oklahoma City
January 15, 1992

PRISONER OF THE RISING SUN

CHAPTER ONE

PROLOGUE: THE SUMMER OF 1941

IN the summer of 1941, I had "the world on a string, and the string around my finger," to quote an old song. That summer, I was only one year out of law school — still wet behind the ears, you might say — when by some inexplicable turn of fate I found myself as prosecuting attorney for Payne County, Oklahoma. At the age of twenty-five, I was a big man in the community of Stillwater, the county seat. And I guarantee you that no one had more self-confidence and pride — "piss and vinegar," as Oklahoma farmers used to say — than I had.

In the summer of 1941, the air was filled with patriotism. I could breathe it. I could feel it. I had it in my bones. When I listened on the radio to the fireside chats of President Roosevelt, I, like millions of other Americans, was inspired. "As president of a united and determined people," he said in a rhythmic cadence, "I solemnly swear that we will reassert the ancient American doctrine of the freedom of the seas." Roosevelt tapped out the rhythm of the sentences on the table with his closed fist: "We are placing our armed forces in strategic military positions." *(Thump.)* "We will not hesitate to use our armed forces to repel attackers." *(Thump.)* "Therefore, I have tonight issued a proclamation that an unlimited national emergency exists and requires the strengthening of our defense to the extreme limit of our power and authority." *(Thump.)*

In the summer of 1941, I couldn't help being caught up by the stirring voice of Winston Churchill during the dark days of 1940 as he reaffirmed that the the British government had but one aim and purpose: to destroy every vestige of the Nazi regime. "We shall not flag or fail. We shall go on to the end. We shall fight in France, we shall fight on the seas and oceans, we shall fight with growing confidence and strength in the air; we shall defend our island, whatever the cost may be. We shall fight on the beaches, we shall fight on the landing grounds, we shall fight in the fields and in the streets, we shall fight in the hills; we shall never surrender." "We shall fight him by land, we shall fight him by the sea, we shall fight him in the air, until with God's help we have rid the earth of his shackles and liberated its peoples from his yoke."

In the summer of 1941, Hitler had already gobbled up Czechoslovakia, annexed Austria, polished off Poland, subjugated France, seized Denmark and Norway, and even now was invading Russia while amassing forces on the English Channel to cross over to England—all as part of his grand goal of establishing the German people as the super race and the German nation as the Thousand-Year Reich.

In the summer of 1941, Mussolini was embarked on his goal of reestablishing the Roman Empire with his party of Black Shirts. Already he had celebrated the bimillennium of Augustus Caesar, the founder of the Roman Empire, in whose role and image he cast himself. He had laid claim to parts of North Africa, Greece, Albania, and some of the Balkan territories.

In the summer of 1941, fired by the sacred mission of extending their dominion over twelve million square miles of the Pacific, the hordes from Japan surged south and east on a rampage of destruction. Names like Shanghai, Saigon, Hainan, Hanoi, Bangkok, Taiwan, Pescadores, Mandalay, Cambodia, tolled out like notes of a funeral dirge. Unless these forces were brought into check, the Pacific Ocean would soon turn into a Japanese lake.

In the summer of 1941, the United States finally woke up from its long sleep of isolationism, and the people of America determined that they were not going to sit idly by and watch evil forces rule the world. As a nation, we decided that we were going to come to the aid of our friends, resist oppression, defeat the Axis

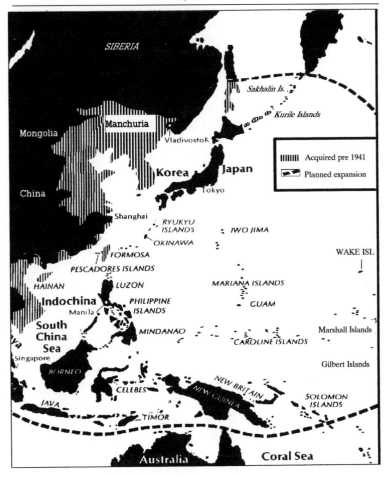

In September 1941 the leaders of Japan decided upon a major gamble to seize control of the riches of Asia by expanding their empire to the limits indicated by the dashed line. Map by Jim Alexander.

powers, and restore peace and harmony and brotherhood to a sore and troubled world.

In the summer of 1941, this spark of fire caught my insides and I was filled with a burst of patriotism. Even though I was automatically exempt from the draft as county attorney, I couldn't stand it any longer. In my new role I had already signed up hundreds of brave young men into military service. Now I too hungered to be a part of that proud tradition.

In the summer of 1941, I thought I had the world on a string; but it turned out I had a tiger by the tail. And I couldn't let it go.

So in the summer of 1941, I resigned my draft exemption as county attorney and applied for a commission in the United States Navy. On September 3 I received two letters in the same mail from the U.S. Department of the Navy: one was my commission as an ensign, as a reserve intelligence officer, and the other was my orders to report to "Cavite, P.I." The first letter I understood, the second one I didn't. It wasn't until I looked it up in an atlas that I determined that "P.I." referred to the Philippine Islands, and that Cavite was a U.S. Navy base located on Manila Bay.

I was extremely proud to be an American. And when I put that uniform on, I felt I was nine feet tall. I wanted the world to know that the United States and I were ready to go to war.

At the time I was sworn in, I had no training, no military background. I didn't know navy regs. I didn't know the bow of a ship from the stern, the starboard from the port, that a sailor doesn't go "upstairs" and "downstairs," or even what a bulkhead was. Naval terminology was a foreign language to me.

When I went aboard the USS *Indianapolis* in San Pedro, California, in transit to Honolulu, I was feeling pretty self-important. This was a real, honest-to-goodness warship, steeped in tradition. Stepping off the gangway onto the cruiser's quarter-deck, I saluted the officer of the day as I was supposed to do—he was an ensign like myself—and requested permission to come aboard. Then, so he wouldn't think I was completely ignorant, I asked, "Do you have a yeoman who can carry my bags for me?" ("Yeoman" was a word I'd heard somewhere and it sounded pretty "navy" to me, and I thought I would impress him with my seagoing lingo.)

He looked at me kind of funny and said, "Not a *yeoman*. Yeomen don't perform those duties! Maybe I can find you a mess boy around here." (Much to my chagrin, I found out later that yeoman are like ship's clerks.) Anyway, I ended up sheepishly carrying my own luggage to my assigned quarters.

After a thirty-day layover in Honolulu, I was put aboard the SS *President Harrison*, a converted passenger liner, for the final leg of my journey to Manila. The trip stretched out over eighteen days as we island-hopped through the South Pacific. As events turned out, the *Harrison* was the last liner to make the trip from Hawaii to Manila, and that trip turned out to be the last voyage of the *Harrison* under a U.S. flag.*

From the moment that I was sworn in as a naval intelligence officer, it was repeatedly impressed upon me that the intelligence service was a secret assignment—strictly confidential. Under no circumstances was I to let anyone know that I was an intelligence officer. Naturally, my lips were sealed. I was puffed up with a feeling of great importance; it was as though I had been specially chosen to carry out some sort of secret mission. So throughout the voyage I didn't let on what my assignment was. I didn't know which of the other officers on the ship, if any, were intelligence officers and I didn't try to find out.

When the *Harrison* pulled up to the passenger terminal in Manila and we all started off-loading, my cover was blown. Standing on the dock atop a stack of pallets was an self-important-looking, over-the-hill lieutenant commander with a megaphone in his hand. He raised the megaphone and shouted loud enough for anyone within a six-block area to hear: "All you intelligence officers line up here." About a dozen of us fell into formation, plainly visible to anyone who cared to see what an intelligence officer looked like. So much for Berry's "secret mission."

That little episode was my introduction into the ways and wonders of the U.S. Navy. Over the course of time, I was to discover that the navy was chock full of little surprises like that.

---

*After leaving Manila, the *Harrison* was cornered by a Japanese cruiser. Unarmed and unable to outrun the foe, the captain beached his ship hard onto a reef on the China coast. The crew was rescued and interned by the Japanese. Later, the Japanese refloated the *Harrison* and sailed her under their flag until she was sunk by an American submarine.

CHAPTER TWO

THE BATTLE FOR MANILA

MONDAY, November 17, 1941 marked our arrival in Manila. The Bay of Manila, one of the finest natural harbors in the world has rightfully been called "the Pearl of the Orient." Because it lay directly athwart the lines of communication between Japan and its objectives in the South Pacific, whoever controlled Manila controlled the gateway to Southeast Asia.

Guarding the entrance to Manila Bay from any seaward attack were the four "fortified islands" of Fort Drum, Fort Frank, Fort Hughes, and Corregidor. By far, the most formidable of these islands was Corregidor, sometimes referred to as "the Gibraltar of the Pacific."

Hearkening to the winds of war, the U.S. War Department in July 1941 had chosen to fortify the Philippines, confident that a strong and sufficient force would deter the Japanese from any further expansion in the China Sea. Gen. Douglas MacArthur was appointed to the post of commander, U.S. Army Forces in the Far East (USAFFE), with headquarters in Manila. Both MacArthur and the War Department shared the assumption that no Japanese attack would be forthcoming before April 1942 at the earliest.

The Philippine Islands themselves were of no great economic importance to the Japanese. They were a poor nation, and because the Philippines traded mainly with the United States, they were out of step with the "Greater East Asia Co-Prosperity Sphere." Their importance was strategic more than economic. So long as the Philippines lay in American hands, they would pose a threat to the Japanese lines of communication into the oil-rich Dutch East Indies. Hence, elimination of the American forces in the Philippines became a prime concern for the Japanese.

The day after our arrival, Jack Woodside, my cabin mate aboard the SS *Harrison*, rented an apartment in the city, and he invited me to move in and share the rent with him. Woodside had been in the Philippines before and knew the area. Our apartment was on the fourth floor of the Admiral Apartments, located on Dewey Boulevard, about a mile from the port area.

Life promised to be good in Manila. Even on a lowly ensign's pay of $125 a month, we were able to afford a Filipino houseboy to launder our clothing, press our uniforms, and keep the apartment clean. That was a lot less money than I had been making as county attorney in Stillwater, but it went a long way here in the Far East. Evenings would usually find us down at the Army-Navy Club, a magnificent facility much nicer than most country clubs I've seen. Mostly, we sat around sipping iced drinks and talking in the enormous bar.

All in all, Jack and I found it easy to slip into the relaxed tropical routine.

To be truthful, I never did quite figure out what the functions of the District Intelligence Office were—or what I was supposed to be doing there, for that matter. All I know is that when I showed up for duty on my first day, someone shoved some papers in my hand and said, "Here, deliver these." Mostly, I shuttled papers back and forth between the Naval Intelligence Headquarters and the Army Intelligence Office. Back and forth I would go, a kind of glorified messenger boy.

The District Intelligence Office was located in the Marsman Building on the Manila waterfront. The building was also the headquarters of the Sixteenth Naval District, headed by Adm. Thomas C. Hart, commander in chief of the Asiatic Fleet. Hart was seldom there, however, preferring to maintain his personal office across the bay at Cavite. Hart was MacArthur's opposite

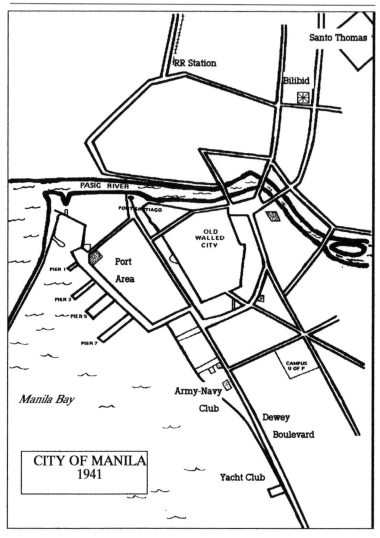

City of Manila, 1941. Map by Jim Alexander.

number. Our office was situated in the midst of the bustling port facility, maybe a hundred yards or so from the docks. The whole area was crisscrossed with railroad tracks leading to and from the various loading piers.

With an easy job in a beautiful setting, I could have found Manila to be a tropical paradise if it hadn't been for Lt. Comdr. Tom Lowe. He was the burr under my saddle.

Lowe, as it turns out, was the guy who met us at the dock with the megaphone. That episode characterized his style: he was a crotchety, dogmatic sort of person who seemed to think that people didn't accord him the proper respect he felt he deserved. Graying, balding, somewhat pudgy, about fifty, Lowe was probably the oldest lieutenant commander in the entire United States Navy. He was what we called a "retread;" that is, a person who had previously been on active duty, was mustered out, and now has been called back to active duty. Back near the end of the First World War, Lowe had graduated from the Naval Academy at Annapolis, but during the peacetime years he had been passed over twice for promotion; this, according to Navy regulations, meant that he had to resign his commission. In other words, what we had here was an officer who couldn't cut the mustard, a situation that had to have been a humiliating experience for an academy man. Nevertheless, he still thought of himself as being a cut above the reservists.

Lowe took me on as his personal project. I think he resented my being little more than a civilian poured into a military uniform and given a commission in the United States Navy. The full extent of my military training—if you could call it that—was a year at the Missouri Military Academy in Mexico, Missouri, as a ninth-grader and a semester of ROTC at Oklahoma A&M, where I had learned little more than how to march and do the manual of arms. Lowe made up his mind that, by golly, he was going to make up for my deficits by personally indoctrinating me into the ways and customs of the U.S. Naval Academy. So that's the way he treated me every day, as a new plebe.

When I first started running documents, we just carried them loose in our hands. Maybe because of my legal background, that didn't strike me as a particularly professional or secure way to carry important military papers. I suggested to Lieutenant Commander Lowe that we ought to get a pouch. Typically, Lowe wanted to do things by the book, and he told me to submit my idea on paper. I thought it was somewhat ridiculous to go through the formality of writing a proposal for such a piddling matter, but I went ahead and wrote it up. Believe it or not, I soon was issued an old, worn-out mail pouch. Lowe offered his congratulations: "You done fine, Berry. That was a great suggestion."

In the course of my duties I became acquainted with Col. (later Gen.) Charles Willoughby, who was in charge of the army's G-2 operations in the Philippines. G-2 is the army intelligence unit. Willoughby was very close to General MacArthur. Now, he was the kind of person you could sit across the desk and talk to. And unlike Lowe, he always found time for me.

Colonel Willoughby asked me one day if I had ever met General MacArthur. I said, "No."

He said, "Would you like to?"

"You bet I would," I replied, being very much in awe of General MacArthur.

Willoughby said, "Unfortunately, he doesn't happen to be here right now, but the first chance we get I'll introduce you."

My first meeting with MacArthur wouldn't occur until a few days later, under circumstances much different from what either Colonel Willoughby or I would have imagined.

The naval command at Manila seemed to be populated with more than its fair share of newly minted ensigns like myself, and since ensigns are at the bottom of the social ladder it was only natural that we tended to form a close-knit group. One of the group was Jack Ferguson, who served with me at the district intelligence office. Unlike me, however, Ferguson had graduated from the navy's V-7 officer's training program, and so he was more self-assured than I with regard to navy customs and conduct.

Ferguson was about my height—right at six feet—trim build, dark hair, neatly groomed, and quite good-looking. Indeed, the young ladies in the office seemed always conscious of his presence. But he also had a delightful sense of humor that made him popular among the men as well. From my perspective, however, Ferguson had an even more compelling quality, namely, he came from Dallas, Texas, just a few miles down the road from my home in Oklahoma City. So, there on the other side of the ocean, I felt right at home with his soft Dallas drawl.

A couple of other ensigns I got acquainted with over at the Army-Navy Club were Dick Tirk and Phil Sanborn. They both worked down in the port area but at a different building, and I never did learn exactly what they did. We often bumped into each other at the officers' mess at BOQ or at the Army-Navy Club. Like Ferguson, both Tirk and Sanborn had graduated from the V-7 officer's training program.

Tirk stood about five-ten, very slender, somewhat stoop-shouldered, and rather dark-complected. He told us he was of Lithuanian descent. He had an angular nose, brown eyes, rather high forehead, and dark, straight hair. Tirk had graduated Phi Beta Kappa from Cornell University.

Sanborn was also an Ivy Leaguer, having graduated from Dartmouth. He was about my height, light brown hair with just a slight wave in it, and he had a habit of brushing his hair back with his hand. Sanborn was a pretty happy-go-lucky kind of person who always managed to find the bright side of every adversity, and he generally had some little witticism or antecdote to share. Maybe he got this from his father: his dad was a psychiatrist, and Phil often came up with a bit of his father's philosophy that he would impart for our benefit.

At five o'clock in the morning of Monday, December 8 (December 7 back in the States), I was awakened from the depths of slumber by a loud pounding on my bedroom door. It was Jack Woodside.

"Bill, get up! Get up!" he shouted. "I just took a telephone call from Stanley Lehigh, and he's just announced that the Japanese have bombed Pearl Harbor." Lt. Lehigh was the watch officer when the news came in.

I asked, "Are you sure?"

Jack said, "Frankly, I don't believe it. I think Lehigh's playing a trick, or some kind of joke."

"Jack," I told him, "it doesn't make any difference to me whether he's playing a joke or not. I'm not taking any chances. I'm going down there immediately."

A driver from the District Intelligence Office came to pick us up. When we reported in at the office, we were informed that the message was indeed no joke.

News gradually began to filter in regarding the horrendous losses of ships, men, and facilities at the Pearl Harbor Navy Base and at Hickham Field. From what we were able to gather, the damage was extensive.

Immediately I was put to work delivering correspondence between Navy Intelligence and the Army G-2 office and running various other errands. It seemed to me that everyone had something that needed to be done. I hadn't had breakfast yet, but there was little thought of food in the midst of all this activity.

Somewhere, somehow, someone in the dark recesses of the naval headquarters came up with the idea that since we were now at war, it would be a smart idea to mount flags on the officers' cars, which would signify that these were official navy vehicles. It became my job to go out and find some flags to put on the cars. The first part of my endeavor was an exercise in frustration: no one around headquarters knew whether we had any flags or not, or if we did, where to look for them. So I took it upon myself to foray into the city to see if I could find some appropriate materials with which to make flags.

After a bit of searching, I found a Chinese tailor who had some ribbon that I thought might make dandy little flags to adorn the officers' cars. But the price he asked was more than the amount of money I had on me (I didn't have any official navy requisition). I said to him, "Look, Pearl Harbor has just been bombed, and you're trying to hold up the navy for a piece of ribbon."

I guess I must have come across pretty forcefully, because then he said he wouldn't charge me anything. But I wanted to be fair about the matter, so I insisted, "Certainly charge me something, but just don't try to rob us."

Finally we agreed on a price, and I got one of the Filipino drivers to help me tie the ribbons on the radio aerials of the cars. Apparently that satisfied whoever it was that thought up the deal, because I never heard any more about the matter. That turned out to be my major contribution to the defense of Manila.

We were all issued .45-caliber automatic pistols and told to wear them at all times. But no one bothered to show me how to operate one. As a matter of fact, I didn't even know how to load the cartridge clip.

Of course, not all of the officers were that poorly versed in the use of firearms. In fact, many of them were highly expert. One in particular, a Lieutenant Henry, was well trained in just about every form of self-defense. When he saw me fingering the gun, handling it awkwardly, he said, "For heaven's sake, Berry, here you are carrying around that forty-five and you don't even have a clip in it. If you did have to use that gun, it wouldn't do you any good."

Thanks to Lieutenant Henry, I learned how to pop a cartridge clip into the gun. Still, I never learned how to shoot it.

Then, almost as if waking from a dream, it dawned on me how ill equipped I really was: I had very little knowledge of weaponry, no knowledge of combat techniques, and I was really in no position to defend myself or to fight a war—certainly not a war of aggression. Yet here I was, a stranger in a strange land, among strange people with strange customs, and war was breaking out all around us.

At noon that day, war came to the Philippines. The Japanese began their bombing of Clark Field, which was our number-one air base in the entire Far East, about sixty miles northwest of Manila. It was Pearl Harbor all over again. They managed to destroy most of our air force while it was on the ground.

Here at Clark Field, the situation was not one of lack of preparedness; it was more a case of bad timing. The scenario went something like this: Earlier in the morning, immediately following

the word from Pearl Harbor, our fleet of B-17s had been ordered
into the air as a precautionary measure. The planes circled Mount
Arayat for several hours, but nothing happened. Finally, when their
fuel supply ran low, they were forced to land for refueling.

As conceived, the strategy was correct. The Japanese had in
fact planned an early-morning strike on the Philippines. And if
things had gone according to Japan's schedule, we in the Philippines would have been ready and waiting for them. What we
didn't know was that the Japanese air force was delayed on
Formosa waiting for a thick fog to lift; that delay caused us to
drop our guard.

The Japanese thought that they had lost the element of surprise, and they feared the worst. But as luck would have it, fate
conspired to give them the upper hand. Since it was now noon
and no attack had been forthcoming, our officers were lulled into
thinking that the Japanese were not planning an attack after all,
so our crews were taken off the state of high alert. All of our
B-17s were sitting on their fueling pads taking on fuel and a new
load of bombs. Everything came to a standstill as the whole base
knocked off for lunch. Even the air defense crews, the coast
watchers, and the radio and teletype operators were in the mess
halls taking on food. In fact, things were so relaxed that the
fighter planes—our first line of defense—were sitting on the
ground, lined up like lambs for a ritual slaughter.

The carnage went on for over an hour. When it ended, the
much-vaunted American air force in the Philippines had ceased
to exist as an effective fighting force.

Only a few of our planes managed to get off the ground, and
these were sent south to Mindanao and Australia. What few
surviving P-40s we had were relocated to the airstrip at Cabcaban, near the southern tip of the Bataan Peninsula, directly
across the strait from Corregidor.

As this dreadful day wore on, report after report came pouring
into headquarters. The Japanese were attacking Hong Kong.
Bombs were falling on Singapore, Guam, and Wake Island. A
message was in the process of being received from Shanghai

when it ended ominously in midsentence. The Japanese were on the move throughout the Pacific.

And here we were, sitting in the eye of the storm.

On Wednesday, December 10, it was the Navy's turn. I happened to be on duty at the intelligence office. Nothing much was going on, so a couple of us went over to catch a late lunch at the BOQ, the bachelor officers' quarters. Someone said, "Hey, look, there's a bunch of planes overhead."

A group of us rushed outside to see what was happening. I was able to count nearly sixty bombers, all flying in perfect formation at an altitude of about twenty thousand feet. At that height, the planes looked like little silvery crosses in the sky. We watched the planes, not knowing whose they were, as they first circled Manila and then headed south toward Cavite, the huge naval base directly across the bay.

Soon the planes began dropping their bombs over Cavite. We could see the bombs exploding. Pitiful little puffs of smoke from our antiaircraft shells could be seen exploding ineffectually about five thousand feet below the planes.

Cavite, we later learned, was completely reduced to rubble. What had not been destroyed by bombs was destroyed by fire. Gone were the repair shops, barracks, fuel dumps, and stored torpedoes, as well as nearby ships and submarines. Great clouds of black smoke poured out from the burning fuel storage. All survivors had to be evacuated, as there was absolutely no habitable base left by the time the bombs stopped falling. After the raid, Admiral Hart, who watched it all from the roof of the Marsman Building, notified Washington that Cavite was completely finished as a base.

After the planes finished their destruction, they headed back north in the direction of Clark Field. Whatever bombs they had left, they delivered over that shattered place in a second round of destruction.

That same day, the United States got its first World War II hero. Five B-17s, covered by P-40s, had flown up from Mindanao, in the southern Philippines, to bomb the Japanese ships attempting a landing on the northern part of Luzon. One of these was piloted by Capt. Colin P. Kelly. Kelly attacked and sank what he thought was the Japanese battleship *Haruna*. His plane was shot up badly; the control cables were shattered and the left wing was afire. With no hope of getting the plane back to base, Kelly ordered his crew to abandon ship. All but Kelly bailed out. He piloted his crippled plane all the way down. The *Haruna*, however, was several hundred miles away; the ship Kelly attacked was apparently a transport. Nevertheless, legend has it that he dived into the Japanese battleship.

Reliable intelligence information about the progress of the fighting was woefully inadequate in our office, and each day it seemed to get worse. Part of the confusion stemmed from the many prongs of the Japanese attack. On December 10 the Japanese had made a successful landing at Aparri, on the northern end of Luzon, and the following day they made another landing about eighty miles to the west at Vigan, which meant that they were headed south toward the capital on two fronts. Also, on December 11 they made an unopposed landing at Legazpi, on the Bicol Peninsula southeast of Manila, and were headed toward us from that direction in a viselike movement. Our situation was becoming increasingly critical, yet we didn't have reliable information about what was happening.

Gen. Jonathan M. Wainwright and General MacArthur had rightly anticipated that the Japanese would make their main landing somewhere at Lingayen Gulf, on the west coast of Luzon, about 150 miles north of Manila. But the Japanese didn't land at the exact spot where Wainwright and MacArthur expected them to. On the other hand, the invasion force didn't land where the Japanese commandant, Gen. Masaharu Homma, expected them to, either. Heavy winds, stormy seas, and faulty communications caused the invasion barges to put ashore about eight miles north of their designated target.

The landing itself was a disaster. More than half the men and equipment were put out of action by the heavy seas and pounding

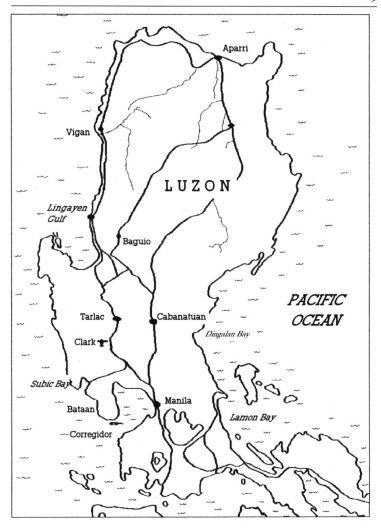

Northern Luzon. Japanese landings were made at Aparri, Vigan, Lingayen Gulf, and Lamon Bay. Map by Jim Alexander.

surf. The only thing that saved the landing from being a total defeat was the lack of opposition from our side on the beaches.

Our only defensive forces in the area was a Filipino battalion armed with a single .50-caliber machine gun. Although the Filipino defenders inflicted heavy casualties, they were not enough to stave off the invaders.

Had we had more men and heavier armament in the area, we might have beaten off the attack. But we had only fragmentary and often conflicting information about the enemy's strength. Initial reports estimated eighty thousand to one hundred thousand troops in the invasion force, more than five times the number that actually put ashore. By the time Wainwright was able to get a complete picture of the situation, the enemy was ashore at several places and the turning point of opportunity had passed.

In the midst of the invasion, it struck me as ironic to note how the stress of war seems to bring out the best in some men and the worst in others. The latter was the case with Lieutenant Commander Lowe, our executive officer. The events of those days showed me why the navy probably cashed him out in the first place, because stress always seemed to bring out his worst elements.

For example, on the day the war started I was on duty for twelve hours straight. At the end of that first watch, Lowe, as the executive officer, came around with the duty list for the next twelve-hour watch. My name was on the list again. Lowe went off to his quarters. That turned out to be a very hectic night—the switchboard continually lit up with traffic, reports of combat activities to be processed, messages to be delivered, and so forth. There wasn't a moment for relaxation.

The next morning, Lowe came in and picked the duty officers for the succeeding twelve-hour watch. "Berry, you stay here," he said. That made thirty-six hours of constant duty without going to bed. Things were still hectic. We were running around like chickens trying to dodge lightning bolts. We hadn't lost our heads, but the intelligence information was fragmented and confusing, and it was almost impossible to get a clear picture of what was going on.

At the end of that third twelve-hour watch, Lowe again selected the duty officers for the ensuing twelve hours. Again he pointed to me and said, "Berry, you stay."

Well, by that time, after thirty-six hours of continuous duty, I was a little wild and more than a little irritated, and I guess it showed. Lowe turned to walk out of the room, and I started after him. I would have struck him, too, if one of the warrant officers had not jumped up and stopped me. "Don't you do that, Mister Berry," he said. "Don't you go in there. Don't you do it."

The warrant officer managed to calm me down. "If you strike a superior officer, you'll be court-martialed," he lectured me. "It will go on your record, and you will never, never survive that."

He went in to Lowe and told him, "Sir, you've had Ensign Berry on duty for thirty six hours now without giving him any relief."

"Hell, let him set up a cot in there," Lyons snapped sarcastically. "He can catch a little nap off and on, if he has to."

That was the only concession Lowe made toward me. And from that point onward, I developed an intense bitterness toward my executive officer, a bitterness that subsequent events would make worse.

As one might expect in the early days of a war—particularly one we were not prepared for—there was a lot of uncertainty and confusion. None of us had been in a war before. We didn't know what we were doing. We had to make up the rules on the run.

Just to give one example, one night one of the officers, a reservist like myself, took a phone call that he didn't know what to do with. It had something to do with a light that was flashing on and off in Manila. He thought it might a clandestine signal— maybe someone was trying to send a message to the Japanese. He called over to Army G-2 to report the situation, but was unable get through to the duty officer over there. Finally, in desperation, he asked to be connected with the commanding officer himself. The CO, infuriated to be bothered with such a trivial matter in the middle of the night, really chewed out that hapless reservist.

I found myself thinking that this was as poor an example of military preparedness as I could think of. We had been caught short. We had lost most of our air force. Most of our ships had been destroyed, and those that survived had pulled out to the safety of the open sea. We were more or less deserted there, fighting an enemy we couldn't see, not knowing where he was, beset by rumors and conflicting information. And our executive officer was off in the sack, leaving a couple of untrained junior ensigns to man the intelligence operations.

The Japanese bombers, now roaring over Manila nearly every day with virtually no opposition, bombed the port area with regularity. All navy personnel were issued gas masks and helmets—old, flat "tin hats" left over from World War I—and ordered to wear them at all times. To be truthful, I must say that felt like an idiot going around all decked out in my pressed white navy uniform, gas mask strapped to my back, tin hat perched on my head, a gun I hardly knew how to shoot riding on my hip, and all the while carrying a ratty little satchel with messages in it.

One day, burdened down with all that gear, I stepped inside the elevator at the army headquarters building, and as I was waiting for the door to close who should walk in but Gen. Douglas MacArthur with his whole entourage of chief aides clustered around him. I was so flustered that I didn't know whether to salute him or what, so I just stood at attention. MacArthur looked over at me with all my paraphernalia on, and with a twinkle in his eye he remarked, "My goodness. This *is* war, isn't it?"

Everyone on the elevator laughed. Everyone but me, that is. I felt like crawling under a rug—if there had been a rug for me to crawl under.

By December 22, the Japanese troops had reached the outskirts of Manila. Japanese planes were conducting savage bombing raids over the city. Occasional Zeros would break out of formation, fly low, and machine-gun the streets. Smoke from incendiary fires was rising from the old section of the city. Most of the department stores and shops had long since boarded up their windows, and the streets were clogged with frightened Filipinos seeking to flee the destruction.

Most naval personnel had been moved out. Sixteenth Naval District operations had already relocated over on Corregidor. With each day that passed, fewer and fewer officers were to be seen around the intelligence office. Our staff of sixty was down to less than a dozen now, and most of these were civilian clerks.

About eleven o'clock in the morning, a formation of Japanese bombers had circled the port area before they went off to unload their bombs at Pasay, an outer suburb of Manila. We suspected they might come back. Lieutenant Commander Lowe said to the office staff, "Come on, girls, I'm going to take you to a safe place." Then he turned to me and said, "Berry, you stay." Personally, I suspected that he was simply looking for an excuse to get himself out of there.

The bombers did return, and they blasted the place to smithereens. We'd been bombed before, but nothing to compare with this. The first bomb that landed shook the building so strongly that I thought it was going to collapse around me. The explosion disarrayed the room, knocked the glass out of the windows, and scattered papers all over the floor. When I finally became aware of what I was doing, I found myself hiding under a desk with a wastebasket pulled tightly over my head. The strangest thing about it is that I had absolutely no awareness how I got there.

After the planes had gone and the all clear had sounded, I went outside and looked around. My eyes were not prepared to see the destruction that had taken place around me. Virtually everything in the port area was destroyed or on fire except for the building I was in. But the thing that impressed me the most was seeing a piece of railroad track twisted and sticking up in the air where the bomb had pushed it out of place. A tiny hole revealed where a bomb fragment had passed right through the solid iron rail. I don't know why that made such an impact on me, but the idea that a bomb fragment could make a clean hole right through a railroad track was simply astounding.

From then on, I noticed that my brave talk didn't sound nearly so brave.

On December 24 the Japanese made another successful landing at Lamon Bay, sixty miles southeast of Manila. There was no artillery to oppose them, and only two Filipino battalions in the area. This latest invasion meant that the Japanese were now advancing on the capital city from four directions.

Lieutenant Meade Willis and I were the only two officers on watch that evening at the Marsman Building. Willis was about five years older than I, tall, straight, dark wavy hair, and very attractive to the ladies. He had plenty of chances to go out with the secretaries, but Willis made it clear that he was fully devoted to a girl waiting for him back in North Carolina and he had no interest in anyone but her.

Mainly, we were just killing time because most of the intelligence operations had already been shut down. We reminisced about our families, and he told me about his girl friend — Anne, I think her name was. Suddenly, an air raid siren went off, and I stopped in mid-sentence and dashed under a middle landing in the stairwell and remained there until the all-clear sounded. No more heroics on my part. I'm not sure where Willis went, but when I made my way back into the intelligence office he was there, undisturbed, as if nothing unusual had happened.

On Christmas Day we received orders to report immediately to the Yacht Club. The city of Manila was being vacated on orders from MacArthur. MacArthur had already evacuated his own staff the day before, but somehow that word failed to get passed on to the navy. So it was almost as an afterthought that we received instructions that all remaining naval personnel in the intelligence office were to be transferred to new duty assignments on Corregidor.

Manila's port area had been thoroughly bombed out by now. And with Japanese planes strafing nearly anything that moved, the Yacht Club, two miles south, was deemed a safer point of departure.

A Filipino driver came to pick up Jack Woodside and me at our apartment, along with Leland Chase, another officer who had temporarily moved in with us. Chase was from Los Angeles.

When Chase found out that Manila was being evacuated, he said, "That's it! I'm getting out." He took off his uniform, resigned his commission, and said he was going to turn himself in as a civilian as soon as the Japanese got there.

That seemed highly irregular to me. "Leland," I told him, "I'm not sure you can do this."

"Well, I'm going to do it anyway," he asserted. We parted later that day in Manila, and that was the last I saw of him.*

Our instructions limited us to only one piece of luggage, along with whatever we had on our backs. I chose a small leather case—not a full-sized suitcase, but a kind of overnight bag that had been given to me by my dad. It was a good, sturdy bag that had my initials carved on it. More important, it had a sentimental value that couldn't be replaced. Still, I didn't relish leaving behind over a thousand dollars' worth of furniture and other items we had purchased for the apartment barely a month before.

Off in the distance we could see tremendous clouds of smoke billowing out from burning oil storage facilities. In a daring solo action, Navy Lt. Malcolm Champlin had set ablaze both the military and commercial storage facilities.

Champlin, a former FBI agent charged with the responsibility of speeding up the evacuation of naval personnel, had discovered to his shock and dismay that the district supply officer had abandoned his post without having first arranged for the destruction of the surplus oil stocks. So on his own initiative, Lieutenant Champlin contacted the local executive from Standard Oil Company and asked him how much oil was in Manila.

"Enough to operate the Asiatic Fleet for the next two years," he was told.

"Holy mackerel!"

---

*Years later I learned that Chase did survive the war and did return to the United States.

"But that's not the half of it," the Standard Oil man continued. "More important to the Japanese than the fuel supplies are all the lubricating oil and the additives used to make high-octane aviation fuels."

The two men immediately got on the phone and started contacting the local representatives of the other oil companies to get their cooperation. The American and Dutch companies were willing to go along with the idea of destroying the oil facilities, but the French and the British were not, pleading that they didn't have the authority to make such a decision. Ignoring the protestations of their French and British colleagues, those two courageous men set in motion the destruction of all the oil storage and refining facilities in the Pandacan area of Manila. And in so doing, they denied a prize that was worth more to the Japanese than the city of Manila itself.

When Woodside and I got to the Yacht Club, it was about ten o'clock in the morning. An admiral's launch was at the dock waiting for us, engine running, with three other officers who had already got there ahead of us. They and the boat's coxswain were impatient to shove off.

General MacArthur had declared Manila an "open city" because he judged it incapable of being successfully defended against the oncoming Japanese forces. MacArthur, finding no merit in seeing the beautiful city he loved continue to suffer devastation by needless bombing, ordered all military personnel to be clear of the city. Otherwise, he feared, the declaration would be violated and the Japanese might continue with their senseless destruction.

To the best of my knowledge, ours was the last navy launch to leave Manila.

CHAPTER THREE

THE SIEGE OF CORREGIDOR

THE boat ride to Corregidor was uneventful, despite the numerous Japanese Zeros buzzing around the harbor. The distance of twenty miles over open water was covered in a little over two hours.

With little else to occupy our attention, the conversation turned to speculation about what might lie ahead for us. Obviously, our situation did not look good. The fate of the Philippines had already been sealed. The navy was gone. The air force was effectively destroyed. The army was bottled up on the Bataan Peninsula. The only issue that remained in doubt was how long we could delay the inevitable.

The strategy that made the most sense to us was that MacArthur would probably concentrate the remaining American forces into the positions that were most capable of being defended, namely, Bataan and Corregidor, where we would try to hold out long enough for relief to arrive from the United States. What we didn't know at the time—couldn't know, as a matter of fact—was that already Washington had decided to divert the promised relief of troops, ships, and arms away from the Philippines and toward the defense of Australia. What little hope we had was unfounded.

Corregidor was enchantingly beautiful. Lush tropical growth covered its lovely hills like a green felt cap. Beneath its verdant exterior, however, lay the powerful apparatus of war. As the boat drew nearer, we could discern big naval guns atop towering cliffs, poking their bellicose snouts out incongruously from amid the gentle trees. Clearly, whoever controlled this "Gibraltar of the Pacific" also controlled access to one of the finest harbors in the Orient.

As soon as our launch touched the dock, I reported to the officer in charge. He checked over his list and said, "Berry, you're assigned to the Inshore Patrol. Take your gear and report to Ensign Russell on Topside."

"Pardon me, Sir, but where's Topside?" I asked.

"Don't worry. There's a driver right outside. He'll take you there."

The driver was a very nice Filipino man. The drive was about three miles, and it gave me a chance to find out something about the island.

From the air, Corregidor looks like a giant tadpole with its tail swung to left. It's about three and a quarter miles long and just over a mile at its widest. The "tail," called Bottomside, contains the two docks, along with the fishing village of San Jose. Farther out toward the narrow tip were the Naval Radio Intercept Station and Kindley Field, a small grass strip capable of handling light aircraft. At the base of the tail is Malinta Hill, high and precipitous, forming a formidable barrier against enemy troops who might be attempting to advance up the tail.

The land west of Malinta Hill is called Middleside. On it were located the hospital, officers' and noncommissioned officers' (NCO) quarters, the Officers' Club, and some schools.

The high and bulbous head is Topside. The headquarters and parade ground were here, along with the famous "Mile-Long Barracks" — a two-story "bombproof" stone building. Most of the big sea defense batteries were sited on Topside.

One of the most impressive features on Corregidor was the extensive tunnel complex that had been blasted through Malinta Hill, heralded as one of the wonders of the age. The main tunnel was 1,400 feet long and 30 feet wide. From the main tunnel, twenty-five laterals branched out from either side at regular intervals. Each lateral was 150 feet long and came to a dead end, except for the one that led to a further complex containing a hospital with three hundred beds.

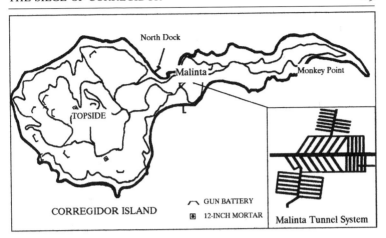

Corregidor Island. Diagram of tunnel system is shown in inset. Map by Jim Alexander.

The tunnels were intended originally for the storage of supplies, equipment, and ammunition. Except for the hospital wing, the tunnel complex was considered too damp and poorly ventilated to house humans.

In addition, there was a long navy tunnel that housed the radios and communication for the U.S. Army Forces in the Far East. A long lateral tunnel connected the hospital tunnel on the north to the naval storage tunnel on the south. Another tunnel, to the north of the main tunnel and at approximately the same level, could store ten thousand gallons of reserve motor fuel.

The island was spotted with huge open gun pits. The main batteries had been installed in 1914, before the onset of the air age, and only modestly improved since then. Nevertheless, the island could present a formidable defense, provided the enemy played by our rules; that is, the enemy must attack from the sea, not use aircraft to drop bombs on the open gun pits, and refrain from deploying artillery on the opposite shore of the narrow channel separating Corregidor from the Bataan Peninsula.

Unfortunately for Corregidor, as for Singapore and some other places, the Japanese didn't play by our rules. The Japanese would attack from the relatively unprotected Bataan side.

The driver deposited me at the base of a signal tower that protruded out from a high point overlooking the channel between Corregidor and the Bataan Peninsula, about two miles away. An observer's platform capped the tower at about eighty-five feet above ground level.

The watch officer leaned over the railing of the platform and called down, "Are you Mister Berry?"

"Ensign Berry reporting for duty, Sir" I shouted back.

"Come on up and enjoy the view," he said with just a touch of irony.

The officer introduced himself as Ens. Bob Russell. He was a friendly, nice-looking fellow, roughly my height—maybe an inch or two shorter—with reddish sandy hair.

My new assignment was to serve as one of three officers who manned the signal tower on a rotating basis. Russell explained to me that our duty was to control the minefields that regulated all of the shipping in and out of Manila Bay. The entire channel was protected by fields of electrically operated underwater mines, and before any ship could enter or leave the harbor we would have to give them passage through the minefields.

The tower was equipped with two-way voice radio and signal lights. Ships desiring passage through the channel would call us on the radio to request clearance. Or if it happened that their radio wasn't working, the ship would use its blinker light to signal us in Morse code. When we were satisfied that the request was legitimate, we'd relay instructions by telephone down to the duty officer in Queen Tunnel, who threw the switch to shut off the mines. As soon the ships cleared the area, we would have the minefields turned back on. We always had an enlisted man up there who could read the blinker light.

By way of underscoring the seriousness of the situation, Russell reminded me of a tragic event that had occurred about ten days earlier. It had been a big story in the newspapers. It seems that the SS *Corregidor*, a Filipino interisland ferry carrying a load of refugees from Manila to one of the other islands, had gone out one night without clearance and struck a mine. The boat blew up and sank within minutes. Nobody really knew how many passengers were on board, because at the last minute before departure a crowd of people seeking to escape Manila had forced their way up the gangplank. It was later estimated that over nine hundred people had been aboard, most of them Filipinos, and that fewer than three hundred of these had survived.

We also had a large telescope up there—eighty- or ninety-power magnification. This telescope was so powerful, in fact, that we could pick out individual buildings in Manila, about twenty miles across the bay; they looked to be about an inch tall. We could even make out automobiles if they were moving. That was kind of fun.

I asked Russell about sleeping quarters. He said he had commandeered one of the vacant officers' bungalows on Topside. After the bombing raids started, the officers had moved down into the tunnels and evacuated their families back to the United States, leaving behind their very nice, completely modern quarters, complete with a golf course and a wonderful view atop the mountain. For the time being, Ensign Russell pretty much had the pick of where he wanted to live. He said I was welcome to share his quarters with him, and I took him up on the offer.

Except for those of us working the signal tower and the troops who manned the gun batteries, everyone else stayed down in the tunnels. The main activity, as far as the navy was concerned, was the Inshore Patrol.

Russell was a likable chap and I respected him a great deal. He was a graduate of ROTC and the navy's V-7 officer training program, and he had been on active duty in the Philippines for a little over six months. Consequently, he was more military-wise than I was and knew a lot more about what was going on. Russell told me that the previous July, when he had been assigned to organize the Inshore Patrol, he had been given a copy of the secret war plans that provided for laying the minefields in the entrance of Manila Bay, moving the dry dock from Olongapo to Mariveles, and establishing the offshore patrol fleet.

The view from our signal tower, some eighty-five feet above the highest part of Corregidor, was breathtakingly beautiful. Not only did we have a view of the entire island, but we could also see for many miles in every direction.

Across the channel to the north of us was Mount Mariveles, an almost perfectly shaped cinder cone mountain that always had a cloud around its head. *Ripley's Believe It or Not* once pointed out how odd it was for this relatively small mountain — I don't suppose it was much more than forty-five hundred feet — always to have a cloud around it. It was perhaps fifteen miles from where we were, and in the clear air it was always perfectly visible from our signal tower.

Corregidor Island looking eastward over Topside. Malinta Hill is in the center, with Monkey Point stretching out toward the east. Courtesy of Dr. Paul Ashton.

We were kept busy trying to keep track of all the ships that were coming and going. Whenever a nonmilitary ship was scheduled to leave the harbor, the port director's office would notify us, so we could in turn notify the gunboats that were on patrol to escort it through the minefields.

On my third day up there, which was December 28—my twenty-sixth birthday, as a matter of fact (though I was hardly aware of it)—I was just coming down from the signal tower after being relieved at noon when I looked up into the sky and saw a formation of some sixty or so planes coming our direction at an altitude of about twenty thousand feet. Then I heard a few anti-aircraft guns popping from down below me, but the projectiles exploded harmlessly about three thousand feet below the planes. If any Japanese planes wanted to dodge our AA fire, all they had to do was fly a little higher.

Because the island's antiquated defenses had seen little up-grading, owing to the arms limitation treaties of the 1930s, all we had to defend against aircraft was a few ancient three-inch antiaircraft guns, which couldn't reach the altitude at which the Japanese bombers were flying. Those guns made plenty of noise, but were absolutely worthless in providing air defense.

Then bombs started dropping on Topside. The planes were making a big, leisurely circle high in the sky, and they would drop a load of bombs each time they passed overhead. It took about ten minutes to make a circle, so every ten minutes we got another load of bombs. That went on for about two hours, although it seemed like months to me. Every ten minutes, wave after wave, the planes flew over dropping their bombs.

We looked around for some place to hide. The bombs made a horrible shrieking sound as they fell. Buildings were being blown up right around us. At first we didn't know what to do. Exposed, we stretched out as flat on to the ground as we could. We could watch the bombs drop, hear their whistle, and feel the dirt and debris drop around our shoulders and faces.

An army private ran up crying and pleading for us to help him. "My buddy has been buried and I need help to get him out."

Russell and I ran over to where his buddy was supposed to be, but the only thing we found was a shoe sticking out of the debris. Just that, and nothing else.

We found a concrete-lined drainage ditch in which a group of soldiers had tried to hide. The big ditch—probably four to six feet wide and maybe five feet deep, I would say—was completely lined with army and navy personnel stretched out flat on their stomachs. We crawled in with them.

The whistle of the bombs was like a steel rod being pushed up into our backbones. We would grit our teeth, close our fists and eyes, and wait for the bombs to land, dropping dirt and debris around us. We were always told that we would never hear the bomb that would hit us. I guess that's because the bomb would arrive quicker than its sound.

Then I got to thinking, *My goodness. This is a big ditch, and it's lined with solid concrete. If a bomb should land anywhere in here, it would throw shrapnel up and down the ditch, killing us all.* I decided staying there was pretty stupid.

Bob Russell and I crawled out and moved over on soft ground. An air corps major went with us. I stretched out on the lowest place I could find, and that's where I remained throughout the rest of the bombing.

The place in which we had taken refuge was a wooded area, but I could look up between the trees and see the planes as they flew over and see the bombs drop. I could hear the bombs whistle and explode.

After the all clear sounded, I found a bomb that had dropped within forty feet of where we lay. Fortunately for us, the bomb didn't go off. I could see the imprint of the bomb where it landed on the soft earth, and a hole in the shape of the bomb where it entered.

The air corps officer introduced himself as Maj. Jack Vance. He said, "Let's go over and see how MacArthur made out."

I said, "MacArthur? Is he out here somewhere?"

"He sure is," he replied.

We rushed over to MacArthur's quarters. Until that moment, neither Russell nor myself had been aware that MacArthur just the day before had taken the bungalow only three or four doors down from ours. It seemed natural that he should have chosen the nicest bungalow up there, inasmuch as he was the commanding officer.

He was standing by the side of his bungalow with his orderly when we got there. He was very calm and didn't appear to be particularly concerned. The two men were pacing off the distance between a bomb crater and his house to see how close the explosion had been. He said, "Well, that must have been a two-hundred-pound bomb that made that explosion."

MacArthur came over and spoke to Major Vance by name. They saluted. We all saluted.

The orderly commented, "I wonder how those people in the tunnel got along."

MacArthur turned to me and asked, "Could you hear those bombs go off down there inside the tunnel?" I guess he thought that I had been the tunnel during the raid.

I couldn't think of what else to say, so I replied somewhat irreverently, "I don't know, Sir. But wouldn't it be nice to be in the tunnel so that we could find out for ourselves?" He chuckled at that.

To be truthful, given the circumstances, I wasn't sure I'd even survive long enough to get down to the tunnel, which was clear down at Bottomside. We were lacking motorized transportation, and the tunnels were two or three miles away down the side of the mountain.

Anyway, I added, "Sir, I hope I live long enough to find out."

MacArthur looked up into the sky at the bombers and commented, "Well, it shouldn't be long before we have a bunch of P-40s that will chase those guys right out of the sky."

Another thing about MacArthur impressed me that day. Referring to the bomb crater by the side of his house, he told us that he and his houseboy had merely crouched down when the bomb came down and exploded. The houseboy took a piece of shrapnel in the leg and needed medical attention, but MacArthur himself emerged unscathed.

I thought to myself, *There you were, Bill Berry, the whole time lying flat on your belly on the ground with your teeth clenched, your fists as tight as they could be, and your hair straight on end; and there was MacArthur merely crouched down as the bomb dropped and went off—merely crouched down.* That quality of MacArthur's made me an admirer of his from that point on.

Our observation tower was destroyed beyond any hope of repair. Ensign Russell and I were ordered to move our gear down into Navy Tunnel in Malinta Hill until a new observation post could be located for us.

Two-tiered bunks lined both walls the full length of the tunnel. There was no such thing as privacy, for activities were going on here twenty-four hours a day. Most of the men assigned here were officers, along with a few enlisted men, mostly skilled technicians. The rest of the enlisted men on Corregidor had been taken off and put on ships that had left as fast as they could.

I would guess that Queen Tunnel, also known as Navy Tunnel, was twenty feet wide and maybe two-hundred-fifty yards long. It was connected by a lateral with Malinta Tunnel, the main tunnel. The inside of Queen Tunnel was semicircular, like a Quonset hut. The walls were coarse and unfinished, in much the same conditions as when they were originally blasted out of solid rock. Of course, at the time these tunnels were carved out it never occurred to anyone that they would someday be used for human habitation.

Sleeping in those tunnels was quite an experience. Conditions were extremely crowded. Big exhaust fans provided the only ventilation we had. When there was a bombing raid, the dust would get stirred up and would be almost choking. The main difficulty was a feeling that I was being slowly suffocated. Nevertheless, being in a protected tunnel with eighty five feet of rock over my head was a pretty nice place to be while there was a bombing raid going on topside.

Dick Tirk and Phil Sanborn had both been assigned to be executive officers of boats in the harbor patrol fleet when we

Malinta Tunnel, inside the east entrance, showing railroad tracks and entrance to Hospital Tunnel. Courtesy of Dr. Paul Ashton.

transferred over from Manila, so we weren't spending as much time together these days. I associated their assignments with their having graduated from the officer's training program, while my lack of military training qualified me for the inshore patrol and not much else. But I was glad for the job.

The new observation post that was rigged up for us was an unused, unequipped gun emplacement that had been carved into the brink of a four-hundred-foot cliff overhanging the water below. From that vantage point we had a full view of the channel all the way from North Dock down on Bottomside to the harbor facilities over at Cabcaban on the Bataan Peninsula. Perhaps this was better for those of us who manned the post, because it didn't stick out as such an inviting target for bombers as had the previous signal tower.

As a rule, the Japanese were fairly predictable in their bombing raids. Usually we could count on them coming over around ten o'clock in the morning and keeping up the bombardment until noon. Then they would stop for a siesta. Along about three o'clock, here they'd come again, usually not quitting until it got dark. After a while we were used to them coming over. If we happened to get caught out in the open somewhere, we'd just get low and find some place out of the line of fire.

Ensign Russell was transferred to a new assignment, to the patrol fleet over on the Bataan side. With him gone, I took over as the senior watch officer. Normally, we had two people up on the observation post at a time: the watch officer and a signalman. The trip to the post was about three miles over winding little roads chiseled out of the sides of the cliffs. Our drivers were always Filipino. Often they couldn't speak much English, but they were nice people, very courteous, and always immaculately dressed. I guess it was because of the difficulty and danger of getting up there that our commanding officer decided to put us on a twenty-four rotation. From then on, our watches were twenty-four hours on, forty-eight hours off.

One of my signalmen had previously served aboard the USS *Houston*. But he missed his cruiser when it sailed from Manila, and before he could rejoin the *Houston* the war came and trapped him in the Philippines. For a long time, he complained bitterly about his misfortune in being left behind in Manila when he would much rather be at sea on his ship. He liked to say that "the worst sea duty is better than the best shore duty." But when word came that the *Houston* had been sunk in a sea battle in the Sunda Strait off the coast of Java, from then on I never heard another yip out of him on that matter.

About the only bright spot on our darkening horizon of ominous reports and diminishing hopes was the derring-do of Lt.

John D. Bulkeley and his intrepid squadron of six PT boats. Bulkeley was a larger-than-life individual, the kind of person who comes along only once in a generation. Although I never met him, I observed him many times on his boat through a telescope. An old "China hand" who had spent several years on gunboats patrolling the rivers of China, Bulkeley turned out to be exactly the person we needed at that fateful moment.

The Patrol Torpedo, or PT, boat was a unique craft in the annals of naval warfare. The boats were intended more to annoy than to destroy, a mission Bulkeley's squadron carried out with gusto. Each boat was made of plywood, seventy feet long, twenty feet wide, and manned by a crew of twelve. Three Packard aircraft engines generated a total force of six thousand horse-power and were capable of driving the boat over the water at speeds in excess of fifty knots. Armament consisted of four torpedo tubes and two twin .50-caliber machine guns firing in pairs from each side. As for armor plating, well, there wasn't any. The crew was protected by only a thin ⅜-inch layer of plywood. In essence, these were high-speed "eggshells" designed to roar in close, launch their torpedoes, and get the hell out of there. Normally, they patrolled at night, when their chief advantages were darkness, speed, surprise, and maneuverability.

Late in January, Bulkeley led two boats on a daring raid into Subic Bay, a well-protected port just north of the Bataan Penin-sula, to take on a Japanese cruiser that had been shelling our artillery positions on Bataan with devastating effect. As usual, the PT boats attacked at night. One of the boats ran onto a reef in the darkness and had to be abandoned, but the other boat made it all the way inside the harbor, where it planted two torpedoes into the side of the Japanese warship, thereby taking it out of action.

Less than a week later Bulkeley's squadron scored big again. While on a routine night patrol along the west coast of Bataan, one of the boats encountered another Japanese ship lying to near the shore. In the darkness Bulkeley was unable to tell what kind of ship it was, but it presented a target too inviting to pass up. When the boat roared in, all hell broke loose: the ship was a baited trap lying in wait. All of a sudden the mystery ship and adjacent shore batteries lit up the nighttime sky with searchlights and a tremendous barrage of shellfire. Dodging big shell splashes, the boat got into a range of about five hundred yards and launched two torpedoes, which either missed or failed to explode. So the crew wheeled around and made a second run, swerving and weaving through the shell splashes. This time they nailed her. Only after Bulkeley got back to base was it reported that they had disabled a Japanese auxiliary aircraft carrier.

These and other exploits of the tiny PT squadron thrilled us. Perhaps more important, they fired the imaginations of the press, which was hungry for some "good news" to report about the war, news that, for a change, would give the folks back home something to latch onto and to cheer about.

From time to time, however, I wondered if those glowing stories might not have a counterproductive effect. That is, I feared the stories might lull people into thinking we were doing better over here than we actually were, and therefore fail to convey the urgency of our desperate need for supplies and relief.

To try to stretch out our limited food supply as long as possible, MacArthur ordered all personnel onto half rations. Meals were dished up only twice a day, at 10:00 A.M. and 4:00 P.M., and even at that they were pretty skimpy. Food supplies were running low and no more were coming in.

Horsemeat was our main meat staple. Initially, I didn't cotton to the idea of eating horse flesh, but it turned out to be quite tasty. Our vegetable was usually asparagus—I guess because we had a big supply of the stuff. After a while, I got to the point where I didn't care much for it anymore. Often we would have canned peaches or apricots for dessert. Our only milk was powdered milk. Tons of it were stocked in the tunnel. There was also plenty of sugar, sugarcane being a principal crop in the Philippines.

Nevertheless, it seemed we were always hungry. We talked about food quite a lot, and the subject often turned to carrots. It was common knowledge around the mess tables that whatever carrots we might get would be earmarked for the airplane pilots alone. Supposedly carrots were good for night vision. Whether or not that was true, that was the scuttlebutt around the mess hall.

Whenever I went up on watch, the cooks would issue me a big No. 10 can of Vienna sausages and a loaf of bread. That was considered enough to feed two men on a full twenty-four-hour watch.

Most of the men who hung around in the tunnels a lot soon became "tunnel rats," fearful of venturing outside at all, particularly during daylight hours. As for me, I couldn't stand being cooped up in the tunnels, and I stayed outside as much as possible, despite the danger. During the bombing raids, of course, I was happy to be underground.

Since my watch schedule gave me forty eight hours off out of every seventy two, I spent a lot of time wandering around. Surprisingly, I had enormous physical energy. My weight was down to about 155 pounds now—some 30 pounds less than the 185 pounds I had brought over with me to Manila. Consequently, I never felt better.

One day in the course of my wanderings, I happened into the mess hall in the main tunnel, Malinta Tunnel. Who should I see but the Philippine president, Manuel Quezon, at lunch with members of his staff and generals Wainwright and MacArthur. At first it took me by surprise to learn that they ate in the regular dining room with everyone else. But as time went on I marveled at the openness and the egalitarianism of the people cooped up together in those tunnels. The age-old barriers of rank and privilege didn't seem to count for as much here.

Many days my buddy Ens. "Moon" Mullins and I would go for a stroll up and down the beach just for the fresh air and exercise, merely ducking down when the bombs started falling. Moon, who got his nickname from the popular comic strip character Moon Mullins, had served in the Coast Guard before he transferred into the navy as an ensign. He knew a lot more about naval customs and protocol than I did.

Mullins also knew of a little bakery shop down in Bottomside, in a little area between topside and Malinta Tunnel where there were several shops and a laundry. The Filipino baker there continued baking his breads and rolls every day even after most of the area was bombed out. For a few centavos, we could go down there and get what he called *bechi bechis*—little pastry balls shaped like twisted donuts, dropped in boiling oil, then rolled in sugar. Mullins and I would buy our *bechi bechis*, then go out and find some nice spot on the beach to sit and eat them, enjoying the view of Fort Drum and the other fortified islands.

Every once in a while I visited Jack Ferguson whom I had been stationed with in Manila. Jack, an outstanding individual in almost every respect, was now commanding officer of one of the patrol boats. His boat was about the size of a PT boat and was armed with a pair of twin .50-caliber machine guns, but, it lacked torpedo tubes and was powered by a single diesel engine rather than the three high-powered aircraft engines that powered Bulkeley's PT boats. The patrol boats carried a crew of seven or eight each. Their principal duty was to patrol the coastline of Corregidor at night and to guard against possible infiltration by Japanese who might try to sneak ashore. Jack was only an ensign like me, but I envied his more invigorating duty.

Many times during my off hours I would find myself taking some kind of special assignment, glad to do something that let me feel I was making a useful contribution to the overall cause.

One day, for example, the submarine *Spearfish* ran the Japanese naval blockade to bring in a load of antiaircraft ammunition that was capable of reaching higher altitudes. There was no way to deliver the ammo over to Bataan except by barge. I volunteered to supervise the job of transporting the ammo over to the docks at Cabcaban, on the Bataan side of the strait. That was my only time ever to set foot on Bataan.

While over on Bataan, I asked about my former colleague Bob Russell. He was now the executive officer on the USS *Mary Anne*, a luxury yacht that had been taken over and converted to a patrol boat. Before the war, the *Mary Anne* had been owned by an American millionaire. It was 120 feet long, powered by twin diesels, and manned by a crew of twenty. Russell was happy to be pulling sea duty—which, I guess, is every navy man's wish.

Not all volunteer activities ended that happily. One that I almost went on turned out to be a disaster. Someone came around asking for volunteers to go across the strait and help clean out a nest of Japs that had infiltrated on Aglaloma Point, a little spit of land jutting out from the western shore of Bataan about ten miles up the coast. Reports had been received that the Japanese had placed a small landing party ashore behind our American and Filipino lines, where they were disrupting the lines of communications.

I was all set to go over and help wipe them out, when the commanding officer, Commander Cheek—the big cheese himself—ordered, "No you don't, Berry! You have your own duties to perform on your watch, and you're not really cut out for what's going on here."

Cheek knew full well that I was not trained for combat—that I didn't even know how to load an army rifle, much less how to fire one.

"Besides," he added, "I don't think it will amount to much, because there aren't many Japs there."

On his first point, he was correct; on the second, he was dead wrong. While the twenty or so navy volunteers selected for the mission may have been adequately trained for naval battles, it's fair to say they were not trained for infantry-style fighting on land. Nevertheless, they were issued rifles and hastened on their way.

It turned out that the Japs were more numerous and better equipped than anyone had anticipated, and our guys ran into an ambush. They were shot up pretty badly before getting out of there. One lieutenant junior grade told me that he had climbed a ridge, looked over, and didn't see anybody, and he was so pooped from the climb that he lay down on a log for a few minutes to rest. His right knee happened to be sticking up in the air, and some Jap over in the woods shot him right through the knee. He had to be carried back, crippled.

Fortunately, some marine troops happened to be in the area, and they were able to call in a couple of tanks and surround the Japanese position. The Japanese were given a chance to surrender, but they refused. When the troops moved in, the entire Japanese position was annihilated except for one soldier who tried to escape by swimming out to sea. He was fished out of the water and taken prisoner. Our wounded volunteers were brought back to the hospital at Corregidor; many of them had lost legs, arms, and the like.

The volunteers discovered not only that there were more Japanese infiltrators over there than they had thought, but also that they possessed much heavier equipment than was probable for a guerrilla operation of this sort. Thus the rumor got started that before the war the Japanese must have shipped in heavy weapons and buried them in anticipation of later use. That rumor was only scuttlebutt — mess hall conversation — because no solid evidence was ever documented.

Lieutenant Commander Lowe, my former exec at the Naval Intelligence Office, and I had another run-in. Some hero he turned out to be! Lowe mostly stayed holed up in the tunnel. Like so many other tunnel rats, he had developed "tunnel phobia" and never could bring himself to venture outside. Even within the protected tunnel, he invariably wore his steel helmet. It amused me to see him wearing that silly tin hat under eighty-five feet of solid rock. First of all, no explosive is powerful enough to penetrate eighty-five of rock; and second, if something were that powerful, a helmet would offer scant protection.

Well, late one afternoon as it was nearing dusk and I was getting ready to go on watch, Mr. Lowe and a Lieutenant Commander Tisdale decided they wanted to go out and get a bit of fresh air, so they told me they were going to ride up to Topside with me and just drive around a little. I said, "Yes, Sir."

Unfortunately, the Filipino driver assigned to us that day was new to the job and didn't know the way. What's worse, he didn't speak a bit of English, and none of us spoke Filipino. Soon we

were lost. To complicate matters, darkness falls quickly in the
tropics, and it turned pitch black before we knew it. All the
while, poor old Lowe was getting more and more fidgety.

Then artillery shells started going off. Poor Lowe had never
before been out in the open when those shells were going off,
because he had always cowered inside the tunnel. Well, he was
scared out of his wits, as if he were going to die right there on the
spot.

Then Lowe started taking out his fright and frustration on me.
He cussed me up one side and down the other. He called me every
name in the book for getting us lost. He said it was all my fault
that the driver couldn't speak English and didn't know where he
was going. Of course, I had no control over who was assigned to
drive, but I couldn't get that across to him. I am convinced Lowe
would have court-martialed me on the spot if he could have found
a way to do it.

When Tisdale had got a bellyful of Lowe's tirade, he jumped
into the fray: "Look here, Tom. Leave the poor guy alone. You
said you wanted to come up here and get some nice clean air in
your lungs, and now you're taking it out on this poor ensign. Why
in the world did you come up here if you're going to jump all over
him? Didn't you know there was some risk out here?"

Lowe sputtered and protested, "Berry should have had sense
enough to check out that driver."

Tisdale told him, "Just shut up and leave him alone."

Eventually the driver found the observation post, and I was
happy to get out of the jeep. It didn't matter much to me what
might happen to them on the way back. Let me take that back: I
did like Tisdale for coming to my defense—it was Lowe I didn't
care about.

To the best of my knowledge, Lowe never ventured out of the
tunnel again after that. And the more I think about it, the more I
am convinced that Lowe was suffering ten times more than the
rest of us—simply because he was so frightened all of the time.
On the other hand, I spent so much time in exposed areas that it
didn't bother me to be out there while bombs were dropping,

because I could see that they weren't dropping where I was standing. And that's all that really mattered.

Strange things happened. I'll never forget the day I was standing watch on the cliff about four-hundred feet above the water when I looked up to see a Japanese plane flying overhead. It dropped a bomb. Now, I was standing in a place that was open to the sky; a concrete parapet in front of me could have afforded some protection against a near miss, but no protection whatever from a bomb dropped directly overhead. And here was this bomb falling from the sky. I could see it — a huge thing, about four feet long and probably two feet in diameter. It must have been a four-hundred-pounder. It came down right past me so close that if I had held my hand out I swear I could have touched it. But it went right past me, and I saw it hit the water just below me. It made a very little splash because of its shape and because it went in nose first. Those are the kinds of things that happened during wartime.

After a while, people got used to the bombardment. We were no longer afraid when the planes or artillery shells would come over. We would just lie there, guts tied up inside into one cold, painful lump. Pretty soon it would be over.

The sad thing is that all our big guns were pointed in the wrong direction. When the island was fortified back in 1914, it was thought that any attack would come from the sea, not over the land. Consequently the gun batteries were positioned to shoot out east over Manila Bay and west over the South China Sea rather than north, in the direction of Bataan. Moreover, the guns were mounted on enormous concrete pads and couldn't be repositioned in a new direction. Sometimes I thought what a difference it would have made if those big guns had been pointed toward Bataan. We might have been able to defend ourselves and Bataan too. Just think what those heavy artillery shells could have done to the Japanese lines if our guns had been pointed in the right direction.

Our artillery pieces couldn't even point high enough to be used for antiaircraft fire. All we had were a few three-inch museum

Battery Hearn, a twelve-inch gun located on Topside, Corregidor, and pointed west, overlooking the South China Sea. Courtesy of Dr. Paul Ashton.

piece AA guns that could shoot up to only ten-thousand to twelve-thousand feet. Later on, after we got some shells that would go higher, the Japanese simply increased their altitude another thousand or so feet and still were able to fly above our AA fire.

What's even more amazing is that, according to reports that filtered in from men who were trying to defend Bataan and other places from the Japanese advance, our troops didn't have any type of mobile artillery. Nor did they have any modern equipment at all. The Filipino troops had been training, but they didn't have any equipment either, not even rifles. Our troops were trying to carry out their orders to defend the Philippine Islands, but for lack of equipment the Japanese were able to capture them and wipe them out.

Without mobile artillery, it's hard to protect troops that are fighting a withdrawing action. And that's what our guys on

Bataan were doing. Army Lt. Tom Harrison, a gunnery officer on Bataan, figured out a way of getting a mobile artillery piece: he simply mounted a field artillery gun on the back of a truck. In that ingenious manner, he was able to provide more effective firepower. Harrison was awarded a silver star for his bravery.

The plain fact of the matter is that we were poorly equipped and ill prepared, while the Japanese had the most modern equipment conceivable. The Japanese brought tanks onto Corregidor; we didn't have one.

I know MacArthur did his best to get supplies over here, but there were none to be had. At the beginning of the bombing, MacArthur addressed the officers with great optimism and enthusiasm about the future of the fighting in the Philippines. He told them that the Japanese air superiority was only temporary. He said new planes were coming from the United States, that twenty-thousand troops were coming to reinforce the units on Bataan, that it wouldn't be long until tons of equipment and all kinds of protection would be over here, and that we would soon launch a counterattack.

Then, while the men were still fighting on Bataan, MacArthur received a radiogram from Roosevelt that no help would be forthcoming. The convoy headed by the USS *Pensacola*, which had been on its way to Manila, was now being diverted to Australia. The radiogram tried to let MacArthur down as gently as possible, but there was no mistaking its import:

THE SERVICE THAT YOU AND THE AMERICAN MEMBERS OF YOUR COMMAND CAN RENDER TO YOUR COUNTRY IN THE TITANIC STRUGGLE NOW DEVELOPING IS BEYOND ALL POSSIBILITY OF APPRAISEMENT. I PARTICULARLY REQUEST THAT YOU PROCEED RAPIDLY TO THE ORGANIZATION OF YOUR FORCES AND YOUR DEFENSES SO AS TO MAKE YOUR RESISTANCE AS EFFECTIVE AS CIRCUMSTANCES WILL PERMIT AND AS PROLONGED AS HUMANLY POSSIBLE.

Nevertheless, MacArthur turned the disappointing news into a message of hope and inspiration. He sent a stirring appeal to the men on Bataan to fight and to hold out: "It is a question of courage and determination," he said. "If we fight we win; if we retreat we will be destroyed."

By the middle of February we were at a turning point in the war, but we didn't know it. The Japanese advance had been stalled. General Homma had lost nearly seven-thousand troops in combat. Beriberi, dysentery, and malaria had disabled another ten-thousand. Three battalions had been sacrificed in futile behind-the-lines landings. Homma feared that if the Americans found out how weak his resources really were, they would counterattack and wipe out what remained of his army. Worse, for Homma, was Tokyo's displeasure with his failure. The Japanese army had been victorious in every place except the Philippines. With tears streaming down his face, the Japanese leader made an open admission of defeat to his staff.

Unaware of these things taking place in the Japanese general's camp, Washington had written off the Philippines. Plans were made to evacuate President Quezon and his cabinet. At the White House, the topic was how to order General MacArthur to leave his troops, for everyone knew that Bataan and Corregidor would soon fall.

The question of reinforcements was on everybody's mind. Many of the people on Bataan believed so strongly that U.S. ships were heading their way, loaded with men and supplies, that they would filter down to the beaches during their off-duty hours and climb tall trees, from which they could look out over the bay in the forlorn hope of seeing the ships as they arrived. But no ships ever came.

Sure, subconsciously we knew we were expendable. But we were not disheartened. Our mission was to delay the sweep of the Japanese forces down through the South Pacific to Australia. The annals of history, when they are finally written, will undoubtedly show that the Japanese were indeed on their way to Australia. And it is an indisputable fact that they were slowed down in the Philippines long enough for the United States to intercept the Japanese fleet and deny them that great prize.

It was on my watch during the moonless night of March 11 that General MacArthur made his historic dash for freedom. President Roosevelt himself had ordered MacArthur to leave the Philippines and establish his new headquarters in Australia. The Japanese had a line of warships positioned as a blockading force outside the entrance to the harbor. Washington wanted to send a submarine in to get him, but MacArthur said no, he thought he'd have a better chance of eluding the blockade if he were on a PT boat.

The duty officer called me in and said, "Berry, what I'm about to tell you is in utmost secrecy and confidence. MacArthur, his family, and a few carefully chosen staff will be going out through the channel tonight in PT boats. We are not going to be able to use the radio, or even signal lights, because we don't want to take any chance that the Japs might find out what is going on and try to intercept them. So I want you to make sure that the minefields are turned off at precisely the right time."

I said, "Yes, Sir."

"Furthermore," he added, "I don't want you to leak any word of this to any of your buddies here on the island or even to act differently in any way, because if people learn ahead of time that MacArthur is leaving it could be very bad for morale."

"I'll do my best, Sir."

So I went up topside and relieved the officer on watch. When the appointed time came, in almost complete darkness, I issued the order to shut down the minefields. Three PT boats from Bulkeley's squadron quietly edged out into the channel, each running only one of its three engines to keep the sound at a minimum. They rendezvoused with a fourth boat just outside the minefield. In the moonless darkness, I could barely make out their ghostly silhouettes. And as the boats idled quietly away into the dark night, I found myself uttering a silent prayer for our commanding general, whom I admired so much, and I wondered if I would ever see him again.

MacArthur received a lot of criticism for leaving—quite unjustly, I think. But when he left, it became even more clear that we weren't going to get out of there.

A lot of people attributed his famed "I shall return!" statement to sheer bravado or showmanship, and certainly MacArthur was capable of that. My own view of the situation, however, is that MacArthur's statement was born of heartbreak—the heartbreak that is felt by a military commander who is being forced to abandon his men. That statement was his promise to us.

Dick Tirk had developed a friendship with Comdr. Melvyn McCoy, the communications officer. Since setting up its headquarters on Corregidor, all communications for the USAFFE was handled through the communications facility in Navy Tunnel. Occasionally we would get together to shoot the bull. McCoy mentioned that he had personally seen the message that President Roosevelt had sent to MacArthur ordering him to get out of the Philippines.

MacArthur himself had wanted to set up his new headquarters on Mindanao, one of the southern islands. But Roosevelt told him he could not be permitted to remain in the Philippines. For if MacArthur, America's greatest war hero, were killed or captured, it would be a tremendous blow to the home front's spirits and a powerful propaganda boost to the Japanese war machine. No, MacArthur had to be ordered out. That was proof that MacArthur did not willingly abandon his troops, despite what some of his critics later intimated. In fact, according to McCoy, on two previous occasions MacArthur had received instructions to leave but had refused the orders.

McCoy said that he had also seen the message that MacArthur sent to the troops on Bataan during the heaviest part of the fighting in which he notified them that American planes and troops were on the way, encouraging them to fight on and hold their ground even if it meant death. At the same time that MacArthur was sending out that message of hope to his troops, however, the War Department was telling MacArthur that he could expect no help whatsoever by way of reinforcements and supplies.

At the time, many people thought it was awful that MacArthur would send out the message to the troops when he knew full well that no relief was forthcoming. Nevertheless, MacArthur's message did help morale and keep the men fighting. And fight they did. Their valiant stand on Bataan and Corregidor was the only spark of pride this nation had in the whole dismal Pacific war to date; this was the only place where the Japanese advance had been stopped.

Moreover, the men did hold out for a long time. And by holding up the Japanese in the Philippines, they gave the United States time to marshal its defenses in Australia, meet the Japanese fleet at Midway and the Coral Sea, and thus turn the tide of battle in the Pacific.

Unquestionably, those five months bought with the blood of the men and women on Bataan and Corregidor served to set back the Japanese timetable of conquest in the South Pacific and thereby altered the outcome of the Pacific war.

CHAPTER FOUR

FALL OF THE "FORTRESS"

AFTER MacArthur left, the days all seemed to blur into one another, each day barely distinguishable from the day before. The routine was always the same: always air raids, always a certain amount of machine gun fire, always artillery shells dropping in from no telling where. It was miserable. Still we generally knew when things were about to happen, and that knowledge enabled us to take whatever precautions we needed to protect ourselves.

One day I was standing outside the battery when a .50-caliber machine gun came tumbling past, dropped from somewhere, struck the side of the mountain, spun around several times, and stopped right beside me. I never did figure out where it came from.

There was another time when a .50-caliber bullet hit the wall beside me, ricocheted, and fell right in front of my feet. Things like that took place all the time. After a while, we learned not to think about our close calls.

There was one fellow, however, who didn't have any respect for the Japanese artillery—or for anything else that was going on. He would go out riding in a jeep during a bombardment, singing at the top of his lungs, as if he didn't have a care in the world. I think maybe he wanted to die. One day as I was looking out over the parapet, I watched him driving up and down the side of the hill, seemingly as happy as a lark, while shells were popping off all over the place. Apparently the Japs could also see him from their position across the channel, because they dropped a bracket of shells around him, and that wiped him out, both him and the jeep.

Sometimes it was hard to convince people that I was actually seeing what I was seeing. One night on watch I spotted through my binoculars some shell bursts coming from an area on the west coast of Bataan, probably some eight to ten miles away. One of our patrol boats had intercepted a Japanese landing barge. I called back down to the tunnel to relay the message to the duty officer so he could be alert to the situation. But he insisted, "No, no, no. That can't possibly be. It's too far up the coast."

"I beg your pardon, Sir," I insisted. "I'm standing here watching it through a telescope, so please don't tell me I can't see it!" The duty officer let it go at that. Later on, he acknowledged that he thought I was talking about Subic Bay, some forty miles further up the coast, where indeed another battle had been going on.

The night that Bataan fell, on April 9, was a gut-wrenching experience. I was at my watch station when the American lines broke. The troops began blowing up all their ammunition dumps. Tremendous bursts of explosives filled the night sky. I couldn't tell you whether there was a full moon or not, because the explosions so brightly lit up the sky. Standing where I was, several miles away, I could feel the tremors from the explosions. There must have been a dozen or more times when the whole side of the mountain would quiver and shake, as though we were having an earthquake.

The situation on Corregidor became much more critical after the fall of Bataan. The Japanese began hauling in artillery pieces to the coast, just two miles away across the strait. From there, they could keep up an unhampered and continuous pounding of our tiny island.

We were trapped. We knew it, and the Japanese knew it. They began pouring it on. Daily, from dawn to noon and again from three to midnight, they poured the shells onto us without interruption.

All structures aboveground were being obliterated one by one. Gone were the air defense shelters. Gone were the beach defenses. Gone were the buildings, the fuel storage facilities, the ammunition dumps, the food depots. Even Corregidor's vaunted big guns were being blasted off the cliffs one by one — sometimes along with pieces of the cliffs themselves. The topography of Corregidor was being inexorably pounded into a lunar landscape.

On the second day of this intensified bombardment, a shell hit my watch post, completely wiped it out. Along with the men who were in it. Thank heavens, I was not on duty at the time. That was the second observation post the Japanese blasted out from under us.

We established a new observation post up at Sunset Battery, on the western edge of the island overlooking the South China Sea. It had one of those big twelve-inch guns that could shoot fifteen miles out into the bay.

In addition to the mind-numbing artillery bombardment, we probably underwent four or five hundred bombing raids in the weeks after Bataan fell. Sometimes there were as many as two-hundred planes at a time. After a while, it got to be a way of life, and we became somewhat fatalistic about it. Once a person understands a few things about how to get under cover and protect himself, a bomb almost has to land right on top of his head in order to mess him up.

That isn't to say that it can't happen, though. That's precisely what happened to Battery Geary, one of our big twelve-inch batteries up on Topside. A bomb or artillery shell, I'm not sure which, came right down through the air vent and exploded in the powder magazine. The explosion killed fifty-six men outright and horribly wounded scores of others. Many of those men died in the hospital.

Seventy Filipinos suffered a similar tragedy. They had taken refuge during a particularly heavy bombardment in one of the partially completed tunnels along the base of Morrison Hill. A salvo of Japanese shells broke loose the overhanging rock and started a landside. The Filipinos were trapped behind hundreds of tons of rock that was blocking the tunnel entrances. Because there was no heavy earthmoving equipment available on Corregidor to mount a rescue operation, the men were entombed there. After a few pathetic days the muffled signals of the trapped men ceased.

Sometimes the experiences verged on the macabre. One morning up on Sunset Battery, the battery officer, Colonel Cohen, called me over to where he was standing. He put a pair of binoculars in my hand. "Look over there," he said. "Do you see that Japanese officer over on the Bataan side looking toward us with field glasses?" With his help, I was able to locate a Japanese officer standing on a stone revetment part way up the mountain side.

Cohen then ordered the gun crew to wheel out a three-inch artillery piece and to blast that fellow off the wall. He handed me back the glasses and said, "Now watch and see what happens when this shell lands over there."

As I watched through the glasses, the first explosion hit a few yards to one side of the Jap officer, and the second about the same distance on the other side of him. Then the third round hit right where he stood and I saw him blown straight up into the air.

Another time, we spotted a big column of dust overhanging one of the roads. Colonel Cohen, believing that the dust was being stirred by a column of Japanese troops coming down the trail, fired several rounds at it. It turned out to be some American prisoners that the Japanese had assembled into a group and were marching down the road.

Sometime afterward a bunch of us guys were sitting around the mess hall when someone brought up the incident. The story got twisted around, and people kind of laughed at the stupidity of our own forces, at our own ineptness. A Lieutenant Scott from Philadelphia, a man for whom I had the greatest respect, informed us that that was no laughing matter, that it was very serious, and that it showed how necessary it was to know who you are shooting at. That shamed all of those who had seen only the humorous element of it. I agreed. There was nothing funny about American troops, acting in good faith, inadvertently killing or maiming their own comrades in arms. Unfortunately, this was neither the first nor the last time this kind of thing happened.

"Moon" Mullins was one of the few navy men on Corregidor to get a medal. It happened on a day that I wasn't with him. In addition to the forces shooting at us from Bataan, the Japanese had brought up some heavy artillery pieces and placed them across the bay on the south shore. From there they would lob shells toward the southern side of Corregidor. Since we were at the outer limits of their range, most of the shells landed harmlessly in the water. Occasionally, however, one would do some damage.

On this particular day, Ensign Mullins watched while a shell landed on the beach and injured several people. Mullins immediately rushed out through the bombardment and dragged the injured people into sick bay. He was awarded a Silver Star for this act.

There weren't many citations handed out, it's true. As one officer wryly remarked, "Losers don't get medals." I guess that sums up the situation: we were involved in a lost cause. It didn't seem to count for anything that our watch station was bombed out three times, that we underwent constant bombardment, incredibly heavy artillery fire, and many, many close calls. We were fighting a losing battle.

An indication that the end was near came the day they asked me to help haul the silver out of the vault and dump it into the bay. Millions of dollars of silver pesos had been stored on Corregidor, and the Philippine government wanted to keep it from falling into Japanese hands.

We carried the silver pesos from the vault onto a lorry and transported them down to the dock, where they were in turn loaded onto a lighter (a small barge). When the lighter was loaded, it was towed out to sea and the silver dumped out in the middle of Manila Bay.

The authorities had decreed that an officer had to be present whenever the silver was handled. That's how I got involved. It became my responsibility to supervise the loading of the silver and to ride with the truck and be there when they off-loaded the boxes onto the lighter.

Each box of silver weighed about a hundred pounds; it took two men to carry a box. I don't know how many trips we made back and forth taking those pesos down to the dock from the storeroom, but it was quite a few. Several times during the loading process the Japanese laid a few rounds of artillery fire over our way; we would merely step off the lorry and lie flat on the ground while the shells burst all around us. No one got hit, but it was a little scary while the loading operations were going on.

If dumping the silver was amazing, that paled into insignificance compared with what took place the following day: We burned the paper money—millions upon millions of dollars in pesos, silver certificates, gold certificates, American currency of every denomination—money brought out to the island from the banks when Manila was evacuated. We had firm orders not to let the currency fall into Japanese hands. So during the midday lull in the Japanese bombardment, we made a big bonfire outside Malinta Tunnel. We had to do the job in daytime; at night the flames would have been so bright that the Japanese artillery could have homed right in on us. We burned it in an open area that we screened in with some fencing. I saw it with my own eyes—millions and millions of dollars, burned.

Some of the guys who were standing around watching this happen made little jokes about slipping some of the bills aside and coming back at a later time to get them. But I don't know of anyone who actually did.

There was also lots of gold on Corregidor—I think about forty-five million dollars' worth. The authorities delayed as long as possible before getting rid of it, hoping not to have to dump it in the bay along with the silver. But as they were trying to figure out what to do with the gold, an amazing coincidence happened: The USS *Trout*, an American submarine, came in carrying another load of antiaircraft ammunition. When the submarine got ready to put back out to sea, the crew found that they didn't have enough ballast. As they were trying to figure out what to use for ballast, someone came up with the idea of using the gold. So they loaded it on. That seemed rather ironic to me—that a precious metal should be used for mere ballast. But that's how the gold left Corregidor and got back to the United States.

Rumors, uncertainty, and misinformation were growing. As a matter of fact, we looked forward to the rumors because hard news was difficult to get. There was a radio station, which from time to time issued news reports, but this news always reported that we were getting along just fine. For example, there were many stories about large numbers of Japanese planes being shot down. I think some of those stories even found their way into the newspapers back in the States. But the fact of the matter is that during the whole time I was on Corregidor—and this included many, many air raids—I saw only one Japanese plane shot down. That was a plane coming in low and doing some strafing, and it was shot down by our gunners. They fished the pilot out of the plane and brought him into the hospital. The story went around that when a thermometer was put into his mouth, he bit the bulb off and committed suicide by swallowing the mercury.

That's one example of how strongly the Japanese felt about being taken prisoner. We heard many stories about how their commanders told them that it was a dishonor to surrender, and that any Japanese soldier who was taken prisoner would face a court-martial by his own people. I don't think our side took more than a hundred Japanese prisoners during the whole battle for Bataan, and it was rumored that many of these had gotten isolated behind the American lines and surrendered for food because they were practically starved to death.

We also had our heroes. We heard about the "Battling Bastards of Bataan," how they would get behind the Japanese lines and all. We heard about the exploits of Capt. Colin Kelly, exaggerated by the press—how he was supposed to have dived his crippled plane into a Japanese ship. We heard about Bulkeley's PT boats and their daring deeds. We heard those stories, and we thrived on them. How much of this actually happened, I don't know. But all those stories fueled our courage. And we needed those heroes.

More and more we came to accept the inevitability of our fate. We knew that our mission was to delay the enemy at all costs, to tie up his army and air power as long as possible, to buy time for

America to rearm itself and position its defenses in the Pacific. We knew that darned few of us would get out of this alive. But our attitude was not that of grim resignation. It was an attitude of rock-hard defiance.

Whenever Dick Tirk, Phil Sanborn, and I would get together, the subject of escape would always come up. I don't know who first broached the idea, but each of us knew that our situation here was hopeless; and if we ever got off this island at all, it would be as a prisoner.

We never talked about inviting anyone else to join us. The way things ended up, it always seemed to be just Dick and Phil and me. We discussed what might happen to us. We talked about the lousy food we had, and how we'd like to sink our teeth into a good steak, mashed potatoes and gravy, apple pie, butter . . . we talked about everything under the sun. But most of what we were doing was just pipe-dreaming; none of us had any real idea of how we might go about it.

Many of the officers I was acquainted with were deeply concerned about leaving their families behind, mothers, fathers, wives and children back in the states. I don't know why I was thinking the way I did, but I rather regretted the fact that I *didn't* have some kind of family to be leaving . . . in the way of a wife and some children, that is.

If we thought we had it bad before, we soon thought otherwise. April 28 began a reign of unmitigated terror as the Japanese began the final phase of their preinvasion bombardment. Overhead, planes were unrelentingly dropping their missiles of destruction. The incredible intensity of the artillery fire from the more than 250 guns positioned against us defied description.

This bombardment continued unabated for eight straight days, much heavier than anything we had endured previously. The noise from the explosions was like being inside a gigantic popcorn popper — an uninterrupted roar, one explosion blending into the next, day and night.

Inside the tunnels everything was in confusion. The pounding of the explosions shook loose the cement on the walls, kicking up a musty, choking, dust that made breathing difficult. People ran through the tunnels with no sense of direction, no aim, no purpose. Some were doing their jobs as a matter of course; others were pacing like caged tigers working aff nervous energy.

I spotted Lieutenant Meade Willis, with whom I stood watch back in Manila, sitting on his bunk in Queen Tunnel with his head in his hands and an open Bible beside him. I couldn't tell whether he was praying or not, so I just went on by. He was not alone. There were many others sitting or praying in their bunks, their faces white with fear.

Nothing could stop the scuttlebutt, the disheartening rumors, the disconcerting alarm about Japanese successes. Word spread through the tunnels that the Japanese had landed on Monkey Point and were gaining ground. We were told that Wainwright carried a bullet that he tossed around in his hand, and in talking with other officers he would say, "This is for me before I allow the Japanese to take this island."

We had heard that MacArthur had given orders to Wainwright that he was never to surrender, that he was to hold out until the last man was killed. Naturally this rumor, along with our already poor prospects for surviving, rang through our hearts like a death knell.

I don't think any of us knew what was really happening, particularly those in the tunnel. They were frightened like chickens. One time a rumor started that the Japanese were inside the tunnel, and I have never seen such panic. It was as though a building had caught fire and everyone rushed against the door. We were all frightened and didn't know which way to go. We were not prepared, not equipped, and certainly not trained for the situation in which we found ourselves.

No one was giving orders. Everybody was seemingly looking out for himself, wanting to get away to protect himself.

Finally the panic subsided, and people gathered their wits. Then it was back to the same old business—long periods of waiting punctuated by moments of fear.

Intelligence sources brought us word that a major buildup of Japanese boats and landing barges was taking place over on the Bataan side. This meant that the anticipated Japanese invasion of Corregidor was now imminent.

I found myself without anything to do. The Inshore Patrol was disbanded. Since no more ships were going in or out of the harbor, our services were no longer needed. As I tried to make myself useful, Lieutenant Commander Lowe, my former exec, thought up something for me to do: he thought I should be put in charge of a stretcher unit that would go out and pick up wounded men from the battle areas.

Now, I knew absolutely nothing about medical procedures. But if this was something that was needed, I was happy to do what I could to help out. Maybe I wouldn't have known how to treat a wounded man, but I certainly would have done my best.

They recruited a group of about fifty Filipino civilians and told me that I was going to be in charge of organizing them for stretcher duty. It turns out that the Filipinos didn't speak any English and I didn't speak any Filipino, so communication was difficult. Moreover, I had only a vague idea of the topography of the island.

Nothing ever became of the stretcher unit. I was issued a rifle and some Red Cross armbands for my group, but then the whole idea was forgotten. We never received any assignments. I asked Lyons about it, and he said he would let me know. But no word came.

The evening of May 5 the Japanese lifted their bombardment. Invasion was now imminent. The Japanese invasion party came ashore about midnight near Cavalry Point, on the north side of the island in the area we called Monkey Point. We also heard that another force had come ashore at James Ravine, out on the western tip. Pandemonium erupted throughout the tunnel. What little information we received was garbled, and nobody really knew how much of it we could believe.

I decided that I would go outside and try to find out for myself what was going on. Sometime previously I had discovered a passageway that led to a ledge above the entrance to the Malinta Tunnel. From there I could watch the battle going on below. A Filipino warrant officer came with me. We could see shell bursts.

All was confusion. The Japanese invasion barges hadn't allowed for the strong incoming tide. The commanders couldn't see the landmarks they were expecting. Swept by the tide, they were landing at the wrong beaches. Our waiting marines slaughtered the incoming invaders as they approached the shore. The Japanese suffered casualties as high as seventy percent while they were still in the water. Nevertheless, about eight-hundred Japanese did make it to shore, managed to land two light tanks, and slowly and doggedly began to move toward Malinta Hill.

Some of those shells began whizzing by pretty close to us, so we crawled under a cover of some corrugated iron and found ourselves in total darkness. It was pretty frightening at the time because we didn't know exactly where we were. But we finally found our way back to the tunnel below.

Jack Ferguson, who was skipper of one of the patrol boats, came into Navy Tunnel looking for me. When he found me, Ferguson said, "Bill, I have my boat all serviced, loaded down with lots of extra fuel and food, my crew is standing by, and we're ready to leave the island. Do you want to come with us?"

"Where are you going?" I asked.

"Well, we're going to try to make it to one of the southern islands, hide in the coves by daytime and travel at night, and hop island by island until we eventually reach Australia."

I asked, "Jack, isn't that desertion?"

He hadn't thought of that. "I don't know . . ."

"Well, Jack," I told him, "I think we're still under orders to stay. There's been no word on surrender yet, and I haven't heard any word that says we are released. So until we're told that we can leave, I'm afraid that we would be classified as deserters. I think it would be desertion if we took off."

Ferguson replied, "Well, I hadn't thought of it that way. But I see no future in our sticking around here any longer. Besides, surrender is only hours away."

"Jack," I said, "I concur with your judgment on that point, but I still feel we're in military service and obligated to remain until told we're released."

Ferguson seemed disappointed as he turned to leave. My parting words were, "Jack, it's my fervent hope and prayer that we'll see each other again after this is all over."

Apparently my words about being a deserter weighed heavily on his mind. Ferguson and his crew never carried through with their planned escape. I was horrified later to learn that Jack sent his crew chief out to the boat to pull the plugs from its bottom and scuttle it.

The sad ending to this story is that not only did Bill Berry pass up his own opportunity to escape the clutches of the Japanese, but apparently he cost Ferguson and his crew that opportunity. It turns out that other people made the attempt and succeeded, and there is every reason to believe that Ferguson might have also. Many times I have thought that if only we had carried on the discussion for just a little longer, both of us would probably have done it . . . or at least attempted the feat.

Just sitting around the tunnel passively waiting for the end to come was not in my nature. So I made my way back outside again. This time, I took one of the laterals out of the south entrance of the Queen Tunnel and climbed up to one of the machine gun emplacements that had been set up to protect the narrow road that wound around the southern side of Monkey Point. From there I watched the unfolding tragedy as if it were a terrible dream.

Corregidor was in its death throes. The Japanese had brought artillery ashore and were using it with devastating effect. The heaviest weapons our soldiers had to counter them with were a few old mortars without sights. Moreover, the Japanese were leading their advance with the couple of light tanks they had managed to wrestle ashore. The Americans didn't have a single tank on Corregidor with which to repel an invasion.

What General Wainwright didn't know—couldn't know, as a matter of fact—was that General Homma was going through a similar agony of the mind. Two thirds of his landing fleet had been destroyed, and he had only twenty-one barges left—not enough to resupply the troops with ammunition or to land reinforcements. His troops had less than a five-hour supply of ammunition and no way to get any more. Homma was sure that he had lost, that his troops would be wiped out, and that he would be sent home in disgrace. He consulted with his staff as to how best evacuate what troops he had left.

By the time the first gray streaks of dawn arrived on May 6, the Japanese could be seen advancing toward Navy Tunnel. The Americans were suffering fearful casualties. Withering fire from well-placed Japanese guns was annihilating the American lines of defense.

Then came the word that struck terror into the heart of every living soul huddled inside the tunnels: *Flamethrowers*. Eight Japanese soldiers armed with flamethrowers and backed up by a tank had positioned themselves across the east entrance to Malinta Tunnel. Hooded in their heavy asbestos suits, they had aimed the nozzles of their flamethrowers right down the main tunnel.

For what seemed like an eternity, the Japanese soldiers and the Americans stared at each other—the Japanese poised with their flamethrowers and their cannons, waiting for word to pull the triggers. Hundreds upon hundreds of American officers and nurses were trapped inside the tunnel and were powerless to stop the Japanese advance. The image of the massacre that would result if the Japanese fired down the length of the tunnel was almost unthinkable. Then, for some inexplicable reason, they lowered their weapons from the ready position. Soldiers continued to guard the entrance to the tunnel, but the moment of grave crisis had passed.

Word was passed to us about ten o'clock in the morning that

Wainwright was going to surrender Corregidor. All firing was to cease at noon. The island was no longer capable of defending itself, and there was nothing to look forward to but complete annihilation. It was better to forgo one final day of freedom than to sacrifice thousands of lives in a hopeless effort. The news came as something of a relief, because so many of us felt so inadequate, so ill-prepared, and so unready for what was taking place.

Nothing was left for us to do now except to get rid of our firearms and wait for the conquering Japanese to arrive. I took out my .45-caliber automatic pistol, which I had never fired—had never been taught to fire, not even a practice round—and threw the bolt over the cliff in one direction and the gun in another. At the same time, I threw away my cartridge belt and holster.

All the men inside the tunnels brought out their firearms—rifles, pistols, submachine guns, whatever—and stacked them up in the road outside Malinta Tunnel. These made a good-sized pyramid.

An army officer came to take down the flag that had been flown proudly over the entrance to Malinta Tunnel every day throughout the long siege. Normally there would have been a little ceremony when the flag was raised and lowered, but this day was different. Today, there was no ceremony. When the flag was lowered this time, it was folded very reverently and tenderly. Then a large pair of scissors was brought out, and the flag was cut into small pieces and scattered in the wind. Men were crying. I regret now that I lacked the presence of mind to pick up one of the pieces and keep it with me as a memento.

Then I sat down in the empty nest of a dismantled .50-caliber machine gun just outside the south entrance to Queen Tunnel—the same spot from which I had viewed the battle the night before. There I awaited whatever fate might befall.

As I sat there on the edge of the machine gun emplacement, I reflected on what seemed to be four major turning points in this war. These were the four points where the scales of fate could have tipped in either direction, for the Japanese or for us. And on each of these occasions the scales weighed against us.

The first turning point was the day they bombed Clark Field; the Japanese thought they had lost the element of surprise, when in fact they gained it. The second turning point was at Lingayen Gulf; the Japanese invasion forces were blown off their intended course and decimated by the rough seas, but they landed miles away from our waiting coastal defenses, which could have pushed them back into the sea. The third turning point came when our War Department decided to abandon the Philippines at precisely the time when a counterattack could have driven back a discouraged and demoralized invader. And the fourth turning point came here at Corregidor where Homma thought he had lost, yet we lacked even the semblance of tanks or artillery that could have finished off his shattered invasion force.

In the midst of my musings, I was jarred to alertness by the sudden sight of a Japanese tank and column of soldiers about a quarter of a mile away coming up the road toward us. The tank was flying a Rising Sun flag, and marching tightly behind it was a column of about a hundred Japanese infantrymen. They were proceeding cautiously up the narrow, winding road carved out of the side of the mountain.

Immediately I stepped inside the tunnel and picked up a phone to call the duty officer. I recognized the voice as Lieutenant Commander Lowe. "Sir," I told him, "we have a Japanese tank and about a hundred soldiers advancing on us up the south road. What shall we do?"

The cease-fire wasn't scheduled to begin for another two hours yet, so we didn't know what this armed contingent of soldiers was up to. Compounding our anxiety, we'd heard rumors that when Bataan surrendered, the Japanese had continued shooting indiscriminately for another six hours. Even as I waited on the telephone, I could hear the occasional rattle of small-arms fire as certain pockets of resistance were still holding out. So at this point, anything was still possible.

All was quiet on the other end of the line. Then Lowe replied, "Berry, go out and meet the column."

As I hung up the phone, I could feel the hair on the back of my neck standing straight up. An enlisted man standing nearby asked me, "What are you going to do now?"

I told him, "I'm going out there to meet that Japanese column."

"I'm going with you," he volunteered.

Now, I didn't know who that man was; I had never met him before, but I did admire his courage. As for myself, I knew that I was extremely frightened at the time, and I assumed that he was every bit as scared as I was. The way I saw it, anything could happen to me. For all I knew, I was walking to my death.

Nevertheless, I walked out there. I had no steel helmet on. Thank goodness for that, or I would have been shot as a combatant. I was wearing my regular officer's hat and fatigue uniform. I carried no sidearm.

I just walked out there. And the enlisted man followed right behind me.

We had walked a couple of hundred yards down the road by the time the Japanese column got up to where we were. I saluted the leader. He was merely a sergeant, but I didn't know that at the time. For all I knew about Japanese military insignia, he could have been a general. Anyway, I saluted and he saluted back. He gave me a little bow and then motioned for me to follow along after him, which I did.

We came to a place in the road where an overturned car had been booby-trapped with a seventy-five-pound land mine. I knew, because I had been watching when the mine was put there. That mine was so powerful that it would have wiped out anything that stood within fifty feet of it. Before I realized what was happening, however, the tank sergeant ordered some of the Japanese soldiers to push the car over the side of the cliff so as to make way for the tank to pass. I steeled myself for the explosion. But thank heavens, the mine did not go off. (I learned later that our guys had disarmed that mine at the same time as the other weaponry.) I'm sure that if it had exploded and somehow I had survived the blast, the Japanese certainly would have finished me off. Anyway, I heaved a tremendous sigh of relief as we watched the car tumble down the cliff some two-hundred feet or so and come to rest by the water's edge below.

The tank proceeded farther up the road until it came to the stack of small arms that we had piled outside the entrance to one of the laterals that went into the Queen Tunnel. It couldn't get past. The Japanese sergeant pointed at me and indicated I should move the guns. I turned to the enlisted man that was with me and asked, "Can we get some help out of that tunnel?"

He replied, "You bet we can." He rushed into the tunnel, and in less than a minute he came back with another four or five sailors. They pitched in and threw the weapons over the side of the cliff so that the tank could get past.

The sergeant looked around, eyed this person and that, then finally settled on me. He pointed directly at me and said something in Japanese, which I couldn't understand. Finally, using gestures, he made it clear that he wanted me to crawl up on the tank and sit on the turret. Why? I didn't know. Nonetheless, I climbed up on the turret and sat there with the Japanese flag — the Rising Sun — flapping over my shoulders.

The enlisted man looked at me and asked, "Sir, why are the Japanese putting you up there?"

I couldn't tell him. I couldn't speak. I tried to form the words, but they just wouldn't come out. My voice had completely left me. It was at that moment that I knew I was even more afraid than I could have imagined.

Then the tank lurched down the roadway with the column of troops following after and me riding on top. I had no idea why they wanted me up on that tank. My mind raced; imagining all sorts of things. I was positive I was going to die . . . at least, I felt that I had reached my time and that I was going to leave this earth. It didn't enter my mind that it could be any other way.

I looked down one side of the roadway and saw a cliff down to the sea; on the other side was a wall of solid rock reaching up several hundred feet above me. On the roadway behind me was more than a hundred Japs, all of them with their guns cocked and in the ready position. And I was perched up against the barrel of this cannon. So I knew I was gone.

Then I said to myself, *Berry, how can you be brave?* I couldn't understand how a person can act so cowardly under certain circumstances and so bravely under others.

As the tank went around a little bend in the roadway that led down to Bottomside, we had a view of South Dock stretched out on one side and North Dock on the other, with about half a mile of level ground. And massed there were thousands upon thousands of Japanese troops.

After we had traveled down the road a little farther, the sergeant called the column to a halt and motioned for me to get down off the tank. I jumped down, and he asked me for something; but not speaking Japanese, of course, I didn't know what he had in mind. Pretty quick, it became clear that he was looking for some kind of souvenir from me. I pulled out my billfold and offered him money. But no, he didn't want money; he wanted a souvenir. Finally, when I couldn't produce one, he just shook his head in disgust and motioned for me to go join the other American prisoners who had already been assembled there.

I was elated to be still alive. I felt a great joy, an immense sense of relief. A few moments earlier I had resigned myself to death, and now I was alive.

The other American captives didn't understand. They couldn't. Most of them were very frightened. They didn't know what was going to happen to them, and they didn't think I had any business appearing so elated. But I was.

It began to dawn on me why the Japanese sergeant had wanted me up there on that tank. Even though General Wainwright had made a surrender offer and had ordered his troops to throw down their weapons, the Japanese had not yet accepted the surrender. As far as this sergeant and his troops knew, they were still fighting the Americans. Therefore, he put me up on the tank to be a human shield in case any Americans should start firing on him.

Reflecting on that experience, a remarkable insight came to me: if you think you're going to die, you can be a hero.

CHAPTER FIVE

MARCH OF SHAME

THE Japanese didn't plan on taking any prisoners. That was not their custom, not their style. In their military code, all soldiers fight to their last breath and never think of surrendering to the enemy. Similarly, they expected the defenders of the Philippines to fight to the last man—as did their own troops whenever they were surrounded. Consequently, the Japanese looked on the American prisoners as cowards and treated them accordingly.

But now they found themselves with ten-thousand prisoners of war on their hands—seven-thousand American soldiers, sailors, and marines, and three-thousand Filipino civilians. Nothing had prepared them for dealing with a problem of this magnitude. They had no plans in place, nor had they any established protocols for dealing with prisoners of war. If we thought we had seen confusion in the tunnels, the situation immediately following surrender was beyond description.

A surprising number of people committed suicide that day rather than be taken prisoner. I don't have the exact numbers, but there were quite a few. Many men jumped off the cliffs. One man found a discarded hand grenade and simply blew himself up.

As first, no Japanese officers were directing or organizing the prisoners of war; no one was telling us where to go or what to do. So with nothing else to do, many of us wandered back into the tunnels, where we could be with what few personal possessions we owned.

We hadn't been back in the tunnels for more than a few minutes until they called us out again. About eighty-five of us were assembled into formation in front of Queen Tunnel, four abreast, making a column of twenty rows or more. Then they marched us back down the same narrow road where I had so recently ridden terror-stricken atop the Japanese tank.

Marching alongside me was Chaplain Trump, a marine chaplain with whom I was already acquainted. He was wearing a little cross on his lapel. Trump leaned over and whispered to me as we were marching along, "Bill, do you think they are going to take us out and execute us?"

"I don't think so," I told him, "but we'll just have to go ahead and see what happens." Trump was not alone in his concern; a lot of people in that column thought we were on our way to be shot.

After we had marched quite a distance down the mountain, with a high cliff on one side and a drop-off to the ocean on the other, we came to a little clearing. The Japanese called the column to a halt and ordered us to take off all our clothes. Why, I don't know. Some people began crying, thinking that this was their final moment, that the Japanese were going to strip us before shooting us. When one officer moved a little hesitantly, and a soldier came over and hit him over the head with his rifle butt and practically knocked him out. The man immediately started disrobing—as did we all. All of our clothing was thrown into one massive pile.

However, no sooner had everybody taken off their clothes and thrown them onto this huge pile than the Japanese ordered us to put our clothes back on again. Immediately, there was a mad scramble as we tried to find our own clothes, which were all mixed up together in the one pile. Seeing that there was little hope of finding my own again, I settled for getting a pair of shoes that were way too big for me, a battered officer's hat that was two sizes too large, and an ill-fitting uniform. I don't think I got back a single item of the clothing I had worn there.

As soon as were were dressed again, they turned us around and marched us back to the tunnels we had just come from. I never did figure out why they made us undress like that, unless it was simply their way of showing us who was boss. Certainly, the humiliating experience made us realize we were captured prisoners who had to obey their commands.

It didn't take us long to discover that the Japanese could be vicious. One of the Japanese enlisted men had commandeered an American colonel to carry his gear for him. By now I had learned to tell Japanese enlisted men from officers. This colonel was an older, white-haired man, very distinguished looking. Why he was still in military service, I don't know; he should have been back stateside in a nice desk job. But here he was loaded down like a pack animal with this Japanese enlisted man's gear on his back, being beaten around the legs and head as he was forced to trot down the road carrying the heavy burden.

Once back in Queen Tunnel, we were left pretty much to our own devices. A bunch of the high-ranking officers had congregated in the mess hall, and I joined them, not knowing what else to do. As they were sitting around, somewhat dejectedly mulling their fate, a short, pudgy Japanese soldier came waddling through, and everyone jumped to attention. I guess this was a natural reaction of being in the service. Anyway, I could tell from his insignia that this guy was only a noncommissioned officer of some type. I said, "Oh, for heaven's sake, he's only a private."

Everybody sat down again as if on command. I thought to myself, *My goodness, I seem to have a lot of authority as a lowly ensign to be able order the top brass around this way.* I guess that in the midst of the confusion and lack of direction, when no one knows what's going on or what's expected of them, any voice of authority is welcome—even if it's from a mere ensign.

This Jap had just raided the kitchen and was carrying out a large No. 10 can of something, which I surmised to be peaches or pineapple. He looked over at us and said in almost perfect English, "I'm sorry, gentlemen, but this is war."

We all laughed at that. I figure he must have been to school in America, because he spoke our language very well.

Phil Sanborn came over to me. "Why don't you have a smoke?" he offered. "It will calm your nerves."

Now, I had never smoked before. As a matter of fact, all my life

I had been opposed to smoking, having been brought up that way by my parents. Also, my religion forbade smoking, and in the past I had thought of myself as being a pretty good church member. Nevertheless, under the circumstances I thought I'd give it a try.

Phil handed me a package of Lucky Strikes, offering, "As a matter of fact, here, take the whole carton."

He had two cartons with him, which he figured the Japanese would probably steal anyway. So I broke open the carton he handed me and stuffed the packs into my clothes.

When I lit up the first cigarette, I puffed away at it very tentatively, not inhaling the smoke. Rather, I just pulled the smoke into my mouth and savored the taste of it. It was amazing, though, how soothing that smoke was and how my nerves seemed less upset, much less tense. I said to myself as I began smoking my first cigarette, *Oh well, I certainly won't let this become a habit.*

We stayed in the tunnel that first night. I even slept in my old cot. Our only disturbance came during the middle of the night when some Japanese soldiers came through to make sure we had no guns. Everyone started scrambling frantically to look under their bunks to make sure they didn't have some forgotten or misplaced weapon lying under there. But that was our only disturbance of the night.

The following day we were ordered to get our gear together and fall into columns. The only thing I carried with me was the little leather bag I had brought from the states, along with a few things I was able to get into it.

The Japanese marched us down the hill and out toward Monkey Point, where the hangar used to be for the navy PBY patrol planes. The planes had long since gone, of course, carrying with them as many evacuees as they could, mostly nurses. And the hangar was no longer there, having been obliterated by the bombing.

On the way, we were accosted by a funny-looking Japanese

corporal in a short-sleeved shirt who had dozens of wristwatches up and down his bare arms. He looked like a character out of the comic strips. As prisoners walked past him, he would say, "Taimu? Taimu?" and point to each of us. If someone had the misfortune to look down at his watch, the corporal would immediately grab it. He wasn't the only one. All along the route, soldiers were shaking down the prisoners for their valuables.

Now, I happened to be carrying with me a Hamilton pocket watch, which was my law school graduation gift from my parents and to which I had quite a bit of emotional attachment. This watch had an enameled white-and-gold case with my initials engraved on the back. At the time I thought it was the finest watch on the planet.

So here was this guy was pointing a gun at me and demanding, "Taimu? Taimu?"

I looked him squarely in the eye and said, "Nope. No taimu." He pushed me aside and went on to the next prisoner.

When we got down to the hangar area, the Japanese herded us into a barbed-wire enclosure that had hastily been erected on bare ground for our benefit. I guess they chose the area because it would be easy to guard. The American prisoners were segregated into one group and the Filipinos into another.

More than ten-thousand of us were herded into this relatively small area, creating a teeming mass of humanity. No water. No shelter. No toilets. No food. Not even a blade of grass. Just bare, flat ground.

The hot tropical sun beat down on us unmercifully. The oppressive heat, made even worse by the extreme humidity, kept us perspiring profusely.

The nearest available water was about a mile back up the road toward Malinta Tunnel. Details were organized to go back and get water to distribute among the prisoners. We scavenged anything that was capable of holding water—canteens, glass jugs, bottles, tin cans, anything at all.

Somehow, Sanborn and I came in possession of two square, five-gallon galvanized cans. My guess is that originally they had held cooking oil or something. The tops had been cut off, and there were no handles. To avoid the awkward task of carrying them in a kind of bear hug, we punched two holes in the sides of the cans and strung some wire through the holes to make bails. We scrounged a pole about six feet long that was strong enough to hold two buckets of water, and we rigged up the pole with one end on each of our shoulders and the two cans slung in the middle between us.

By the time we got to where we were going, there was already a long line of prisoners ahead of us waiting their turn. It wasn't hard to see what the holdup was: there was only one spigot, and the water pressure was so low that it took quite a while to fill up each container. I guess we must have stood in line a good forty-five minutes or more with the hot sun beating down on us before our turn came. Fortunately for me, I still had on that old, battered officer's cap that I had salvaged out of that big pile the day before, and it afforded me some slight measure of protection from the sun's rays.

That wait gave me an opportunity to look around and survey the damage done by the bombardment. I was unprepared for the amount of devastation that had taken place. The bombardment had blown out absolutely everything. Gone were all the utilities, the stone tower, buildings, hangars, and improvements, all the bakery shops, all the shops of the merchants. Before the bombing, this had been a thriving area. Now there was nothing but utter devastation.

As I looked around me, I could see many dead American defenders. For example, about thirty yards away was a marine sergeant, bloated in the hot sun, lying there with his arm sticking up in the air as if he were getting ready to throw a hand grenade when he was struck down. He was all stretched out and looked to be about six foot five and weighing 250 pounds—but that could be deceiving, because his body was so swollen in the hot sun.

The Japanese had already carried away their own dead. Now I could see American details going around to gather up the swollen bodies and bloated corpses of the American dead. I didn't know where they were taking the bodies. I hoped that those brave men would be getting a dignified burial in a military cemetery somewhere and that their graves would be properly marked for the benefit of their families, who might want to visit them someday.

After filling our cans with water, we trudged back the long mile to the compound with our heavy burden. The two cans of water weighed over a hundred pounds. My shoulder developed a painful raw sore at the point where the pole rubbed. I kept trying to reposition the pole to relieve the pressure, but to do so, I would have had to hold one of the cans with one hand and the pole with the other to keep the water from splashing or tipping over—an obvious impossibility.

About four o'clock in the afternoon, the guards wheeled in a big cauldron of rice. That was our only meal of the day. Nothing but gluey brown rice. Several of the prisoners just looked at it and turned away. They were hungry, of course, but they couldn't bring themselves to eat that tasteless glop without any salt or seasoning. (Time took care of our finickiness, however, and it wasn't long until all of us developed a greater appreciation for rice . . .)

Nightfall came, and with it came the rain. And did it rain! We had no shelter or protection of any kind. A few prisoners had been able to salvage boards or scraps of corrugated iron from the demolished hangar, but I wasn't so fortunate. The bare ground beneath our feet turned to a sea of soupy mud. As I stood there ankle-deep in muck and with rainwater pouring down over me, Phil Sanborn came up to me and commented, "One thing, Bill . . . we can't lose our sense of humor. The minute we lose our sense of humor, we'll be dead. So you and I are going to have to laugh."

Then, almost as an afterthought, Phil added, ". . . and when I look at you, I can't help laughing."

The trauma of defeat began to weigh heavily on us. Some men developed acute anxiety attacks, causing them to shiver and shake uncontrollably, even to vomit.

Exacerbating the agony were the primitive conditions under which we lived. The area had no sanitation facilities whatsoever. Initially, whenever a man needed to relieve himself, he would just find an unused patch of ground. But with thousands of men crowded into such a confined area, that practice soon became untenable. The ground everywhere was littered with human waste, and the flies that this waste attracted were everywhere and in everything. A few enterprising individuals foraged some materials that they could use as primitive shovels to hack out open-air straddle trenches. Those trenches were a godsend, because so many of the prisoners had by now contracted diarrhea and dysentery. Men had to wait in long lines for the privilege of using the trenches; however, when one has dysentery he cannot wait very long—and he may go wherever he happens to be.

From time to time teams of men were called out by the Japanese to work on burial details. The groups were sent out with handcarts to collect the American dead—a grisly task, for by this time the bodies were grotesquely decomposing in the tropical sun and they stank horribly. Bodies by the hundreds were gathered from where they had fallen along the shoreline, at the inland defense positions, and outside Malinta Tunnel. The corpses were stacked up like cordwood in an open area, doused with a flammable liquid, and burned without ceremony.

Mingling with some of the members of General Wainwright's staff, we got the true story about the shameful and humiliating way Wainwright was treated by the Japanese commander, General Homma, when he tried to surrender. According to the reports, General Wainwright had sent a message to General Homma saying that he wished to meet with him and work out the terms of surrender. Simultaneously with his message to Homma, and fully expecting acceptance of it, Wainwright ordered the troops on Corregidor to haul down the American flag and to destroy their weapons.

Despite this message, and even though only the formalities of surrender remained to be worked out, the Japanese guns did not cease in their bombardment of the island, and Japanese troops continued their advance toward Malinta Tunnel. So Wainwright requested an immediate face-to-face meeting.

Homma refused to accept Wainwright's offer to surrender, saying that unless it included all of the American forces in the Philippines, he would continue his assault on Corregidor. Reportedly, he flew into a rage and stormed out of the meeting when Wainwright insisted that he had command of only the garrison on Corregidor.

With Homma's rejection, Wainwright was faced with a terrible choice. The American forces on Corregidor had already destroyed all their weapons and were now totally defenseless. If Wainwright refused, the lives of more than ten-thousand people hung in the balance—many of them already survivors of Bataan—and they would face almost total slaughter.

In the end, Wainwright acceded to Homma's terms. He surrendered all of the American forces in the Philippines. Then as an act of further humiliation, Homma forced Wainwright to make his surrender to a junior officer.

When I heard this, it made me all the more jittery about the foolhardiness of my walking down the road to meet the Japanese tank and troop column. Not only had the tank commander not been informed of Wainwright's surrender, but Homma had actually rejected Wainright's offer. As far as the Japanese were concerned, we were still officially at war.

We existed for about ten or eleven days in the mud and filth of this crowded area. *Existed* is hardly the word for it. *Survived* might be the more appropriate term.

Dick Tirk came over to me and asked, "Where's Sanborn? Have you seen Sanborn?"

I said, "Not lately. Why?"

"Well, we need to talk."

"What about?" I asked.

"Escape, that's what!"

We located Sanborn, and the three of us found ourselves a spot where we could be alone and talk out of earshot of other prisoners.

Dick said, "I've been thinking. If the future we've got to look forward to is anything like what we're experiencing here, then we've got to figure out a way to get out of here. This is no way for human beings to exist."

Phil said, "Well, we can't leave from here. There's no place to hide on Corregidor; they'd find us in half an hour. And there's no way we can swim off the island."

"I don't mean for us to leave from *this* place. The Japs aren't building any permanent facilities here, so that means one of two things: either they're going to shoot us or they're going to transfer us. The way I have it figured, sooner or later they're going to have to transfer us to some more permanent facility. That's the time we need to make a break for it."

"Well, do you have any suggestions?" I asked.

"Not yet, but if we're ever going to make our escape, it'll have to be early in the game, before we get settled into a prison routine. Once people get into an organized prison routine, it becomes very difficult to escape. The best time to escape is when there's a lot of confusion, like when we're being transferred from one place to another or something like that. So we need to be making our plans now, and we need to be looking for opportunities, so that when the right opportunity presents itself we'll be able to recognize it and be ready to take advantage of it."

Dick was doing most of the talking up to this point, while Phil and I were doing most of the listening. But what he said made a great deal of sense.

"Where would we go, assuming we were successful in breaking free?" Phil asked somewhat skeptically. "We don't know anything about the geography, we don't know the language, we don't even look like the people—we'd stick out like sore thumbs at a poker party."

"I don't really have the answer to that question. Not yet," Dick said. "But I do know this: If we don't have a plan, we're going to fail. If we do have a plan, we've got a chance."

The more we talked about it, the more convinced we became that we did want to escape.

Having now made a tentative decision to escape, we thought it prudent to avoid creating suspicion by spending too much time together, so we agreed that we would not to be seen together any more than necessary. After all, there was no way of knowing whom we could trust. As a further precaution, we agreed to guard our secret from even our closest friends and not bring anyone else in on the deal.

"Remember," Dick said, "he who fails to plan, plans to fail."

On our last day there, the Japanese rousted us out before dawn, gave us a rice ration, and lined us up in columns to march down to the dock area. Three ancient and rusting Japanese freighters were anchored a few hundred yards out in the bay. We were herded aboard barges and ferried out to the ships, where we were shoved into the holds with the hatches battened down behind us. It took nearly all day to complete the loading.

It was crowded and uncomfortable down there, and very, very hot. No food or water was provided, of course, but fortunately we did have plenty of air and we didn't suffocate.

We spent the night there.

Apparently this freighter had previously been used to transport Japanese troops, because there were a few bunks up against the sides of the hold. These so-called bunks were little more than bamboo slats, but at least they gave some of the men a place to stretch out. I lucked out and got one of them. And even though the slats creased into my bony body, it felt good to be able to lie down in a horizontal position — something I was not really able to do on the beach.

Of course, we didn't know where the Japanese were taking us. We didn't know what was going to happen. We were down in the dark hold of the ship, where we couldn't see anything. So the rumors got started. Some people thought they were taking us to Japan. Others thought we were going to Formosa. Some even thought they were hauling us out to sea to dump us over the side.

The next morning, the engines started up and the ship got underway. A couple of hours later the throbbing of the engines ceased. We didn't know if we were out at sea where they were going to dump us, or what. We didn't know where we were. Pretty soon the battens were lifted off the hatches and guards prodded us up into the blinding sunlight.

As my eyes adjusted to the light, I could make out that we were back in Manila. Instead of coming into the port area, which one would expect, however, we were anchored a few hundred yards offshore near the Yacht Club. This placed us about two miles farther south, at the end of Dewey Boulevard.

The prisoners were ordered to disembark down cargo nets over the side of the ship onto lighters. The lighters would haul them to about fifty feet from shore, where they were forced to jump into waist-deep water and wade the rest of the way to shore.

As soon as I saw what was happening, I tried to take off my shoes before going into the water so as to keep them from getting wet. Somehow, I seemed fixated on the idea that getting my GI shoes wet would ruin them, and I certainly did not want to spend the rest of my time in prison without shoes. Unfortunately, I had barely loosened the laces on my left shoe and got it half off before I was unceremoniously shoved over the side. Once in the water, I managed to jam my foot back down into the shoe again and was thus able to avoid losing it altogether as I waded toward shore.

After arriving on dry land, I tried to bend down and retie the laces, but the guards never allowed me to do it. I must have looked a sorry sight with that wet shoe flipping and flopping when I tried to walk.

It was nearly noon by the time they got all of the prisoners ashore and into the assembly area. We were formed up into columns of four abreast and paraded through the streets of Manila in what was intended to be a "March of Shame."

The purpose behind our being dumped in the water and forced to wade ashore became abundantly clear: the Japanese wanted the Americans to look even more bedraggled and pathetic than they already did. Obviously, the intent of the Japanese was to denigrate and humiliate us in front of the Filipinos in a great propaganda effort to show off their military invincibility.

Up Dewey Boulevard we marched and through the heart of the

city for five or six miles. Hundreds of thousands of Filipinos lined the streets.

The planned humiliation didn't succeed, however, because thethrongs of Filipinos who lined the streets cheered and made "V for victory" signs as we marched past; countless others simply stood there with tears streaming down their faces, and a few even tried to pass us food.

As we approached the center of Manila, someone started singing "God Bless America." That song was picked up and carried down the whole column. Pretty soon we were all singing at the top of our voices. I tell you, that was really something! Honestly and truly, I was never more proud to be an American than I was at that moment.

On and on we went, singing at the top of our lungs, with the Filipinos cheering us on both sides and the Japanese getting angrier and angrier. Japanese soldiers standing with the crowds were infuriated. Some took out their fury by striking the Filipinos; others vented their anger on prisoners by slinging out their rifle butts and hitting them on heads and arms, often drawing blood and occasionally knocking one down. But we went on singing anyway.

After marching five or six miles, shoes full of wet sand, feet aching and bleeding, knees feeling like rubber, and dizzy from the hot sun and lack of food or water, we staggered into Bilibid Prison. My left foot was in such agony from the constant rubbing of the loose shoe that I could hardly walk any longer. That wet, floppy shoe had rubbed a giant blister on my heel, which had burst from the unremitting walking.

We were not put into cell blocks; rather, the soldiers simply herded us into what I would describe as a holding area. Within that crowded arena, however, we were pretty much free to move around as we wished. There must have been five thousand or more of us shoehorned in an area designed to hold no more than eight hundred.

I inquired around to see if there happened to be anyone else from my state of Oklahoma. On the occasions when I did find a fellow Okie, it was like old home week. We'd swap stories about our respective hometowns, or colleges, or mutual acquaintances. A lot of our jabber was sheer bravado to keep our courage up, and it helped to take our minds off wondering about what was going to happen to us next.

Later, we were dished up a scanty meal of sour rice, the only food we'd had all day. Drinking water was plentiful, but there wasn't any place to wash or shave. No furniture or personal amenities of any kind were in this area; on the other hand, the place was dry and sheltered from the sun, and one could usually find a space to sit down or stretch out on the concrete floor.

I still carried with me the little leather bag of personal items that I had brought with me out of the tunnel on Corregidor. Thank heavens I hadn't tried to bring out a lot of stuff, or by now it probably would have been lost or taken away from me. The items I did carry were a safety razor and blades, comb, tooth-brush, and small bottle of iodine. For some reason, I had two white sheets; I don't know how I happened to have them, but they were easy to carry and I guess I thought I might make use of them. There were one or two other little necessities and a framed picture of my mother.

Not many guards were in evidence. Half-jokingly, I asked Tirk if maybe this was the opportunity we were looking for.

"Not yet," he said, "The prison walls are solid concrete and sixteen feet high, and they're topped with high-voltage wires carrying a lethal dose of electricity. We'll just have to bide our time, but I don't think our time is far away."

In this pressure cooker environment, the friendship among Phil Sanborn, Dick Tirk, and myself ripened rapidly. Why we felt so drawn to each other, I don't really know; probably it had something to do with our being three kindred spirits who found themselves facing the same set of adverse circumstances. We tended to have similar values, similar outlooks on life, and we tended to look on our situation pretty much in the same way. And whether we liked it or not, we seemed to be destined to share the same fate, whatever that fate might be.

Phil was easy to talk with, congenial and friendly; he never had a bad word to say about anyone or anything. As long as I knew him, I don't recall ever hearing him use a curse word.

Dick was a little this way too. Maybe not as outgoing as Phil— he didn't talk as much or laugh as much. Rather, Dick was the more serious and intellectual member of our threesome.

None of us knew what was out there on the "other side," but we were all three firmly of the same mind—that almost anything was preferable to spending our lives in a Japanese prison. Already we could read the handwriting on the wall; it seemed to be saying to us, "Escape or die."

Bilibid Prison was a fortresslike structure built a hundred years or so ago by the Spanish to house murderers and rapists and other dregs of human society. The prison was located in the heart of Manila and covered an area of about six square blocks. The main prison consisted of eleven long, low, one-story cell blocks, one large main building; a two-story administration building, four two-story L-shaped buildings (one at each corner); a separate execution chamber; and a small building that was used for solitary confinement.

The prison grounds were laid out in the form of a wheel, of which the round central guardhouse served as the hub and the long, low buildings the spokes. A sixteen-foot stone wall ran around the perimeter, topped by a walk on which guard towers were erected at certain intervals. The Japanese had erected a twelve-foot wall right down the center, which separated the POW section from the MP section.

In addition, a back section was separated from the main prison areas by another twelve-foot wall. Back here was one three-story building that lacked a roof, along with three low buildings that had originally served as barracks but now were converted to prison use.

The walls all the way around the prison, including the interior walls, were topped with high-voltage electrical wires to make sure that no one escaped alive. Definitely, Bilibid was not the place from which to launch our great escape.

Freedom would have to wait for a better day.

CHAPTER SIX

ESCAPE FROM CABANATUAN

ON our second day at Bilibid Prison, about five-hundred men were called out for transportation to Cabanatuan, about sixty-five miles north of Manila. Tirk, Sanborn, and I managed to go out with that group.

The detail was formed into columns of four and marched through Manila to the railway station, about a mile away. We were crammed like sardines into waiting steel boxcars, 150 men to a car, jammed together so tightly that even if someone passed out he probably wouldn't have been able to fall down. As if that weren't miserable enough, the steel body of the cars heated up like an oven under the hot rays of the sun, and before long we were drenched in our own body sweat and our neighbor's urine.

The train trip lasted about ten hours. Even though we made several stops at little villages along the route, those stops served only served to heighten our thirst and our hunger.

From where I was standing, I had a view through a crack in the door and could see many Filipinos lining the station platforms trying to get a glimpse of the American prisoners. Vendors were going up and down the platforms selling candy, soft drinks, and various other sundries, but the guards never opened the doors or let us buy anything.

It was already dark by the time we got to Cabanatuan City, and a great many of the men were suffering from dehydration and heat prostration. We were all in a sorry and distressed state. Nevertheless, our journey was not yet over. The Japanese made us get into columns and march about two miles away to a schoolyard, where we spent the night. The yard was fenced, and the school building itself, like most rural Filipino structures, was elevated about five feet above ground on bamboo stilts.

The Japanese guards here were some of the fiercest and most menacing I think I have ever seen. Every one of them had his bayonet fixed on his rifle, and they jabbed at us repeatedly with the bayonet points to keep us moving along.

After we had been in the schoolyard about an hour, the Japanese trucked in a big tub of rice. The prisoners all scrambled to get in line for food because we hadn't eaten a thing since before daylight. Unfortunately, the tub didn't hold enough rice for everyone, so those of us who didn't move fast enough didn't get to eat.

Wherever we could find space to stretch out on the ground we bedded down. Hardly had we gotten settled, however, before it started to rain—a veritable downpour. The annual rainy season

Boxcar on siding at San Fernando in which were packed Death March prisoners on the trip from San Fernando to Capas. Courtesy of Dr. Paul Ashton.

was now upon us. Water began collecting in the hollow where I lay trying to sleep, and I had to move. I managed to find sanctuary under the school building. It was strictly standing room only—over five-hundred people trying to crowd into a space scarcely more than fifty feet square and not high enough for a typical American to stand erect. But it was dry, and that's what counted.

Without consciously seeking him out, I found that I was standing next to Phil Sanborn. Phil looked over at me and said, "Berry, you look about as funny as I feel."

We started laughing at that. I don't know why it seemed so funny at the time, but it did. I guess we were giddy. Humor can be a way of controlling fear. Certainly we were making something humorous out of nothing. Again Phil reminded me that we dare not lose our sense of humor.

"Is it time?" I asked jokingly, alluding, of course, to the idea of escaping.

"Not yet," he said solemnly. "But very soon." That expression became kind of a standing joke among us.

Early the next morning they herded us into a loosely formed column of twos and marched us out. By this time I was desperately hungry, not having eaten for more than twenty-four hours, but no one came around with a rice ration. Fortunately, I did have the presence of mind the night before to fill my canteen with runoff rainwater, so taking an occasional small sip of water helped to ease the hunger pangs somewhat.

Of course, I had no way of determining whether the water was contaminated or not, so to be on the safe side I put a couple of drops of iodine in it from the small bottle I carried with me from Corregidor for just this purpose. I hoped that perhaps the iodine might kill off whatever germs might be in the water. We had been cautioned all along not to drink water unless we made sure it was not contaminated in any way. Dysentery was a constant fear among all the prisoners. Many died from it.

We didn't know where we were headed, but it took us all day to get there. About every two hours, we'd stop for a brief rest

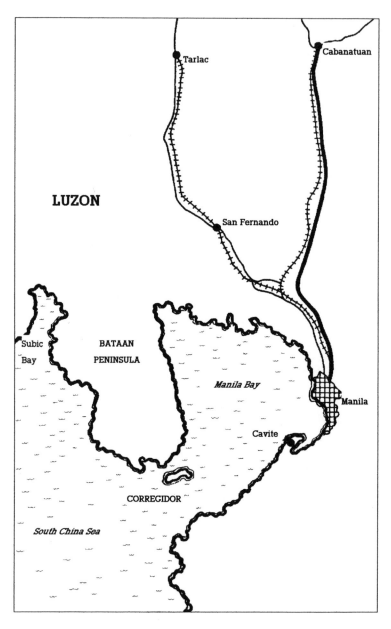

Central Luzon. Death March prisoners were marched from Bataan to San Fernando, transported by railway boxcars to Tarlac, and finally marched again to Cabanatuan. Map by Jim Alexander.

period. The officer who happened to be marching next to me was someone I had previously known, a Lieutenant McGowan, who had been with the naval intelligence office in Manila. McGowan, an outstanding individual, had been very kind and courteous to me. I think I especially appreciated his being a reserve officer who didn't carry an outsized opinion of himself, as many of the academy graduates seemed to do. In my experience, when it came to guts and courage and standing up under pressure, the reserve officers held up every bit as well as did the academy men.

As the day wore on, however, Lieutenant McGowan began perspiring heavily. His shirt and trousers became soaked. And the more he perspired, the more he pleaded for water. Finally, I gave him a little from my canteen. I cautioned him to drink as little as possible. McGowan kept begging for more water, and each time I insisted that he take as little as possible.

It was late afternoon by the time we reached our destination, a partially completed Philippine army training that the Japanese were now using as a POW camp. It was known as Cabanatuan POW Camp No. 2. Much to our shock and horror—and probably to the dismay of our captors as well, who, after all, hadn't wanted to be saddled with prisoners in the first place—the camp had no water supply. Again, that miscue further demonstrated to me that the Japanese had made no plans whatsoever for handling prisoners of war.

At this stage of the game, there wasn't much else for us to do but to spend the night there. Shelter from the monsoon rains was available by crowding inside the barracks, thatched with nipa palms, that had been built to house Philippine army troops. Again, I refilled my canteen with rainwater. This time, not only was I able to dose it with a few drops of iodine, but I was also able to nestle the canteen amid the hot coals of a small campfire and heat the water to the boiling point. As soon as the water cooled sufficiently, I drank every bit of it with gusto and in full confidence that whatever germs may have lingered there were now defunct. Then I repeated the procedure so I could have enough water for the following day.

Sanborn rounded up Tirk and me. We went off to a spot away from the other prisoners. Sanborn was grinning like the proverbial cat that ate the mouse. "Guess what I've got?" he asked, grinning from ear to ear.

"Heavens, I wouldn't have the faintest idea," I replied.

He reached into his tow sack and pulled out a small, thin, battered school textbook. "Look at this," he said proudly, holding it up where we could see.

Dick and I must have looked somewhat perplexed, unable to focus clearly in the fading light.

"It's a geography book," Phil said excitedly. "A grade school geography book. And it's got a map of the Philippines in it."

Now, that was a treasure worth more than gold to us. It was our passport out of prison. With this map, we would be able to plot our path and know where we were going.

"Where in the world did you get it?" I asked in wonderment.

"Under that school building last night. There was a stack of old books there that I guess someone had thrown away. And as I was rooting through them, I came across this old geography book. I couldn't believe my luck."

"Well, don't let anybody get it from you, because we're going to need it," Dick said.

The following morning we were formed into columns of four again and marched back down the same road that we had trudged up the day before. Heat exhaustion and diarrhea took its toll. Many fell out along the roadside, Lieutenant McGowan among them. I tried to help him as best I could, but he was too weak to go on. I hated to leave him behind.

We took it for granted that the fallen prisoners would be bayoneted or shot. Much to our surprise, however, the Japanese went out in a truck and picked up the stragglers. Instead of killing them; they just hauled them in and dumped them in the camp.

After several hours of marching in the heat of the tropical day, with only a couple of rest stops along the way, we arrived at another Philippine army camp. I recognized this camp to be one that we had passed by the previous day. It was called Cabanatuan

POW Camp No. 1. In terms of physical layout, it was nearly a carbon copy of Camp No. 2 — except it had a water supply.

Shortly before the war, the Philippine army had built three of these camps with the idea of using them as training camps. They were all nearly identical and only a few miles apart. Camp No. 3 was similarly converted for use by American prisoners, but to the best of my knowledge Camp No. 2 was simply abandoned after our abortive attempt to occupy it.

Camp No. 1 occupied about fifty acres of land and consisted of a large wooden building partitioned off into small offices, a dispensary building, a guardhouse, and a number of nipa-thatch barracks. Each barracks building had been designed for forty Filipino soldiers, but now each one housed 120 prisoners.

Sanitation simply did not exist. Latrines were dug at the far edge of the camp. But since this was rice paddy area, the water table was about two feet below the surface, and the latrines, never deep enough, kept filling up.

Tirk and Sanborn and I were still talking about escape. I can't say that we had fully made up our minds yet, but it did seem more plausible here than any place we'd seen before.

"Where would we go?" I asked.

"I've got it all figured out," Dick said. "We're up here at Cabanatuan, about a hundred miles north of Manila. The map shows the area east of here to be 'unexplored territory.' I figure that if it's unexplored on this map, then it must be unexplored to the Japs as well. If all goes well, we should be able to make our way over to the east coast, which is only sixty miles away, and then follow the coastline down to the southern end of Luzon. Our biggest danger will come when we pass Lamon Bay, because that's where the Japs made a landing, and they probably still have troops in the area. I don't think we'll find many Japs once we get down to the southern tip of the island. From there, we ought to be able to hire ourselves a boat to the other islands and eventually find our way to Australia."

"Well, Dick, how do you know we can make it?"

"To be truthful, I don't know. But I think we've got a pretty

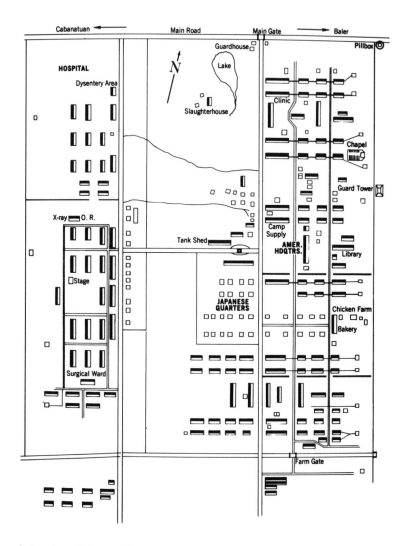

Cabanatuan Prisoner of War Camp No. 1, plan view. Courtesy of Dr. Paul Ashton.

good chance. Right now, the Japs are not very well organized. From what I've seen, they're masters of disorganization — both here in the prison camps and in their administration of the islands. The Filipinos hate them. So our best chance is to take advantage of the confusion and disorganization, and that time is now."

I persisted. "But Dick, we don't know what's out there. We haven't the faintest idea of what we'll be getting into. How do we know that we won't be jumping out of the frying pan and into the fire?"

"Bill, look at it this way, how long do you think we'd last in this camp? Not very long! And we'd be miserable doing it. As I see it, we really don't have a meaningful alternative."

I said, "Dick, let's sleep on it."

The next morning, the conversation started again. We saw the Japs stringing barbed wire around the perimeter of the camp. When Tirk saw the barbed wire going up, he said, "If we're going to go, we're going to have to do it tonight."

I was really beginning to have second thoughts about the wisdom of whole idea, and I told him how I felt. Just three days before we arrived, three American enlisted men had wandered away from camp, headed down the main road toward Cabanatuan. When they were picked up and returned to camp, one stated that he was planning to get a job in Manila, the second was planning to go to Australia, and the third thought he would hide out somewhere until the U.S. forces returned. The men were beaten and tortured for eighteen hours, then executed.

That sobering fate awaited us should we fail to make good our escape.

The thing that finally made up our minds was the sight of the survivors from Bataan who were being trucked in from Camp O'Donnell. Camp O'Donnell was the terminus of the Bataan Death March. Back on Corregidor we had heard rumors of how badly they were being treated, but we were unprepared for the shock of what we saw. Those guys all had malaria and dysentery and were so skinny that they looked like walking skeletons with skin hanging from their bones. There was absolutely no hope in their eyes. These were relatively young men in their late teens and early twenties—people who only a few months before had been in prime physical condition. But now they looked so old. So downtrodden.

We asked every prisoner we could what things were like at Camp O'Donnell. We found out that they were dying at the rate of sixty to seventy men a day. At that rate, the whole camp would die off pretty fast.

The terrible appearance of the survivors from Bataan—gaunt, jaundiced, emaciated from malaria and dysentery, utterly without hope—swept away any lingering doubts that Tirk, Sanborn, or I may have had about whether we were willing to spend the war in captivity.

Dick said, "It's tonight or never."

I agreed. Death in the quest for freedom was preferable to life in spiritless captivity.

There was no backing out now. I felt my stomach get weak. Butterflies, or whatever you call it when you are overwhelmed with anxiety—I had them.

We agreed to meet at the latrine. The best time to leave would be at dusk, when there was still a lot of movement and noises around the camp but the guards' eyes would not yet have adjusted to the darkness.

We tried to be careful not to be seen talking together too much so as not to arouse suspicion. Our biggest fear was that someone might catch onto our plans and report us to the Japanese. We didn't know who we could trust; we didn't even tell our senior officers what we were planning to do or try to enlist their support. Our obsession for secrecy was so extreme that I didn't even tell my bunkmate, Jack Woodside, my old apartment mate from Manila.

Woodside made the suggestion that I ought to donate the two sheets I was still carrying in my leather bag to the new prison hospital that some of the medical prisoners were planning to set up within the camp. Being fearful that if I gave them away too readily someone might put two and two together and come up with the idea that we were planning to escape, I told him that I would keep the sheets tonight but would let the hospital have them tomorrow. I knew, of course, that the next day the sheets would still be there but I would be long gone.

Time passed agonizingly slowly as we whiled away the hours waiting for night to fall. This was absolutely the hardest decision I ever had to make. Previously, when I had been in life-threatening situations, the danger had been imposed suddenly from without; the only control I had had was in how I controlled myself. This time, however, I was choosing to put my life in danger. No one forced me into it.

I used what little time I had left to sort through my few possessions to see which I needed to take with me and which I could leave behind. Because it was fairly common for prisoners to finger through their keepsakes and dream of happier days, my activity wasn't at all unusual and attracted any unwanted attention. Naturally, we would have to travel light. By some streak of good fortune, I found a gunnysack that someone had discarded. By looping a cord around its neck, I could make it almost the ideal thing to carry my gear in—lightweight, pliable, immensely practical, I would be able to carry it any number of ways—on my arm, slung over my shoulder, or even tied to my waist. I packed the small, brass-framed picture of my mother, which she had given me when I was thirteen or fourteen years old. I also took along an old army blanket, some medication, matches, and three or four hundred American dollars in paper money (called "American gold" over there), which I had sewn into the collar of my shirt. I think both Dick and Phil had about the same things.

As it began to get dark, I eased my way out of my bunk as if I were going to the latrine. By leaving my sheets there along with a few other personal possessions, it would look as if I'd be coming back. Woodside didn't even stir. As casually as I could, I walked toward the latrine, carrying the gunnysack nonchalantly in my hand as if it were a toiletry kit or something. I planned to say, if anyone had asked why I was carrying my ditty bag, "Because they steal things back there."

There was barely enough light to see the shadowy figures of Tirk and Sanborn. We met at the corner of the latrine. There didn't seem to be anyone else there at the time, which was so much the better for us. We tried to keep our voices low because we didn't know how far away a Japanese guard might be.

After a few whispered last-minute instructions, Dick said, "Let's get out." And he crawled out. The plan was that Dick would crawl out first, followed by Phil, and then me. The area we would be passing through was a low swale with grass grown up to about the height of a crawling man's back. After about a minute's wait, Phil crawled out after Dick.

Then it was my turn. My heart was pounding. I don't know what kind of courage it took, but it took more courage than anything I had ever done in my life for me to step off into the darkness. By this time the next day, I would be either a free man or a dead man.

Phil and Dick went first. They crawled out along a ditch. They got to the far edge of the camp and waited for me.

I decided I wasn't going to crawl; I was going to walk out of there as fast as I could. It was practically total darkness and no one could see anything. Then I hit a strand of barbed wire that I didn't know was there. I tripped and fell. I made such a tremendous noise that I thought anyone within a hundred yards could hear me.

Nothing happened. No one yelled. I jumped to my feet and started running.

Dick or Phil hissed at me, "Berry, get down. Get down."

I hissed back, "If they didn't hear me fall, they can't hear us running. So get up, and let's go."

So we took off. We ran and we ran. We didn't know exactly where we were going, but we wanted to put as much distance between us and the camp as we possibly could.

We ran hard for hours. There was no trail, just jungle and swamp. We hit things, we stumbled over things, and we fell. My face and arms were badly battered from running through brush and vines, which we couldn't see to avoid in the dark. If I hadn't been honed down to such fine physical condition on Corregidor, I probably wouldn't have had the stamina to do it. Certainly, if we had waited a few weeks in prison camp, we wouldn't have had enough strength left.

A gibbous moon, about a quarter past full, was now rising in the east. The moon gave us both a sense of direction and a fair amount of light to see our way. We wanted to keep going east.

After the first few hours we settled into a comfortable dogtrot. Whenever we came across a jungle trail that was headed our direction, we would follow that until it veered off in another direction. It was a lot easier and less hazardous when we had a trail to follow. When we ran out of trail again, we'd cut out across country through the underbrush. By now we were in the foothills of the mountains, the Sierra Madre, so the going was getting much tougher.

We kept up this pace all through the night, resting only for brief periods to catch our breath. By daylight, I guess we had put fifteen to eighteen miles between us and the camp. That distance may not seem like much to someone who has never traveled through the jungle, but considering the rugged country and unfamiliar terrain, we didn't think it was too bad.

Shortly after daylight, we noticed that a little Filipino man was following along not too far behind us. He followed us for quite a while. When we would stop, he would stop. When we speeded up, he would speed up. But he never came any nearer. We didn't know whether he was friendly or not, but we couldn't seem to shake him.

Along about midmorning, we came upon a barrio—a small Filipino village in a clearing in the jungle. There were six or eight *baihais*, which were charming little bamboo houses built on stilts about six feet off the ground and covered with nipa palm. The natives seemed friendly but a little afraid of us. We had no way of knowing what their attitude was toward the Japanese, or even if they knew about the Japanese up here in the jungle, but we decided to take a chance.

We made motions like we wanted to eat something. We picked out a couple of chickens, and even though we didn't speak the language, they seemed to be communicating something like, "Take them and get out of here." I guess we frightened them. Or maybe they feared reprisal from the Japanese if we were found there. So on impulse, I took out the picture of my mother and showed it to them. I don't know what they thought it implied, but they softened up toward us and began to show a little warmth. Someone brought out some rice to go with the chickens and a little pot to cook it in. We gave them some American money, and they seemed to be very happy to see us leave.

We trudged on up the mountainside a couple more hours until we came to a nice clearing, where we thought would make camp and spend the night. By now we had been running for eighteen hours straight and were dog tired.

Dick volunteered to cook one of the chickens for us, and Phil said he would cook the rice. I said that would be all right with me. What I didn't realize at the time was that Dick was a city boy who had never seen a chicken's head taken off before. He didn't have the faintest idea how to go about the task. I guess he thought that chickens came already dressed. Anyway, he got out a razor blade, stretched out the chicken's neck, and carefully slit the jugular vein. That chicken jumped up and flew out of his hands, spewing blood all over the place. It took off and found refuge high up in a tree where we couldn't reach it. Poor Dick was beside himself trying to figure out what to do.

I told him, "Well, let's just wait awhile and pretty soon that chicken will come down all by himself." Sure enough, the chicken slowly bled to death, began to totter, and finally toppled out of the tree.

"Dick," I said, "next time, I'll show you the right way to kill a chicken." I was raised in a small town and I grew up knowing how to kill a chicken. All you have to do is take it by the head and give it a quick snap of the wrist, and the head will jerk right off.

The little Filipino man who had been following us all day was still with us. He sat hunkered down near the edge of the clearing.

We decided that he meant us no harm, so we motioned him over. We offered to share our food with him, and he seemed very happy. Of course, we didn't speak his language, but he had picked up a few fractured words in English, which, with a lot of gesturing, enabled us to communicate after a fashion.

Macario was his name. He came from Mindanao, one of the southern islands. That meant he was of a different race and a different language from the Filipinos around here. As best as we could decipher it, Macario had been drafted into the Philippine army, but when the army surrendered to the Japanese he took off and escaped rather than be captured. So in a sense, he was in the same boat that we were.

We slept on the ground in our clothes. It might be more accurate to say that we just conked out. Our bodies were bone weary after a night and a day of running.

The next morning we started out again. Macario wanted to carry our gear. He was short but strong, and he insisted on doing it. He seemed to want to do it, and quite frankly we were happy to let him.

Macario carried a banjo. He wasn't much of a singer, but as we went along he would strum on his banjo. I think he knew only four words, "Every evening, Saturday night." He would sing those same words over and over again as he changed the tune. But somehow, he managed to make it sound like an American song.

We came to a place where the trail forked. We weren't sure which direction to take. Macario said something about the Philippine army, but we couldn't figure out what he was trying to tell us.

Anyway, we took the left fork, which eventually brought us to a big bamboo forest. I had never been in a bamboo forest before. It was like a fairy wonderland. Walking through it was like being in a giant asparagus patch. Bamboo is classified as a grass, but I had never seen any grass that grew to be six or eight inches thick and thirty or forty feet high—like trees, but without any branches. The foliage was green, but the trunks were yellow.

We went through a couple hundred yards of forest and came

out into a little valley that had lots of *baihais* in it. The people came out and greeted us. One kind woman said we could stay with her, and Macario was taken in by another family. So the three of us stayed and she cooked a meal for us. I can't tell you how wonderful that was. We tried to pay her, but she wouldn't accept any money. We slept in our clothes on bamboo mats on the floor, and the temperature was so comfortable that we didn't need even a blanket.

Breakfast the next morning was rice with mushrooms, and I swear, it was one of the most delicious breakfasts I ever tasted. Of course, we were already half-starved by the Japanese prison diet, and we had burned up a lot of energy running through the jungle, so our appetites couldn't possibly have been greater. Food never tasted better than it tasted now.

We took the time to look around a bit to see where we were. The *baihai* consisted of a single room, about twelve by twelve feet, with thatched roof and sides, and elevated about five or six feet off the ground on bamboo stilts. The family's pigs and chickens were kept under it. We had to climb up a bamboo ladder to get into the room. The floor was made of split bamboo with the slats spaced far enough apart so that crumbs and leftovers could sift down to the pigs and chickens below.

All of the family activities took place in this room. In one corner was a crucifix and a religious shrine. Evidently, this family was Catholic. There were a few basic necessities of life, such as pottery and clothing, and a large container in which the wife stored her rice. This woman had a large wooden box, maybe three by four feet, in which she stored a stalk of bananas. I learned that the bananas were cut green, then stored in the dark to ripen. Those were the smoothest, sweetest bananas that I can ever recall eating. Outside the baihai at ground level was a firebox where the family did its cooking.

As we were talking, and maybe relaxing a little too much, I happened to look out the window and saw a column of soldiers — rifles, uniforms, and all — coming right toward me. So I jumped out the opposite window and hit the ground running. I ran as hard as I could. The village happened to be located at the bottom of a little bowl-shaped valley with steep hills on each side. I clawed and scrambled up the side of a hill as fast as I could. I began to wonder why none of the soldiers were shooting at me, so I looked around. There they were, all standing and laughing as hard as they could.

Then it hit me like a brick: these were *Filipino* soldiers, not Japanese! And it was funny to them to see me so frantically clawing and scratching my way through the underbrush in a desperate attempt to get away. They knew I was an American, of course, and they knew that I thought they were coming to get me, so they found it highly amusing. When I saw that, I turned and laughed too. Never mind that my hands and feet and my knees were all scratched and bleeding from trying to get away, I realized how ridiculous and foolish I must have looked, and it suddenly seemed funny to me too.

Sheepishly, I came back down the hillside to where the Filipino soldiers were standing. It turns out that those fellows were very gracious and hospitable. They were members of a guerrilla band that was harassing the Japanese and causing all kinds of trouble. We learned that they were a part of a fairly large and well-organized resistance movement. There was a Communist group called the *Hukbalahap* in the area, but we didn't know if these people were part of that group.

We spent one more night in the village. We told the soldiers that we wanted to get out of there if we could, so they pointed out to us a route across the ridge of a mountain, telling us that when we came out on the other side we would be near the coast.

The next morning, the three of us were all ready to set out on our journey again with Macario, but the soldiers asked us to wait for a little while. They said that Marcos was coming. The name meant nothing to us, but they kept saying, "Marcos come, you wait. Marcos come, you wait." They seemed quite insistent, so we agreed to wait around and see who this Marcos was.

Sure enough, Marcos came. He was a pleasant-looking person and he spoke English quite well. He introduced himself to us as

Ferdinand Marcos and said that he was the leader of the Filipino resistance forces in that region, which was the Nueva Ecija Province. Marcos chatted with us a couple of minutes, then moved on to attend to some business with his own troops. A couple of hours later he left the camp in the company of a fairly large contingent of soldiers.

It dawned on us that the village we had stumbled into was actually a secret guerrilla camp for the resistance forces. Considering the number of soldiers around the area, it's a wonder we weren't shot at before being recognized.

We never found out why the soldiers wanted us to stay around to meet Marcos. He didn't pump us for any information, and he didn't ask us to join him, which was just as well, because we had had all the fight we wanted at that point. We just wanted to get as far away from there as possible and join our own forces in Australia. Our dream may have been far-fetched, but we had convinced ourselves that we weren't doing anything in that prison camp but watching people die, and we had already seen enough of that. We were sure that whatever evils may lie ahead for us, they couldn't possibly be worse than what we had already seen back there in the prison camp.

So we set off again on our journey across the mountain, but this time we were heavily laden with provisions that the villagers had given us. We went single file. Dick led the way up the mountain trail, Phil Sanborn and I followed along carrying a bamboo pole with our provisions between us, and Macario brought up the rear. Phil carried one end of the pole on his shoulder, and I the other end. Tied in the middle was a cage with a chicken inside it, a bag of rice, our cooking utensils, and a few other things our hosts thought would be useful to us on our journey.

Just as we were most exposed in crossing the top of the ridge, a Japanese observation plane flew over. Of all the rotten luck! Trapped out in the open with very little tree cover and no place to hide, we had to restrain the strong temptation to run. Running would only attract attention to ourselves. So we did the only thing we could do under the circumstances, and that was to try to pass ourselves off as Filipinos. From the air, maybe the pilot wouldn't be able to tell the difference. Fortunately, we weren't wearing any recognizable military uniforms or headgear, so we just ducked our heads down and waved at the plane as it flew past. We hoped the pilot would think we were a little a group of Filipinos crossing the mountain down there. I suppose it also worked to our benefit to have Macario along with us, because that made us into a group of four rather than just the three who had escaped. Anyway, for whatever the reasons, the Japanese plane passed over us and flew on down the ridge.

We didn't take any breaks for lunch or rest because we were anxious to cover as much distance as possible. At one point Phil happened to notice that our chicken had laid an egg in its cage. "Let's eat it," he suggested.

"Fine,", I said, "but what about Dick?" Tirk was twenty or thirty yards ahead of us up the trail.

Phil said, "He's too far up there anyway, so we'll eat it and he won't know the difference." So the two of us ate the egg and didn't tell Dick. That was the first time I can remember eating a raw egg, but it tasted delicious. It's amazing how good food tastes when one is hungry enough.

It was still daylight when we made it down off the ridge of that mountain. We were now back in deep forest. When we came upon a small pond, we decided here was a good place to put up for the night. Dick looked down into the water to see if there were any fish or shellfish to supplement our diet. The only thing he found was a bunch of small, snail-like creatures that had cork-screw-shaped shells, kind of like Christmas tapers. They looked to be edible, so we fished out several of them and boiled them in a pot to go with our rice.

The only way we could figure out how to eat them was to break off one end of the shell and suck out the insides. There was lots of dark, muddy-looking stuff along with the chewy meat, but we ate it all anyway along with our rice. I must confess, however, that even as hungry as we were, the food did not taste as good as the raw egg had. Nevertheless, we had burned up lots of energy and needed the protein, so we ate it anyway.

Darkness came very quickly, as it always does in the tropics. The only covering we had was one shelter half that the Filipinos had given us. A shelter half is one half of a pup tent; ordinarily, soldiers hook two shelter halves together to make a pup tent to sleep under. But in our case we only had one shelter half among the three of us. Macario curled up in his clothes. As luck would have it, it began to rain—very hard. We were in a thick forest with heavy foliage all around us, but that didn't protect us from the falling rain. So the three of us crowded together on top of one another under our lone shelter half, and that's how we spent the night.

The rain ended the next morning, and as soon as the sun came out we forgot all about the hardship we had endured the previous night. Dick cooked up a little rice and we got back on the trail.

Along about midafternoon we came to a clearing near a paved road. I didn't think we should venture out onto the road, but Dick insisted, "Come on. Let's go. We can make better time this way."

We hadn't been out on the highway more than fifteen or twenty minutes, however when we were spotted by a group of Filipinos. We eyed them warily, because we had no way of knowing whether they were friendly or hostile. They watched us, and we watched them.

Finally I couldn't stand it any longer, and I blurted out, "My gosh, if they wanted to capture us it would be easy to do. We can't outrun them, and even if we did manage to lose them, they could find us in the jungle. So let's try to get them to come over and see what they want."

We motioned for the Filipinos to come over, and they did. Their leader, a fellow named Juan, spoke a little English. Luck was still with us, for these people were friendly toward the United States. As yet, the Japanese army hadn't been in the area to indoctrinate and intimidate them.

Juan led us to their barrio. It was a village of some fifty or sixty huts, all built on stilts. The whole town turned out to welcome us.

What a feast! They put on the most elaborate meal one could possibly imagine in such a primitive setting. The people were all barefoot, but the men were neatly dressed in trousers and shirts. The women wore skirts. The married women were bare on top, but the unmarried women wore a covering over their breasts.

The people escorted us into a central area where the cooking was taking place. The first thing they served us was popcorn. I never expected to get popcorn out here in the middle of the jungle. Then they started bringing out ears of sweet corn that they had roasted in a pit. A bowl of warm coconut oil was set before us; we would dip the ears of corn into the oil, then sprinkle on some salt and eat them. Dick and Phil and I ate corn as if it were going to be our last meal on earth. I would guess that among the three of us, we must have put away a good two dozen or more roasting ears.

Then they said, "Now we're going to feed you." We were ceremoniously led into one of the largest of the *baihais*, where the women had already prepared a meal and laid it out for us. There was every kind of Filipino food imaginable: fried foods, boiled foods, fruits of every variety, camotes (a kind of sweet potato), abundant rice and numerous side dishes to go with the rice. The meat dishes were boiled shrimp and crispy fried fish fillets.

We were then introduced to a new dish, which the Filipinos call *balut*. This was a duck egg that was fertile and near to the point of hatching. The Filipinos boiled them and served them like hard-boiled eggs. Inside you could see the head, beak, body and legs. About a third of it was yolk. It was a disgusting-looking thing, but it was supposed to be a tasty treat, and I hated to disappoint our hosts. So I poured a lot of salt on it, closed my eyes, screwed up my courage, and bit in. Really, it didn't taste half bad.

After all this they brought out fried bananas for dessert, sliced thin like potato chips and deep-fried in coconut oil.

It was late in the day by the time we finished eating. Several of the men said they were going to take us to a place where we could hide out. My stomach was full of that good food, but all of a sudden it tied up into a knot. During those wonderful festivities, I had temporarily forgotten the fear of the Japanese that remained constantly with us. Now that fear came back.

The men led us up a cliff that overlooked the little valley where the village lay. We had to climb practically straight up at certain points. I was so weak that I couldn't climb, and two Filipinos had to pull me along to get me up the trail. I didn't realize it at the time, but I was coming down with a fever.

Finally, after a couple of hours we got to where we were going. The view over the valley was magnificent. We could see the highway like a black ribbon running right down through the middle of the valley. The setting sun bathed everything in a magical, otherworldly light.

Macario came with us. I had forgotten all about him during the banquet. He hadn't been with us in the *baihai* where we ate. I suppose he had been over in some other part of the village and had been well taken care of.

There was a small *baihai* up there that we could use as a temporary shelter. The men left us plenty of food, so we could take care of ourselves. A small spring flowing out the side of the mountain provided us with fresh, pure water.

We bedded down for the night, exhausted. I slept well.

The next morning I was too weak to get up. Dick Tirk was already cooking rice for breakfast, but I could hardly move. My head hurt terribly, as though two red-hot pokers had been stabbed behind my eyeballs, and every joint and muscle in my body ached. I was dizzy and running a fever.

I had dengue, a jungle fever the GIs called "dingy fever." Dengue's symptoms are similar to malaria, and like malaria, the infection is spread by mosquitoes. The major difference is that dengue isn't as incapacitating and it doesn't come back on you in future years.

I managed to get up enough energy to go down to the spring for water. The spring was down below our camp a few dozen yards. The cold water on my face and hands felt refreshing. On the way back up the trail, which was a steep incline of fifteen degrees or more, I was balancing a tin of water in my right hand and walking gingerly up the incline when I noticed a stubby little brown snake, maybe eighteen inches long and three quarters of an inch in diameter, coming down the path toward me. I didn't have any shoes on, but I stood there transfixed. I didn't know what to do, so I remained as motionless as I could while the snake passed between my bare feet and continued down the trail.

Later, when the Filipinos came up to look in on us, I asked them what kind of snake it was. Based on my description, they said it was probably a rice snake, which is a species of cobra and quite deadly.

This encampment was only a temporary stop for us. We probably could have stayed there longer by persuading the Filipinos to look after us, but we didn't want to get them into trouble. Frankly, we didn't think the Filipinos really wanted us there either, because we could have been a terrible liability to them. If the Japanese came around and discovered that they had befriended us and were provisioning us, that would have been a capital offense. Anybody caught helping us would have been executed on the spot without any semblance of a trial. Maybe even the whole village would have been destroyed.

This danger weighed heavily on our minds, as I am sure it did theirs. We felt that they should be protected, and we appreciated all that they had done for us.

So after a couple more days' rest, we started off again. Macario didn't go with us. He said goodbye and went his separate way. I still had the fever; my legs were weak and I was dizzy when I attempted to walk, but with considerable help from our Filipino friends, I half-staggered and was half-dragged on down the trail toward the next stage of our odyssey and—we hoped—our eventual freedom.

CHAPTER SEVEN

LOOSE IN THE JUNGLE

THE safest time to travel was at night. The difficulty was the darkness. It was so pitch black that we couldn't see a blessed thing. If it had not been for our Filipino friends helping us we never would have made it. It's a mystery to me how they managed to find their way in the dark. On top of that, they literally half-dragged me along the way, one Filipino on each side of me, because I was so weak.

They led us through a pass in the mountain range toward a place on the east coast called Dingalan Bay. They thought that there we might be able to hire a boatman to paddle us on down the coast.

Most of the way we followed a highway through the area. The traveling wasn't too difficult, but each step we took was under the constant worry and threat that the Japanese might drive up the highway at any time and flash their lights on us. Whenever we saw or heard anything that even remotely resembled a car we would scatter and hide alongside the road as best we could.

It was the wee early hours of the morning when we finally reached Dingalan Bay. The villagers were asleep, of course, and our friends were not acquainted with any of the families who lived there, so rather than attempting to wake anyone up we simply dropped to the ground from exhaustion and slept the remainder of the night.

The next morning the villagers befriended us and took us in. Our friends from the mountain village solemnly shook our hands and left. They had been kind and gracious to us and seemed genuinely concerned about our safety and welfare, but I think

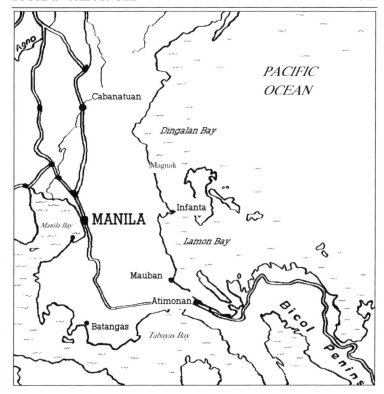

Eastern Luzon. The author's escape route led from Cabanatuan to Dingalan Bay, Magnak, Infanta, and Mauban. He was recaptured between Mauban and Atimonan while attempting to cross the island's narrow isthmus. Map by Jim Alexander.

they were also relieved to be able to turn the three escaped Americans over to someone else's care and keeping.

The villagers told us about a band of pygmies that lived near there, and they insisted on taking us to see them. I didn't really want to go, but I didn't want to disappoint our hosts. So we went over to the pygmy village.

The pygmies were perfectly shaped human beings, but I don't think any of them stood more than three and a half feet tall. The men carried long bows that were twice as long as they were tall. On their chests and foreheads the men had threaded tufts of cotton under the skin to form designs. Some of the women and a few of the children had done the same.

They were friendly, and seemed just as curious about us as we were about them. I would guess that none of them had ever seen a white person before. Belying their almost childlike appearance, we were told that the pygmies could be extremely ferocious at times, especially if somebody mistreated them in any way.

By the time we got back to our first village, someone had found a boatman for us. They took us to a young fellow who had a banca, an outrigger canoe with a sail. We offered him ten dollars to take us down the coast.

Our goal was to go down the coast as far south as Infanta, on the narrow waist of the island of Luzon about seventy miles east of Manila. Shortly below Infanta, the island narrowed to only about eight miles wide. We planned to cut across the island at its most narrow point and then work our way on southward.

I was very sick with the dengue fever. Most of the trip I spent flat on my back on a board stretched across the outrigger. The sea was calm and we hugged the coastline, never more than a couple hundred yards offshore. It would have been a fantastically beautiful trip if I had been in a condition to enjoy the scenery. The coastline was fringed almost all the way by virgin forest—no roads or highways. Occasionally would we see a Filipino *baihai*, but for the most part it was palm trees and mountains that came right down to the sea.

Finally, my condition deteriorated so badly that we had to stop. Our boatman found a little inlet on the coast with a tiny fishing village, Magnak, where he could put in to shore. I would guess we had traveled some thirty or forty miles down the bay from our starting point. The boatman even located a Filipino family who agreed to put us up for the night.

We were introduced to Eulogio Solleza, his wife, and his daughter, Maryanna. We Americans had a difficult time pro-

Typical Philippine banca (outrigger canoe). Courtesy of Dr. Paul Ashton.

nouncing the name of Eulogio's wife, but it sounded something like *Reyena*, which, according to Dick Tirk, was close to *reina*, the Spanish word for "queen." He said that was a flattering term, so we called her Mom Reyena. We never saw anything in writing, so we had to guess at the spelling.

My friends helped me out of the outrigger canoe and took us up to Eulogio's house, where we stretched out on the floor. The house was a typical Filipino *baihai*, built on stilts about five feet off the ground, and one had to use a bamboo ladder to get up there.

Of course, the house had no indoor plumbing. When Dick or Phil or I had to attend to Mother Nature, it was quite a chore. We'd have to crawl over sleeping bodies, climb down the ladder, find some place to relieve ourselves, then crawl back up the ladder to our assigned sleeping place. We slept on a bamboo strip floor, the strips spaced about a half inch apart with the cracks open to the ground below. It made for good ventilation, and I suppose easy sweeping of the floor.

Later I found out that the Filipinos didn't bother crawling out over people and waking them up the way we did. When Mother Nature called, they simply found a crack in the floor and relieved themselves to the ground directly underneath.

When morning came I was unable get up, my fever having got so bad. After some anxious consultation, it was decided that Eulogio and his family would look after us until I got well enough to travel again.

No one had a thermometer, of course, but Dick guessed that my fever must have been somewhere around 104 or 105 degrees. The thought of food held no appeal for me whatsoever.

Eulogio said he knew how to cure my fever. He brought in a deer antler and took out his bolo — a knife with a blade about two feet long and as sharp as a razor — and he proceeded to scrape off the outer layer of the antler into a pan of water. Then he placed the pan over an open fire and brought it to a boil. As soon as this decoction had cooled down enough to sip, he brought it over to me and helped me get it down.

It tasted bitter, but I had no difficulty swallowing the liquid. At that time I had no idea whether it would help my fever or not, but I was at the point of trying anything. So I forced it all down.

I noted that the family was Catholic, which was not surprising, because the Spanish had been there some four-hundred years or so before the Americans had arrived. As the days wore on, however, I noted that Eulogio also practiced a lot of nature medicine and ritual. I suppose it's fair to say that he observed a mixture of Catholic and native religions.

My first several days there were a haze to me. I had little consciousness of the passage of time because of my delirium. Gradually, however, my appetite started to return and my strength started coming back. I was feeling better and able to eat more.

The villagers ceased calling us by our American names and gave us Spanish names like their own instead. I became known as

Guillermo, Dick as Ricardo, and Phil as Felipe. I guess that was a sign that we were accepted.

A Catholic priest came up by boat from Infanta. The trip was a full day's journey in a banca. He had received rumors that there were Americans up here that were reported to be ill, so he brought some quinine to fight the fever. He thought that I had malaria, but it didn't really make any difference, because quinine is an effective treatment for dengue too.

While he was there he held a baptismal service for the village. All the children who had been born since his last visit were brought for christening, some of whom were three or four years old at this time. Dick, Phil, and I were all asked if we would be godfathers. My godson was christened as Welfredo Torres. He was about four years old.

Phil's godson was much younger, less than a year old. Like all young Filipino boys, he didn't wear any covering over the lower part of his body. As we were standing there holding our children and the priest was going through his ritual, Phil's godson suddenly felt the call of nature and had to relieve himself, which he did—all down Phil's front. Phil held the baby a little away from him, and we both started laughing. The priest went right ahead with his ritual without interruption, but Phil and I never stopped laughing. The Filipinos, I'm sure, were somewhat amused by it also, but they didn't let on that anything was happening.

After the baptism was over, the villagers gathered for a fiesta—at least I would call it a fiesta, although I am sure the Filipinos had a different name for it. This was a wonderful occasion. They were celebrating the priest coming up there and christening the children, and at the same time Dick, Phil, and I were also honored for being godfathers to the children.

We filled our bellies on roast pig that had been cooked in a pit in the ground. Absolutely delicious! The rice was of the variety called field rice, which cooked up particularly light and fluffy, not gummy like the more common swamp rice. Also we had camotes, crispy fried fish, and coconut meat. Coconuts grow wild along the seacoast and are in plentiful supply. The Filipinos eat the meat of the coconut when it's soft and moist, not hard and tough like the dried coconuts we get in the States. I think we also had some shark fin.

And bananas. If I were asked to name the food most plentiful in the Philippines, I'd have to say it was the banana. Wherever we went in the villages, bananas were served with every meal, eaten as snacks between meals, and prepared in an infinite variety of ways.

We found out from the priest that it was a fortunate thing I had been too sick to continue our journey down the coast. The boat that brought us here from Dingalan Bay had continued on down to Infanta, which was our original destination. When it landed there, a troop of Japanese soldiers was waiting for it. The soldiers examined everything on the boat, looking for some sign of the Americans. My bout with dengue fever proved to have a silver lining after all, for once again our lives had been spared.

I went to bed that night with a full belly and a warm feeling in my heart. It had been many, many days since I had relished the taste of food or enjoyed myself so much.

One night while we were asleep, a loud commotion brought Dick and Phil and me to a completely wideawake and upright position. There was a lot of excited shouting going on, but the only word we could decipher was the Filipino word for "snake." Eulogio climbed down into the cooking area and gathered up bunches of grass, which he wound tightly around one end of a short pole, and proceeded to light like a torch. Then he began to climb a coconut tree that stood right next to our *baihai* by crouching down with both feet close together, gripping the tree with his feet, and holding on with his right arm, all the while carrying the torch in his left hand and clenching his ever-present bolo knife in his teeth. (Of course, it helps that coconut trees grow outward at an angle rather than straight up.)

As he reached the lower fronds, about ten or twelve feet off the ground, he came face to face with a huge snake. Its head was about the size of a man's head, and its body was a good ten inches in diameter. The snake was staring straight into the torch and flicking its tongue. Eulogio held the torch about two feet from the snake's nose, clutching the tree with only his two bare feet, and very slowly reached out with his bolo knife in his right hand. Then with a quick flip, he flicked the snake's head right off. He did it so quickly that I could hardly see his hand move. That also shows how sharp he kept his bolo knife.

When Eulogio unwound the snake's body from the tree, we could see that it must have been twelve to fourteen feet long and weighed a hundred pounds or more. I hadn't realized it before, but apparently the snake had been eating the villagers' chickens, and they had been on the lookout for it.

It's my understanding that the neighbors cleaned the snake and ate it as they would any other meat. But thank heavens they didn't serve me any. At least, I don't think they did.

One day when I was almost well enough to travel, the three of us were talking about where we were going to go. Eulogio went out and cut a length of rattan. He brought it back, carefully measured it, and examined it thoroughly. Then he sharpened one end with his bolo knife and trimmed the other off to a squared end. Very solemnly he would talk into one end of the stick, then turn it around and put the other end in his ear as if he were listening to something. He repeated this two or three more times.

Finally, he told us that he knew we were thinking about leaving but that the "listening stick" told him we shouldn't leave, because it was very dangerous out there. He said our chances of getting caught were very great.

Eulogio told us that whenever we did decide to leave, he wanted to go with us to look after us. Probably, the smart thing for us to do would have been to let him come with us. But we knew it would be too risky for him and his family if we were to be caught by the Japanese while he was with us. Naturally, we were deeply touched by the genuineness of his offer, but we knew he had a family, a wife, and several others that were depending on him for their survival in that primitive setting. Besides, we thought we could do all right on our own.

Mom Reyena thought I should have a wife. She thought it strange that I had absolutely nothing to do with the native women at any time in the way of a personal relationship, other than simply to be courteous and pleasant. But a wife was the furthest thing from my mind, and actually I thought her concern was quite amusing. I purposefully avoided forming that kind of relationship because in the back of my mind was the thought that if we upset their traditions, customs, and way of life, it might end up having serious consequences.

We were in constant fear of being recaptured by the Japanese. Not only did we fear that Japanese soldiers might be lurking about and chance to happen on us, but we also knew, thanks to the priest, that the Japanese had posted a handsome reward to any Filipino who turned us in. In fact, the reward was large enough that any poor villager who collected it could look forward to spending the rest of his life in relative comfort. Moreover, rumors had reached us that bounty hunters were in the area. Obviously, we wanted to be circumspect and avoid doing anything that might trigger someone's wrath. And while we didn't feel we had anything to fear from the people here at Magnak, a romantic entanglement was the last thing we needed under those circumstances.

Eulogio wanted to show us the local sights. He said he wanted to take us to see the "monkey people." We meandered through the forest until we came to a little lean-to. It was a horrible-looking place, a kind of cave in the side of the mountain, with leaves and branches brought over the top to keep the rain from getting in.

Outside the cave was a family, the likes of which I had never seen before. The man stood about five feet tall, stooped over, with a scraggly beard and scales on his hands that looked like he had never washed. The woman sat there in a squat position preparing food of some sort. She was holding onto one squalling baby, and several other tots of various ages were crawling and rolling around. But what seemed most incredible was that the man was carrying a club or pole of some sort, like a caveman. I could swear that we were looking at a drawing right out of some archaeology book.

My strength had come back sufficiently that we were able to travel. We had been laid up for more than a month now. Eulogio and his family knew we wanted to leave, and when they couldn't persuade us to stay any longer, Eulogio arranged for one of the outrigger canoes passing down the coast to carry us as far as Infanta. Once we got there, we hoped to find someone who would carry us down farther, or perhaps guide us across the island to the other side so that we could travel on down the Bicol Peninsula, which is the southern half of the island of Luzon.

When we arrived at Infanta, a barrio of several thousand people, we could tell that the villagers were nervous about our presence. They didn't want us there. It was obvious that Japanese troops had been there and effected an attitude change, because the traditional Filipino hospitality was completely nonexistent. People even seemed frightened to be seen talking with us.

The villagers did nothing to hamper our escape, but at the same time it was clear that they wanted us to get out of there as quickly as possible, so they arranged for a young man with a small outrigger canoe to run us on down the coast. He was probably eighteen or nineteen years old, and of a very slender build. Each of us took a paddle, and with him in the stern, or steering, position, we resumed our journey southward. I don't think our boatman was thrilled with the idea of having us on board his boat, because he was sullen and would barely communicate with us. In fact, he wouldn't even give us his name — possibly out of fear of retaliation if we were ever captured by the Japanese.

After we had gone about ten miles, he insisted on putting us ashore. Dick argued that he should take us farther, and indeed we offered to pay him more, but he wanted to get rid of us as quickly as possible. He said this was as far as he would take us. When we argued, the young man pulled his bolo knife from his belt and made threatening gestures like he was ready to attack us if we didn't get out of the boat. Of course, the three of us could have easily overpowered him and taken over the boat and continued on our own—in fact, Dick or Phil, I forget which, said we ought to do that.

But I argued, "Let him live. He was nice enough to take us this far. He hasn't done anything to harm us, and it isn't worth taking a human life." So we paid him the money that was promised and went ashore on a sandy beach.

Unfortunately, the area where we were put ashore was Lamon Bay, which had been one of the previous Japanese invasion sites. We knew that there was a strong likelihood that Japanese soldiers were thick in the area and, as a result, the natives would not be very friendly toward us. In fact, it was probably that fear that drove our young boatman to put us ashore on this beach rather than carry us farther on down the coast as intended. From now on, we could expect to see only mistrustful or hostile natives.

We thought we should try to get out of the area as quickly as we could by journeying inland and crossing over to the other side of the narrow isthmus of Luzon. At first, we tried to work our way through the jungle, but we couldn't find any trails, and the thorns and vines and underbrush were so thick and impenetrable that we couldn't make our way through it.

Not only did we have the jungle to contend with, but we were also surprised to learn that a precipitous range of mountains ran down the spine of the island a couple of miles inland. Our schoolbook map hadn't shown their existence, and we found that they formed an almost impenetrable barrier. We were unable to spot any passes that would let us cross through. So, with no other alternative, we had to take our chances on working our way down the coast and hope that we could find a pass through the mountains to the other side of the island.

Finally, we came upon what appeared to be an opening that would let us turn inland. We followed this little valley for two or three miles until we came upon a *baihai* in a little clearing. It was abandoned, but we could tell it hadn't been vacant for very many weeks, because the garden still had lovely, purple breadfruit growing on a vine. We decided to spend the night there.

We had learned from the natives how to cook breadfruit by slicing it and frying it in coconut oil. Moreover, our friends up north had provisioned us with a little coconut oil, along with our rice and kettle. Dick fried the breadfruit, and it made a tasty dish to go with our rice.

The next morning we started out again. We followed some trails until they came out on a highway. This road led toward the town of Mauban, a fair-sized habitation on the coast. That was a place we wanted to avoid, because we could be reasonably sure that Japanese soldiers would be around. Moreover, we felt that by staying on the highway—even though the mode of travel was easier—we would be in too much danger of being seen. So we we cut off the main road onto another trail that led farther inland.

As it was getting along toward evening, we came upon another *baihai*. First making sure there were no soldiers lurking about, we went up to the hut and spoke to the woman who lived there, who was able to speak a little English. It was clear that she was frightened by our presence and didn't want us around. Nevertheless, she did feed us graciously and then urged us to be on our way.

Upon leaving her place, we followed a trail that led through some shoulder-high grass. This looked like as good a place as we were likely to find to spend the night. We turned off the main trail and went into the high grass for perhaps a hundred yards or so, then circled back a little ways and made our camp. We thought that no one would be able to track us, particularly in the dark, but we were wrong.

Just as we were settling in for the night, we saw some torches coming up the path from the same direction we had come. A group of maybe sixty to seventy Filipinos were coming right up the path we had traveled just a few minutes before. We were frightened and apprehensive, but we still thought we were safe. After all, we had no way of knowing whether they were out looking for us or just happened to be on their way to somewhere else. It turned out that they really were good trackers, for despite the darkness they found the place where we had cut off from the main trail.

When we saw the men turn off the trail and begin tracking toward our location, we decided that we'd better hightail it out of there as fast as we could. Gathering up our stuff hastily, we ran up another little path that we found. It was pitch black and we couldn't see a thing. Dick was leading the way with Phil right behind him, and I was bringing up the rear, carrying my gunnysack with the medication and various other things in it. We were hoping to put as much ground as we could between us and the Filipinos who were pursuing us. But every time we looked back, there were the torches, still following us.

Because I couldn't see where I was going in the darkness, I accidentally stepped off the edge of a concrete culvert. I fell perhaps a dozen feet straight down, landing in a ditch. As I fell, I banged my chin on the edge of the concrete abutment, then landed in the ditch with my legs twisted under me. Momentarily, I blacked out from the pain.

As I regained consciousness, I began to struggle back up to level ground. My chin was cut wide open where it had struck the concrete and was bleeding all down my shirt, and my left leg wouldn't carry any weight. My right leg seemed to function all right, but I found it difficult to stand up.

In the dark and with the pursuers on our trail, I didn't have time to hunt for the sack that had my gear in it, so I had to leave it where it had fallen. Fortunately, I had tucked a few things away in my pockets. Included among those items were my mother's picture, about three-hundred in paper currency sewn into the collar of my shirt, and the watch that my parents had given me. The watch, however, was broken by the fall and rendered useless. My razor, toothbrush, medication, and the other valuables that had been with me since Corregidor were now gone.

Phil and Dick helped me out of the ditch, and we struggled on our way with me dragging my left leg. The pain was terrible, but we were in such fear of our pursuers that I had to go on despite the agony. Still, there can be no doubt but that I slowed them down quite a bit.

We pressed on all through the night. Finally, about dawn we

were so exhausted that we had to stop and get some rest. We managed to find a little secluded area on the side of a hill, crawled in there, and managed to steal a couple of hours' sleep.

Continuing on our way the next day, we came upon a Filipino farmer working in his field. He looked at us warily. Phil went up to him and asked him if he was a *soptolista*, which was a member of a Communist group. If he had been, he would have befriended us. Instead, the man became frightened of us, which in turn made us apprehensive. We were sure he would notify the authorities where we were.

Phil grabbed him, and I think he may have been ready to kill him. I said, "For goodness' sake, Phil, turn him loose. You can't do anything with him except tie him up, and you wouldn't want to kill him or injure him." So Phil let him go, and the fellow beat a hasty retreat down the valley.

We did our best to go in the opposite direction from the way the farmer had gone. On and on we went, and eventually we found that we had circled back onto the very path we had been on the previous day when the Filipinos started chasing us. We stayed on this path for a little while until we caught sight of some *baihais* in another village up ahead of us. We thought we'd better turn off there, so we doubled back on our tracks, then carefully picked our way into a clump of tall grass, doing our best to avoid leaving any trail that could be tracked.

Before we knew it, here came a bunch of Filipinos up the path. Perhaps the farmer had informed them, we didn't know. However, we noted that they were coming from the direction opposite that from which we had come, so we were hopeful that their appearance now was a pure coincidence and that they didn't know we were there. With little choice left open to us, we remained hidden in the clump of tall grass and hoped for the best.

Darkness hadn't yet set in when we saw the group creeping up on us like a posse. The grass was so tall that we could barely see over the tops. But we could hear them whispering to each other. Dick told us that he recognized the Filipino word for "gun." All of a sudden, Phil said, "They've got a gun out there and they're pointing it straight at us."

We tried to shush him down, but he said, "I'm going to stand up."

"Phil, don't stand up," Dick pleaded. But Phil stood up anyway, and I stood up with him. So with little choice, Dick got up also.

The Filipinos came over, and they were about as afraid of us as we were of them. It turned out that they didn't have a gun after all; as a matter of fact, they thought we had a gun. That's what they were whispering about. Had we continued to lay low, they probably would have maintained an appropriate distance but continued to follow us until the Japanese soldiers arrived.

In that respect, I guess we were pretty lucky. Had the Japanese soldiers caught us themselves, they probably would have performed an immediate execution.

The whole band came up and gathered tightly around us. I didn't take count, of course, but I would guess that there were seventy-five people or more in the group — mostly men, but with a few boys tagging along. All things considered, they were nice to us: they didn't treat us roughly, or anything like that, but they did want us to know that we were captured. We were fully aware that we would be turned over to the Japanese as soon as they arrived on the scene.

Our captors tied us up so tight that the circulation almost stopped in my arms. At first our legs weren't tied, but later on, when they prepared us to sleep on the ground, they bound our legs as well. To my complete surprise, someone returned my sack of gear to me. I guess they found it back by the bridge where I had fallen and, in simple honesty, felt that they should return it to its rightful owner. I was not able to take an inventory of its contents, but it did appear to me that most of the items were left intact, including our medication.

Long before, while we were still at Dingalan Bay, the three of us had thrown away our dog tags and every other form of identification. Always anticipating the possibility that we might be recaptured, we wanted to be in a position to claim that we were not escaped prisoners. Rather, we concocted the story that we were Americans who had never been captured. The story we made up was that we had paddled in inner tubes across the channel from Corregidor to Bataan, then worked our way up the peninsula, around to the east coast, then on down the coast to the place where we now were. We had our story pretty well together and had rehearsed it many times so that we could be sure each of us would be telling the Japanese the same story, particularly if they were to interrogate us separately.

Also, we took the precaution of choosing new identities for ourselves. We could be pretty sure that the Japanese, as haphazard as their record-keeping system was, would have our names on a register somewhere, and if we gave them our real names they could easily check whether or not we were lying about our escape. Further, rather than simply making up names out of the blue sky, we appropriated the names of three fellow officers whom we knew had been killed in the fighting back on Corregidor. Again, we surmised that the Japanese might be in possession of some captured documents that listed a roster of officers on Corregidor; we felt it was unlikely, however, that they would have an accurate listing of all the people killed during the final days. Even if they did have such a list, we felt we could at least make the claim that we had thrown away our dog tags and deserted, and that's why the officials reported us as dead.

The main thing was that we didn't want the Japanese to find out that we had escaped from one of their prison camps. Escape was a capital offense. We knew that they routinely shot any prisoner who had escaped or who was caught trying to escape.

Our Filipino captors took us to a large town. We never did find out the name of it, but I figured it had to be either Atimonan or Mauban, because those were the only two large towns in that province.

A truck full of Japanese soldiers was waiting for us when we got there. Several enlisted men jumped out of the back of the truck and surrounded us menacingly, and the two officers climbed out of the cab and came up to look us over. When they got to me, what they saw first was blood still dripping from the gash on my chin down onto my shirt, coagulating with the dried blood that was already caked there. The wound on my chin was about three inches across, open to the bone, and still dripping.

A soldier ran up with a machine gun and started poking me with the barrel of it. The officer started jabbering away at something that I couldn't understand, and I think they were ready to shoot me, when one of the Filipinos started shouting, "No, no, no, no." I sensed that the officer wanted to know how I had been injured, so I pantomimed as well as I could that I had fallen off a bridge. Apparently, the officer had inferred that I had been injured in a struggle with the Filipinos while resisting arrest, and that was very offensive to him. He glared at me for a while, and then gradually he settled down.

The soldiers loaded us aboard the truck and drove us across town to the building where their office was. They tried interrogating us, but since none of us spoke Japanese and none of them spoke English, the attempt was not very successful. Finally, they found an older Filipino gentleman who could speak a little Japanese and another who could speak a little English, so they carried on their interrogation through this cumbersome process—from Japanese to Filipino to English and back again.

When they were through with the interrogation, the Japanese loaded us onto another truck and hauled us up into the mountains. After a couple of hours of jouncing around in the back of the truck we arrived at a camp that had previously been a famous resort area before the war. When we had a chance to get out and look around, we were surprised to discover that the camp overlooked Manila Bay, and off in the distance we could see the island of Corregidor.

It appeared to us as if the Japanese army were in the process of converting this resort into some kind of training camp. Most of the soldiers here seemed young and inexperienced. A small detail of soldiers was at work building a beautifully landscaped flower garden, and in the very center of it they had molded the soil to form a small model of Corregidor. I was sure that in time it would turn out to be a beautiful scene. They certainly seemed to have a particular talent for working with flowers.

Many of the young soldiers seemed curious about us. I got the impression that none of them had ever been exposed to the Americans in battle. Dick Tirk, who had a fantastic ability with languages, tried to make conversation with some of them. These kids were generally pretty ignorant and poorly educated, and by our standards they seemed pretty backwards. Yet they were fanatically loyal to the emperor and completely dedicated to the objective of creating a "Greater East Asia Co-Prosperity Sphere."

They wanted to talk with us and to learn about America. They would go out and buy stuff for us. But after one of the Jap sergeants gave them hell, they weren't so friendly anymore.

We were put into a building that looked like a mess hall. It had tables and chairs but no other furniture. The floor, like the barracks at Cabanatuan, was bare dirt. That evening they served us chow. It had been two days since we had eaten. The main dish, as always, consisted of rice, but along with it they brought in some fish. These fish were about ten inches long, I would say, and cooked in hot oil until they were crispy. Apart from being gutted, the fish were served whole. We even ate the heads and tails, we were so hungry. We slept on the tables that night, and we were so tired that they didn't seem hard at all.

The next morning we were taken into a large town and put in the town jail. Here, again, the Japanese soldiers—young kids, really—seemed quite curious, and we began trading things with them. I think we were probably the first real Americans they had ever seen. We would slip them a little money in exchange for favors. Once again, an officer came and yelled at them and they took off. He let us know in no uncertain terms that we were forbidden to communicate or try to be friendly with the Japanese or let them do anything for us, that they weren't our servants.

I still hadn't received any treatment for the cut on my chin, and it was really quite painful. Of much more concern to me was the knee that I twisted when I fell; there were times when I could hardly bear to put weight on it.

Dick busied himself learning Japanese, just as he had previously learned Tagalog (the Filipino language in this area) and several other languages. His method was to write down various words the way they sounded and to repeat them over and over again until he could say them correctly. I admired his ability to do that.

In so doing, however, Dick made a nearly fatal mistake. One day, he uttered one of the Japanese words he had learned, and quick as a flash an officer took him out of the jail cell to interrogate him. I thought then that we were goners.

When the soldiers brought Tirk back after questioning, he filled us in on what had happened. He said that they had tried to trip him up every way they could. The interrogator said, "Oh, you've been a prisoner before. You're an escaped prisoner."

Tirk said, "No. Why do you say that?"

"Because you know the special army word for 'rice.' You wouldn't know that word if you had not been a prisoner."

Tirk explained, "Well, I have this notebook, and every time I pick up a word I write it down in the book." He showed them where he had written it down, along with some of the Filipino words that he'd written down previously.

"I heard somebody use this word," he said, "and one of the enlisted men told me what it meant, so I wrote it down."

That seemed to mollify them.

Still, our constant concern was what the Japanese were going to do with us. We had no idea what to expect. The uncertainty was terrible. Our great hope and desire and prayer was that sooner or later things would come to a resolution. The only consolation we had was the knowledge that each minute was bringing us that much closer to the end of the whole matter, one way or another.

That night we slept on the floor of our jail cell. Unlike our quarters the night before, the town jail had a concrete floor. I guess they didn't want prisoners trying to dig their way out.

They served us breakfast the next morning and then tied us up as securely as possible. Even our legs were hobbled. Then they brought in a Filipino soldier with a two-wheeled donkey cart, which I think was called a *carremata*. This kind of cart was used for all kinds of transportation in the Philippines. In the tourist cities, for example, one would pay a peso to take a ride in one of these *carrematas* and have his picture taken; but among the villagers it was their basic mode of farm transportation.

The three of us were piled onto the back of the cart, bound securely hand and foot, and trundled on down a dirt road. Up front, alongside the driver, was a young soldier toting a big rifle and zealously guarding us as if his life depended on it. For all we knew, this may have been his first time guarding American prisoners, for he seemed to take the assignment very seriously. We passed through village after village, where we were quite a curiosity.

I felt the call of nature and tried to convince the guard that I needed to urinate, so I kept repeating the word *benjo*, which was the word for "toilet." He waited until we got to a big town, then let me off the cart and said, "OK, benjo." I motioned for him to untie my hands, which he did.

We were in the town square with hundreds of Filipino citizens gathered around to see what was going on. I looked around for some kind of public toilet, but there wasn't any. Frankly, I had never before had the experience of relieving myself in front of so many watching people, but on the other hand, I was feeling terrible discomfort. The guard repeated, "Benjo, benjo," and seemed amused by my embarrassment.

It only took me a moment to make up my mind. The thought was running through my head that after all, the Jap soldier was the law in this town; his gun gave him charge over these defenseless people. They couldn't do anything about it, nor could I. Also I recalled that the Filipinos weren't overly modest. Men and women who needed to relieve themselves would simply widen their legs, separate their feet, and just let go right there. To be sure, they might step off the path a little, and a man might hold his hands over his private parts. But apart from that, they never gave any indication that what they were doing was in any way embarrassing. So under those circumstances, I did likewise and relieved myself. I secretly expected people to applaud, but no one did.

The more embarrassing moment came, however, when Phil indicated that he had the urge to go also. The guard refused to untie Phil's hands. So, inasmuch as my hands were still untied, Phil asked me to undo his fly. But I guess the shock and embarrassment were too much for poor Phil, because he wasn't able to go.

From that place we were taken to some kind of government building. The guard went inside while another soldier stood watch over us. When our guard came out a few minutes later he was carrying a receipt showing that he had delivered us, along with some other papers that I assume detailed our capture and set forth the circumstances thereof. Then he did something that I thought was very strange. He came very close to us and out of the earshot of the other soldier he asked us for some money. Apparently, he knew we had some money on our persons but didn't know where we had secreted it.

Phil said, "We better give him some money." Dick didn't say anything, he just stood there watching Phil and me.

I argued, "Phil, this man has had every opportunity in the world to rob us—or do anything else he wanted to with us, for that matter—and as far as I am concerned we don't owe him a thing. If he doesn't know that he has the power to take it, I certainly am not going to give him anything."

With that, we told him no. He went away without bothering us anymore.

The next we knew, we were loaded us back onto a truck and driven about two hours to another camp that overlooked the bay. This was south and west of Manila. We stayed here several days and shared basically the same food that the Japanese soldiers ate. This camp was situated on a narrow point of land that had sharp cliffs falling off on both the north and south sides. I toyed with the idea of whether it might be to our advantage to make a break for it and jump off one of the cliffs just to see what would happen. We had the crazy idea that perhaps rather than a sheer drop to the rocks below there might actually be a sloping area that we could slide down and escape. But the more we thought about it, the more ludicrous the idea became.

We reconciled ourselves to the thought that our fate was no longer in our hands.

CHAPTER EIGHT

SOLD DOWN THE RIVER

Regulations Concerning Concentration Camp

Chapter XI. Miscellaneous Rules

ART. 51. *Prisoners will keep at least 2 meters away from the fence surrounding the concentration area.*

ART. 52. *Prisoners will—so far as possible—answer calls of nature between sunrise & sunset. After sunset no one will be allowed to leave his barracks without permission of the section leader.*

ART. 53. *Prisoner Officers of the Day & runners will wear specified arm bands on left arm.*

ART. 54. *Prisoners will, on all occasions, salute the Nipponese soldiers and corps.*

ART. 55. *All work details will be assembled by 8:00 a.m. every day. Whenever necessary, special instructions in connection with the work details will be issued at time.*

ART. 56. *Penalties to be inflicted on prisoners will be decided by the Commander of the Concentration Camp.*
Penalties will be of the following 5 classes:
(1) Shooting (2) Confinement in the Guard House
(3) Food reduction (4) Additional work (5) Reprimand

ART. 58. *The penalty for attempting riot, attempted or actual escapes will be death by shooting.*

ART. 59. *Penalty for opposing the orders of Nipponese Soldiers or insulting the Nipponese Corps & Soldiers will be death by shooting.*

ART. 60. *Each barracks will organize squads of about 10 men and in case a member escapes the squad to which he belongs will be jointly responsible, and the squad leader and all members of the squad will be shot.*

ART. 61. *Violations of any of the various regulations may result in death by shooting or in confinement to the guard house.*

ART. 62. *In addition, according to the nature of the offense, punish-*
ments will be inflicted as sanctioned by the Commander of
the Concentration Camp.

—*Report on American Prisoners of War Interned by the Japanese in the Philippines,*
Office of Provost Marshal General, Nov. 19, 1945.

When we returned to Cabanatuan, those were the rules we
found waiting for us. Article 58 was the one that especially
concerned us: *The penalty for . . . attempted or actual escapes*
will be death by shooting.

Tirk, Sanborn, and I hoped to avoid the death penalty by
passing ourselves off as Americans who fled directly from
Corregidor without ever having been captured. And for this
reason, we gave our captors the new names we had established
for ourselves. I, for example, became "Bill Lloyd"—an officer
who I knew had been killed back on Corregidor.

In many important respects, Cabanatuan POW Camp No. 2
was no longer the same camp we had left three months earlier. It
operated in a much more organized and efficient manner. The
barbed-wire enclosure was now securely in place, with menacing
guard towers punctuating the perimeter. There was a lot more
bustle and activity: about ten thousand men now inhabited the
three-quarter-mile square compound, as compared with the few
hundred or so disoriented and disorganized early arrivals at the
time of our escape.

Much of the reason for the efficiency, we soon discovered, was
that the Japanese had learned how to turn the Americans'
organizational genius to work for them: the camp was now
administered by the U.S. officers. The camp staff included an
American camp commander, an executive officer, an adjutant, a
supply officer, a commissary officer, a work details officer, and a
few other officers appointed by the commander to specific
duties. The pattern of organization carried on down to the
barracks level. The camp officers were not required to go out on
work details, yet they were issued a full food ration.

This system led to a higher level of operating efficiency within the camp and it probably saved quite a few lives; however, it also meant that fewer Japanese soldiers were required to police the camp, hence freeing up more for the combat effort.

The Japanese maintained a perimeter guard around the barbed-wire fence that encircled the compound. The guards were posted in watchtowers about twenty feet high. Inside the fence, however, the Americans maintained their own perimeter guard. It was the duty of these guards to prevent fellow Americans from approaching the main fence and to apprehend anyone who tried to escape.

All in all, as long as the American camp administrators maintained discipline and no prisoners tried to escape, the Japanese didn't intervene much in the daily routine of the prisoners. Over the course of time, the Japanese came to the point of giving recognition to the best administrators.

The three of us were delivered to the receiving compound, where new arrivals were processed before being assigned to permanent quarters. They told us we would have to remain in this reception area until we were assigned to a prison unit.

At this time, the Japanese still thought we were first-time prisoners who had somehow managed to elude capture until now; they weren't aware that we were escapees from this very prison.

The receiving compound was not a restricted area; other prisoners had access to it. Jack Ferguson and another ensign came to visit us. I think they had heard that there were some new arrivals and simply came as a welcoming committee. Jack was genuinely surprised to find out that it was us. We quickly explained to Jack and his friend what our situation was and asked for their help in covering our true identities, which they readily agreed to do. Asked about the nasty cut on my chin, now scabbed over but not yet completely healed, I explained how I fell and not only cut my chin but also damaged my knee. I said the knee pained me more than the chin. Jack saw we were walking around barefoot, so he brought over some shoes. I never asked him where he got the shoes, but I suspect that shoes and other reusable items of clothing were stripped from dead prisoners before burial.

Dick Tirk took it upon himself to give Ferguson ten dollars in American money in exchange for the shoes. My first reaction was to be somewhat annoyed by his act of generosity, since this was money that we had pooled together and Dick hadn't consulted us before making the expenditure. But soon I began to feel remorseful for having allowed myself to think those thoughts, because Ferguson certainly did deserve the money and I certainly did appreciate having some shoes.

As much as we hated the thought of being brought back to prison, I must confess that there was a kind of nostalgia connected with seeing some of our old friends again. And it felt absolutely wonderful to get those ropes off our arms and hands and feet.

While we were in the cell waiting to be processed, we looked out through the bars and saw a platoon of Japanese soldiers who had been out on a detail. They came marching into camp, carrying the heads of Filipinos on their bayonets. The word spread around that the soldiers had cleaned out a guerrilla camp up in the hill. I counted four or five heads—a gruesome sight.

An orderly came to tell us that we were being taken to the American POW headquarters office. This turned out to be located in one end of the administration building. There to greet us was none other than Lieutenant Commander Tom Lowe, my old executive officer, along with a contingent of other senior officers. Lowe seemed to be the spokesman for the group.

Lowe was not at all friendly toward me. In fact, he lectured me sternly, "Berry, you know that escaping is a very serious thing, and you have been recaptured and brought back here."

"Yes, Sir," I said, not quite knowing in which direction he was headed, whether we were going to get a commendation or a condemnation. After all, we were well aware of the *Bluejacket's Manual*, the basic handbook for all navy men, which explicitly stated that "if you are unlucky enough to be captured . . . you are to occupy yourself by thinking about the possibility of escape."

Lowe asked, "Were you guys involved with any guerrilla activity?"

That question caught me by surprise. "No, Sir," I replied.

"Were any of you involved in gathering arms and men?"

"No, we were not!" I was beginning to dislike that line of questioning. "Why are you asking me this?"

"Well, we've been getting some stories back here in camp that you guys were out there organizing a guerrilla band, that you had gathered a cache of arms and ammunition, and that you were planning to conduct underground warfare against the Japanese."

"Where did you hear such poppycock?"

"They came to us from some Filipinos," Lowe said.

"Mister Lowe, that is pure hogwash!" I informed him.

"Do you mean it's not true?"

"I'm telling you, it is not true. Those are false rumors."

The officers went off to huddle together out of our earshot for a couple of minutes. Then Lowe resumed his role as spokesman for the group.

"We can't protect you," he said. He seemed agitated. "We can't keep the Japanese from discovering that you were prisoners who escaped. You've managed to put all of us here in jeopardy. There are stool pigeons here in the camp, and if you are found out it will mean not only punishment for you but a serious reprisal on the rest of the camp as well."

I still hadn't caught the full import of what he was saying. I knew it wasn't good. But I was totally unprepared for what Lowe said next: "The three of you are hereby ordered to turn yourselves in to the Japanese and inform them of your true identities."

I could hardly believe I was hearing those words from an American officer. Nothing that I had ever read or heard in my military manuals even remotely prepared me for an order like that.

Tirk was defiant. "What if we refuse to turn ourselves in?" he asked.

"We can't protect you," Lowe asserted again. "There are stool pigeons here in the camp, as I have said, and we *won't* protect you. That is an order!"

Lowe informed us that the senior officers had met, and it was their collective judgment that this was for the welfare of the camp. The three of us had no choice in the matter.

I asked sarcastically, "Are these officers aware that this will result in an almost certain death sentence for us?"

"They are," Lowe assured us. Again, he explained that their concern was for the welfare of the camp and that our wishes didn't matter. Lowe was talking to us in a condescending tone of voice exactly as if we were little boys who had been caught doing something naughty.

"Well, I'll be goddamned," Sanborn said in the strongest language I ever heard him use. "I never thought I would hear this from an American officer!"

A U.S. marine lieutenant colonel, who spoke Japanese fluently and served as the Americans' interpreter to the Japanese, seemed to be more helpful than the others. He advised us that before we were taken in to appear before the Japanese commanding officer, it would be wise for us to sit down and write out whatever we had to say about our escape and recapture. He said that we should tell why we escaped, what conditions we found out there, and why we came back. If we did all that, he said, maybe the Japanese would show some sort of mercy toward us. I got the impression that he thought this was going to be our last will and testament, and that the best we could hope for was a merciful death.

We were put in a little room and given pencil and paper. Very quickly the three of us agreed on a strategy of saying that we had voluntarily turned ourselves over to the Japanese. We had reason to believe that no narrative had been sent in to describe the actual circumstances of our recaptures, and certainly no one was there to contradict any statement we made. But we had to take that chance. So each of us separately drafted a paper in which he said that we had returned on our own volition because we had found conditions on the outside so deplorable that we wanted to come back.

There were certain things we didn't want to divulge. We didn't want to indicate in any way to the Japanese that the Filipinos were disloyal to them. We wanted to leave the impression that the Filipinos would turn us in. And I certainly did not wish to disclose that I was a naval intelligence officer.

At this point we were desperately trying to save our lives. We hoped that in some fashion this argument, flimsy as it was, would be palatable to the Japanese—palatable enough, at least, to forestall our execution.

As soon as we had finished writing our confessions, we were taken into another room, put in front of the Japanese interrogators, and made to stand there while our confessions were being translated. It was early evening and just beginning to get dark.

A little later we were taken into the office of the Japanese commanding officer. At this point, the Japanese were still under the assumption that we were new prisoners. When it was revealed that we were escaped prisoners giving ourselves up to the Japanese, however, their demeanor changed dramatically. Immediately, we were grabbed and our hands were securely tied behind our backs.

We were forced to sit in a kneeling position. Soldiers were standing around with clubs in their hands. *This is it*, I thought.

The interpreter said, "Tell the truth. If you lie to us in any way, you will be severely punished before we execute you." The obvious inference, of course, was that we were destined for execution in any event—the only question being how much misery we would be put through beforehand.

A commotion of some sort broke out in another part of the camp. Within a few minutes, whoever or whatever was causing the commotion was brought into the adjacent room. Everyone except the interpreter and one guard rushed over to the other room. Tirk, Sanborn, and I were ordered to sit quietly.

Tirk whispered to me, "If I had a razor blade I would cut my wrists."

I whispered back, "No, let's wait a bit and see what happens."

Viciously, the Japanese guard kicked Tirk in the small of his back so hard that it knocked him over. The interpreter snarled, "Quiet! Keep quiet!"

We focused our attention on what was going on in the next room. Through the paper-thin wall, we could hear the Japanese questioning three American officers. As the story unfolded, it turned out that these three officers—army lieutenant colonels Briggs and Breitung and navy Lieutenant Gilbert—had been caught attempting to escape. They had tried to crawl out a trench that had been dug through the camp to drain off excess rainwater. Unfortunately for them, there happened to be two other Americans—one a former football player and the other a master sergeant—standing alongside the trench and urinating into it when these three officers came crawling along.

The two guys up on the bank called out, "What are you doing?" One of the officers became belligerent and said, "We're officers, and we order you to be quiet." At that point, the officers got up and started to run. The football player tackled one of them and threw him to the ground. Nearby prisoners rushed up to restrain the other two from getting away.

The football player said, "Look, our lives are at stake if we let you go, and we're not about to lose our lives just to let you escape."

All they wanted was for the officers to give up their escape. But hearing the hullabaloo, a Japanese guard came rushing over to find out what was going on. From this point on any thought of escape was a lost cause; but neither could they go back and pretend that no attempt had been made. One of the officers started swinging a club that he had made with heavy wire wrapped around the end of it. It wasn't clear to me whether he was swinging at the Americans or the Japanese, but in any event he injured a Japanese soldier. That was absolutely the wrong thing to do: injuring a guard while trying to escape is probably the most serious offense that he could possibly have committed. I wondered if perhaps he hadn't been trying to provoke the Japanese into shooting him on the spot, thereby getting a merciful death right then and there.

As the interrogation wore on, the navy lieutenant, Curt Gilbert, spoke up and said, "Look, conditions in this camp are horrible, and we have a right to escape. So that's what we were doing, trying to escape."

Immediately, the Japanese stopped the interrogation and ordered the officers outside. They were made to stand in a column of light that was emanating from the window of the room where we were kneeling. From our positions, Tirk, Sanborn, and I could see plainly everything that was going on outside our window. One by one the officers were beaten across the head by two Japanese enlisted men. One of the officers wore glasses, and when he was struck his glasses shattered all over his face. With each blow, the Japanese would say, "Down America!" Then they would punch the poor soul again and shout, "Up Japan!"

For what seemed like a half hour or more, we witnessed this beating: "Down America. Up Japan. Down America. Up Japan." Their heads were a bloody mess, noses broken, ears torn off, teeth bashed in. When the officers could no longer stand by themselves, they were tied to a stake and made to stand there all night. The next morning they would be shot, and their heads cut off. That was to be the fate of those three would-be escapees who were exposed by their fellow prisoners.

Minutes after we witnessed the beating, when it came our turn to be questioned again, it was with this admonition: "Don't lie, or you will be punished severely before you are executed."

We knew what they meant.

The interpreter asked which one of us was the ranking officer. We weren't sure. All three of us were ensigns who were commissioned about the same time—I think maybe my commission was a few days junior to the other two, but that wasn't the issue. Seeing that we were all three of the same rank, he then asked, which one of you is the oldest? Since I happened to be older by a few months, I volunteered, "I am."

They led me into the room where the previous interrogation had taken place. A dozen or more Japanese soldiers formed a circle around me, glaring menacingly as I was forced to stand with my hands tied behind my back. Several of the soldiers were carrying a club or weapon of some sort. Standing in the midst of them were the two enlisted men who just minutes before had so savagely beaten the three Americans, bloody clubs still in their hands, as if to say, "You're next."

The interrogator started peppering me with questions. It was expected that I have answers for everything. I tried to answer the questions as best I could without revealing anything I didn't want them to know. For example, they wanted to know which Filipinos had befriended us during our three months of freedom, but I didn't want to divulge their names. So I told them that we had been afraid to expose ourselves to the Filipinos, but that one Filipino soldier had taken care of us. We would give him money and send him various places to buy food and bring it back to us. I said we had tried as hard as possible to avoid contact with any Filipinos. That answer seemed to satisfy them, because they wanted to believe that the Filipinos loved the Japanese and were co-operative with them. After all, it was Filipinos who brought us in.

Our strategy was to tell them things they liked to hear without revealing any information that was detrimental to either the United States or our Filipino friends. We discovered that the Japanese were easily persuaded when they heard things they liked to hear.

They wanted to know where we had gone when we first escaped from the camp. I told them that we had gone out of the camp because there was no fence up, had gone over a range of mountains, and then had come down through a pass and traveled down the coast. They understood that.

They wanted to know if I had seen any guerrillas. I said no. They said, "Well, you went right through an area where the guerrillas were." I said we had been with a Filipino deserter—I couldn't remember his name, but we called him Macario—and he had steered us around all Filipino habitation, so we never knew if there were any guerrillas there or not.

Then they said, "Describe the road you took."

I said, "If you'll untie my hands and give me a piece of paper and a pencil, perhaps I can draw you a map." I visualized a map, took my pencil and made a few wiggly lines on the blank page, and handed it back. They seemed to be satisfied with that.

Next they wanted to know why I had escaped. My first remark was to say that Americans had been dying all around me, and I had thought in order to survive I would have to get out of the camp. (Of course, the real reason was that we were trying to go south and join up with other Americans, but it would have been a terrible mistake for me to have said that. I was convinced that the Japanese were trying to latch onto any excuse that they could put into the books and say this is why we were executed.)

They persisted with the question, "Why did you escape?" Again and again I said, "We were trying to get out because people were dying."

I could sense the tension rising in the room, and I wondered why. Then it dawned on me that my statement was causing them discomfort; I was causing them to lose face by suggesting that they had been letting the Americans die. They didn't want to hear that from anybody.

I don't know what prompted me to do it, but instinctively I reached into my shirt pocket and pulled out the picture of my mother that I was still carrying after all this time. (Fortunately, my hands were still untied from drawing the map.) I showed my mother's picture to the interpreter and said, "I wanted to go home to my mother."

When that statement was translated into Japanese, the whole room of Japanese soldiers burst into laughter. I was not sure whether they laughed because my statement was ridiculous or because it struck some sort of responsive chord with them. Anyway, it broke the tension. Maybe every one of them identified with that sentiment. No heroes in here, just a bunch of boys in uniform who were all a long way from home, all wanting to see their mothers.

From that point on, the entire atmosphere was different. The colonel told the enlisted men they could leave, and they all

Harriett Virginia Berry. Actual photograph in its original frame as used by the author during the interrogation by Japanese officers following his recapture. From author's collection.

trooped out, including the two who had done the beating. I was left alone with just the colonel and his executive officer and the interpreter.

Tea was brought in and I was served a cup. The colonel also asked if I'd like a cigarette, which I gratefully accepted. Smoking the cigarette helped me to relax. I had started smoking the day Corregidor fell and found that it seemed to ease my nerves.

The colonel was cordial and courteous. He let me sit down and we had a friendly visit. He talked at length about a Christian church someplace in Japan and how they would ring the bells with a rope braided from human hair.

After the interrogation, we were taken back over to the American headquarters and put in the guardhouse. Right away it became apparent that this was not merely a holding area but a place of punishment—a prison within a prison. It was under the control of the U.S. officers, and the sergeant in charge was an American MP who had been a prison guard in civilian life. The other individuals in here were not exactly the most desirable people in the camp; each one had committed an act of violence, thievery, or some other offense on fellow prisoners and was incarcerated here for punishment or isolation. One, I know, had killed another prisoner in a fight over a can of sardines. That was the kind of people we were thrown in with. Apparently, Tirk, Sanborn, and I had committed the most serious offense of all, namely, we had dared to escape.

We were assigned a bunk about five feet above the ground, and we had to crawl up a bamboo ladder to get there. Remarkably, each of us still had our gunnysacks of gear containing the few things we were able to keep with us. I think I still had some medicine, a couple of cans of sardines, and a small bag of brown sugar that I had acquired along the way. We all still had some money stuffed in the collars of our shirts, but we didn't disclose this to anyone.

We weren't in our bunks long before we had some other visitors: bedbugs and lice. I fought half the night with the bloodthirsty little critters, itching and scratching and rubbing myself raw. In the end, the bedbugs won and I got very little sleep.

Late the next afternoon, the American sergeant in charge of the guardhouse came to us and told us, "You guys better get yourselves ready. The Japs are coming for you."

Phil asked, "Why are the Japs coming for us?"

"You guys are going to put on a 'floor show.'"

He explained that about once a week, the prison chaplains had been in the habit of arranging amateur theatricals and skits for the entertainment of the POWs. Since this was the only form of entertainment the camp had, these "smokers," as they were called, were well attended by both the prisoners and the Japanese.

Word had been put out through the camp that the entertainment for that day had been canceled and that instead there would be a special "show" put on by the three returned escapees. The Americans were looking toward this "show" with deep foreboding, not knowing which turn it would take.

With great apprehension we made ourselves as presentable as we could under the circumstances. If our last earthly act was to be dancing at the end of a rope, we were resolved to do it with bravery and dignity.

Almost before we knew what was happening, the guards had arrived, put ropes around our necks, and were leading us out. Each of us was escorted by two armed guards, one on each side. Our hands were not tied. They marched us to an elevated platform in the center of the compound that stood four or five feet above the ground. We had to climb a little ladder to get up on it.

It seemed as if the entire body of POWs had been called to assembly. I don't know how many were massed there in front of the platform, but the number certainly ran into the many hundreds, perhaps even thousands. Overall, about seven-thousand prisoners were incarcerated in the camp, but a great many of them were sick and incapacitated. I would judge that most of the able-bodied prisoners were in attendance.

Atop the platform stood the commanding officer of the camp, the Japanese colonel, who had questioned me the day before. The colonel was neatly dressed in his starched uniform, complete with a white collar and a helmet covered with some kind of canvas camouflage. With him was an interpreter and two guards standing at attention with their rifles and fixed bayonets. I looked for a gallows but didn't see one. I wondered how they were going to carry out the execution.

When we reached our positions on the platform, the three of us in unison gave a polite bow, which was a Japanese courtesy and custom—a kind of salute. The colonel returned the bow smartly.

I was called on first. The guard brought me forward, the rope still around my neck. I was fearing for my life. The interpreter placed into my shaking hands the "confession" that I had written the night before at our interrogation. I was instructed to read it loud enough so that everyone could hear.

There was no PA system, and the audience was very large. So in a strident, high-pitched voice, stretched an octave or two higher than my natural voice because of the strain I was under, I tried to convey to the assembled throng what was written on the paper.

I told them that we had escaped because we saw so many people dying around us and we didn't want to suffer a similar fate, and we thought our chances for survival would be better in the jungle.

"We hid out. We found this Filipino soldier Macario who would go and buy food for us. But we stayed out in the jungle and we scrounged for food. We did everything we could, but we didn't have any money and we were desperate." Actually, the Japanese knew we had three or four hundred dollars in American money because they saw it when they went through our things. But here I was, telling them how desperate we were.

"We were afraid of the Filipinos," I said. "In our minds, we were afraid the Filipinos would turn us in."

It was the Japanese colonel to whom we were playing, not the American prisoners. We hoped that the other prisoners would see through our ruse. At that point, we didn't think we were being disloyal; I thought that after all, we were up there fighting for our lives. We wouldn't have been on that platform if we hadn't been ordered to turn ourselves in when we had expected our senior officers to protect us. We thought they had an obligation to us.

"After we had escaped," I went on, "we were sorry that we had. The conditions out there were deplorable. The conditions were horrible. We went for weeks without food, the jungle water was infested with bugs and poisonous insects, and we were continuously attacked by venomous snakes and ferocious wild beasts. We were in a state of perpetual starvation, we were in constant fear, and nothing could be any worse than that. And we felt that the Japanese would have a certain amount of sympathy if we would turn ourselves back to them, which we had done voluntarily."

Apparently, my "confession" had the desired effect, because after I finished reading it the colonel issued some admonitions to the prisoners and then indicated that the assembly was dismissed.

We went back down the ladder with the ropes still around our necks, and then we were led back to the guardhouse.

That afternoon we were visited at the guardhouse by Jack Ferguson. He reported, "Everybody got your message when you told them how tough it was out there. None of the Americans were fooled. Even with your bruises from being kicked around and beaten, you guys looked to be in far better condition than any other prisoner in the camp." I was happy to learn that the Americans had received one message and the Japanese another.

Ferguson always had a pleasant manner about him, a way of making you feel good about yourself. I sometimes thought that he would make a good minister or chaplain someday.

Jack brought us up to date on the scuttlebutt floating around the camp about the progress of the war. No one had any hard news, of course, but stories were going around that MacArthur had stopped the Japanese advance toward Australia; the vaunted

Japanese navy had been crippled in a battle off Midway Island, and fighting was going on with the U.S. navy in the Solomon Islands. We eagerly lapped up that kind of information.

Ferguson also told us that we had a lot of friends in the camp and they absolutely could not understand why the senior officers ordered us to turn ourselves in. We could have been shipped out to Davao without the Japanese knowing our true identities.

"You know why they made you do that, don't you?" he asked.

"No."

"They had to."

"What do you mean, they had to?"

"Because you guys were heroes."

"That's crazy! In what way were we heroes?"

"Look at it this way. Suppose that you were camp administrators charged with the responsibility to maintain peace and order within the camp, and that your own well-being depended on how well you did that job. Then three of your guys jumped ship and make good their escape. Sometime later, rumors start floating back that they're up in the hills gathering up men and arms to conduct guerrilla warfare against the Japs."

"That's nonsense."

"Wait. Hear me out. You guys were a threat to them. As long as people here at camp *thought* that the real Berry, Tirk, and Sanborn were out there in the hills setting up an underground army, you were an inspiration to every prisoner in here. You gave them hope. Because you could do it, that meant they could do it too. So as long as the myth existed that Berry, Tirk, and Sanborn were out there, then there was the strong possibility that others would try to escape and join you."

"But I still don't see why they made us tell the Japanese our true identities. Why wouldn't it have been OK for the fictional Berry, Tirk, and Sanborn to remain in the hills, so to speak, while three new guys named Lloyd, Rawlins, and Williams were hauled into camp?"

"You still don't get it, do you? You guys had become a symbol. Lowe and his bunch had to destroy that symbol if they were going to keep others from trying to emulate you by hightailing it to the hills. Just look at those three souls who tried it last night and got caught. So you guys had to be sacrificed. That's the reason they had to tear you down and denigrate you in front of the entire camp."

In other words, it was the camp administrators who stood to lose if the Japanese found out about us, not the prison body as a whole.

Nevertheless, we were continually dismayed by the attitudes that some prisoners held toward those of us who had escaped.

"You dirty bastards," one person said, "don't you know you might have gotten a whole bunch of us killed?"

Another day, as I was getting a haircut from the prison barber, he put a razor to my throat and said, "You son of a bitch, if you so much as twist your head you're liable to get it cut off."

"What are you talking about?" I asked.

"Anyone who would escape from this camp ought to have his head cut off," he snarled.

The truth of the matter is that the prisoners were afraid for their own lives, afraid for their own safety, afraid for the condition of the camp and for the fellow prisoners who might suffer reprisal because of someone's escape. On the whole, I was made to feel like an illegitimate child at a family reunion. They didn't care for us.

It wasn't hard to figure out why: we had created a problem. During our absence—and largely as a result of our escape—the Japanese had developed the policy of organizing the prisoners into what came to be known as "blood groups." This was a diabolical stratagem on their part to control escapes.

The blood groups worked like this: All prisoners were organized into groups of ten, and they were even allowed to choose their own groups. That's why they came to be called blood groups—each group became something like a family. Thereafter, if any member of the group escaped, or even tried to escape, the remaining members of the escapee's blood group were summarily shot, no questions asked. The idea, of course, was to create a powerful incentive not to escape. Hence, anyone who even dared to think about escaping was perceived as an immediate threat to the whole community.

The next morning, I discovered my brown sugar was missing. I made quite a fuss about it and asked some questions, but I didn't accuse anyone. That incident demonstrated to me a sad truth, that we had sunk to a new low.

It was obvious that we were penned up with a dangerous and unsavory lot. Dick, Phil, and I made a pact that if any one of the three of us were attacked or abused in any way, the other two would take his part. Happily, nothing of the sort happened, but we did not relax our vigil.

Sometime later we had another visitor, an American enlisted man named Sontag whom the Japanese trusted to run messages and drive a truck outside the camp. The way he became so trusted by the Japanese is kind of interesting: While on a work detail outside the camp one day, some Filipino guerrillas had stopped the truck and killed all the Japanese on it. They tried to talk Sontag into going with them, but he wouldn't go. Instead, he loaded all the corpses back onto the truck and hauled them back to camp. From that time onward the Japanese looked upon Sontag as a model prisoner of war and gave him pretty much the run of the whole place.

Sontag dropped in to see us three or four times over the next few days. We couldn't figure out why he took a liking to us. Maybe it was because he was an outcast too. Sontag was considered by the other prisoners to be a buddy of the Japanese, and they didn't like him. Bit by bit Sontag began passing little tidbits of information on to us that he had been able to glean from his easy access to the Japanese offices.

Through Sontag's good efforts, we learned that we were scheduled to be shipped to Manila to face a military court-martial. Moreover, he said, the colonel was writing a letter to the court-martial board saying that he had in mind not executing us.

According to Sontag, the colonel's letter outlined seven good reasons why we should be spared execution. That was welcome news to us, and, if true, we prayed the colonel's arguments would carry some weight.

In any event, we had survived another round.

CHAPTER NINE

TRIAL BY TRIBUNAL

THE day came when we were removed from the guardhouse at Cabanatuan and transferred to Manila for trial. Bright and early one morning, six prisoners — Tirk, Sanborn, and myself, along with three others — were trucked down to the railway station in Cabanatuan City, where we were placed aboard a regular civilian passenger train.

How different this journey was from the crowded boxcars that had hauled us up here! We got to sit on real seats — with cushions on them, no less! The six of us occupied a pair of seats that faced each other, three to a seat, while the two armed guards hovered over us, nervously watching our every move. Bound and shackled, we weren't going anywhere, but I guess they thought we were dangerous prisoners who might try to escape. Vendors came up and down the aisles hawking their wares, and the civilian passengers — mostly Filipinos — ogled us curiously, particularly when the train pulled in at a station and people could peek in through the open windows. But we weren't allowed to buy anything or even talk to them.

Bilibid Prison presented a dismal and ominous face to us when we arrived. We were thrown into a different section of it; one we had not seen before — the execution chamber.

The execution chamber was a free-standing building located near the center of the compound. There was no furniture in the death chamber; just a bare concrete floor with a raised platform in the middle. Its electric chair had been removed sometime earlier; however, the markings from where it had previously sat were still plainly visible. Just being there filled us with a profound sense of doom and foreboding.

We had no idea why they put us in the death chamber. Did that mean we were slated for execution? If so, when? Would they come in the wee hours of the morning and take us out to be shot, as the French did when they took someone to the guillotine? Would we be allowed to write letters home? These and other kinds of questions raced through my mind as I tried to get a grasp on the situation.

The days and the nights were uncomfortable both physically and mentally. As far as physical comforts were concerned, there weren't any: not only was there a complete absence of furniture in the chamber, but we had no bedding or blankets either. We had to sleep on the bare concrete floor; and when we would wake up in the mornings, we would find big splotchy bruises wherever our bones had stuck out and made sustained contact with the hard concrete. And as for the mental comfort, we labored under the constant anxiety of not knowing what the Japanese were going to do to us . . . or how . . . or when.

A lot of my time was spent thinking about my mother back in Stillwater, Oklahoma. I couldn't help wondering if she had ever received any information about me, if she knew whether I was alive or dead, a prisoner or free. And I wondered about my dad, whether he was still alive. His health was poor when I left and had been for a long time. Obviously there was no way I could communicate with either of them, inasmuch the last mail had left Corregidor some five or six months earlier. I do remember having asked an American war correspondent who was scheduled to be on one of the last planes out of Corregidor if he would please get in touch with my parents and tell them I was still alive, but of course I had no way of knowing whether or not he actually did so. I hated the thought of the pain and the anguish and the uncertainty that they must be suffering on my behalf.

The terrible strain manifested itself in various ways. For example, I still had one tin of sardines left in my ditty bag that I

Execution chamber at Bilibid Prison. The author was incarcerated here while awaiting court-martial for escaping from prison camp. Courtesy of Dr. Paul Ashton.

had managed to hoard all the way through captivity (the other one had been stolen at Cabanatuan); I was saving it with the thought of having some kind of "feast" with my buddies Tirk and Sanborn whenever the right occasion came along. But one morning I awoke to discover that the tin was missing. That made me extremely angry, perhaps as angry as I had ever been in my whole life — the thought that here we were on death row, probably all of us were going to die, and one prisoner had the gall to steal from another prisoner in the same cell.

Now, seven prisoners were lodged in the cell at the time, including myself, so I knew it had to be one of the other six. What made it more galling was that I could look out the barred window of the cell and see the emptied tin lying on the ground below where the thief had tossed it. I knew it couldn't have been Dick or Phil because we had already pooled our resources, so it had to be one of the other four. Finally, I settled on the most likely culprit and confronted him with my accusation; but nothing came of the episode except a lot of bluster because, really, there was little that could be done about it at that stage. Nevertheless, the hard feelings persisted, and it still rankles me every time I happen to think about it.

We were held in the execution chamber for ten days, then taken out and put into a special cell. We were on a cell block with other prisoners, but we were isolated in a section all to ourselves. A soldier stood outside our door twenty four hours a day with bayonet fixed to make sure we didn't cause any trouble or try to escape. The guard changed every hour. Nevertheless, conditions were a little more comfortable in here. Although we didn't have regular beds or anything so comfy as that, we were each given a straw mat to sleep on and a blanket with which to cover ourselves. That was heavenly compared to sleeping on the bare concrete floor.

A Catholic priest came to see us one day. He, too, was a prisoner of war. We appreciated his words of encouragement; but I must say that the mere fact of his visit raised a new level of anxiety. We couldn't help fearing the worst. Indeed, I wondered if there might be some special reason why a priest was sent in to see us.

From time to time, however, other prisoners were allowed to come by and visit us. The American prisoners who visited us seemed to show a lot of respect for—indeed, take considerable pride in—the fact that we had tried to escape. Unlike the officer corps back at Cabanatuan, who, I'm ashamed to say, tended to view escape as an act of treachery, here at Bilibid many of the prisoners looked upon escape as an act of bravery.

One day the Japanese brought in some postcards and told us we could write to our families at home. At the same time, however, we were advised that whatever we wrote was going to be heavily censored. So there really wasn't much we could say except that we were alive and well. But that in itself was wonderful, just being able to tell someone we were still alive. I labored hard and long about what I would write in the small space provided for us on the card. In the end, I didn't say much. I informed my mother that I was a prisoner of war and that I was in Manila. (I wasn't permitted to tell her that I was soon to go on trial for my life.) I also said that my health was good and that I was much better off physically than most of the other prisoners. (This was true, because I had managed to keep up my weight fairly well while living among the Filipinos, and even though I was now down to about 140 pounds I was still in better physical shape than those who had subsisted on a prison diet for the entire time.)

Fervently I prayed that this card would get delivered, that we weren't being deluded. (Unfortunately, as I was to learn later, it took another eighteen months before my card finally arrived in Stillwater, and until then the only communication my parents had received concerning me was a vaguely worded letter from the Navy Department informing them that their son had been on Corregidor, that many prisoners were taken by the Japanese, and that there was a chance that their son might be among the prisoners. My card, which did not reach them until the late spring of 1944, was the first word my parents received telling

Bilibid Prison, aerial view. The prison comprised eleven buildings radiating out from a central guardhouse. Courtesy of Dr. Paul Ashton.

them definitely that their son was still alive and had not been killed on Corregidor.)

At this time our clothing consisted of just a G-string and a blue denim jacket issued to us by the Japanese. The jackets had originally been used by the Philippine army, and even though Filipino soldiers were ordinarily much smaller than the Americans, we had lost so much weight by this time that we didn't have a problem with their size. The G-string consisted of a cord threaded through the hem of one end of a twelve-inch by thirty-inch cloth. You put it on by tying the cord around your waist with the cloth hanging down in back; then you would reach back and pull the cloth between your legs, loop it up and over the knotted cord at your waist, and let the flap hang down in front.

We'd been in the special cell about six weeks when the Japanese came in to interrogate us. Mostly, they wanted to know how and why we escaped. They gave each of us a sheet of paper—used paper, of which we had to use the back side—and told us we were to write of what we thought about the Japanese, about our experience in some battle that we had been in, and what we thought of our present condition. Now this seemed to me to be a strange assignment, because we knew pretty well that we were awaiting a court-martial by the Japanese army. Nevertheless, we did write, and this is what I wrote on the back of that sheet of paper.*

Three short weeks before the present conflict between Japan and America. I landed in the Philippines. Not until the 29th day of December did the reality of war come to impress itself indelibly upon my senses. For upon this date shortly after noon did several waves of Japanese bombers appear high above Corregidor and unload high explosives. I found my way to a shallow ditch and there waited for this bombing to cease. For more than two hours these planes came roaring over amidst booming anti-aircraft. At last the land batteries were silent. The attackers had fled. I arose from my place of refuge to discover bombs had landed every direction from me—one only a few feet away.

I had many other trying experiences from this date until the fall of Corregidor but this one stands out most clearly—perhaps because it was the first encounter.

At present I console myself with thinking of that distant future at which time I can return to America. This period in concentration camp has taught me how great and wonderful my country is.

After we finished our writing, the Japanese took up our papers, then they brought our gunnysacks of gear into the cell and distributed them to us. We were told that we would be going to court-martial the following morning and that we were to dress the best we could.

*This document was found in Japanese war records and returned to the author several years later.

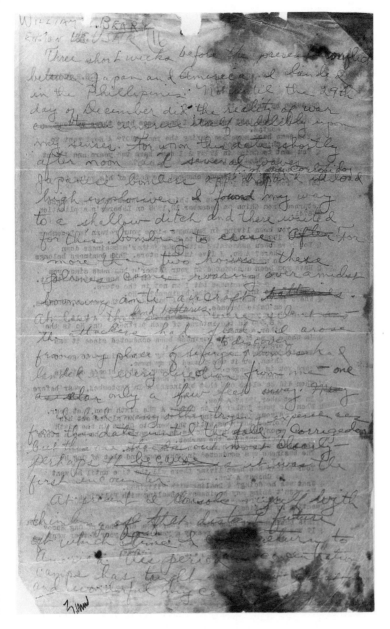

The author's statement written at Bilibid prior to court-martial. This document was found in Japanese war records and returned to the author several years later. From author's collection.

Apparently they were viewing this court-martial as a formal occasion, because they gave us fresh haircuts and even let us have our razors so that we could shave. Some of us had pretty long beards by then. And when I say haircut, I mean that they cropped our hair down close to the skull so that we looked like skinheads.

Of course, we didn't have proper military uniforms to wear. The only clothes we had were the tattered and threadbare khaki trousers and shirts that had served us all through our escape and captivity. But we washed them that night so that they would at least be clean and a lot more presentable than the G-strings and denim jackets we were accustomed to wearing.

That was a difficult night. Sleep was hard to come by, worrying all the time, as we did, about what was going to happen to us. But eventually morning did come. We were taken out, hobbled so that we couldn't take steps more than twelve inches long, our hands securely tied behind our backs, and led out of the prison.

That was an amazing ride we had. We were loaded on the back end of an army truck, Japanese guards around us with bayonets fixed on their rifles. We drove through the streets of Manila. I didn't recognize any of the buildings we passed. I was confused, bewildered, knowing perhaps that we had come to the end of our road. We hoped not. We didn't talk about it among ourselves, but we had the deep anxiety that this could be the end.

Finally, we stopped before a large building. I didn't recognize this building either, because I really wasn't all that familiar with Manila, having been there such a short time. The sergeant went inside with our papers, leaving us still in the truck guarded by the three or four remaining noncoms.

Phil leaned over to me and whispered, "Where do you suppose we are?"

I shrugged my shoulders. "Beats me. It looks like some kind of a military headquarters building."

"You don't suppose this could be General Homma's headquarters?" Dick whispered back, half-jokingly.

Phil snickered at the idea. "Boy, if it is, I sure hope I meet up with the old bastard, because there's a thing or two I'd like to tell him!"

The guard was anything but amused. *"Karuf!"* he barked, meaning for us to keep quiet, as he menacingly banged the side of the truck with his rifle butt. We got the message.

A continual stream of Japanese officers was flowing in and out of the place, and we were conscious of being something of a minor curiosity. From time to time one of the officers would pause to ask our guards a question. Even though I didn't speak any Japanese, I surmised that the questions must have been something like, "What did these guys do?" Then they would laugh at the answer. Obviously, their laughter didn't do much to enhance our comfort.

Shortly, the sergeant came back and marched us inside the building. We were taken to a waiting area and made to sit down. They placed blindfolds on us. There we waited for quite a period of time, still in our shackles and bindings. Some kind of activity was going on in the adjacent room, but we couldn't tell what it was. I surmised that there was another court-martial going on ahead of ours.

Finally, our turn came. Tirk, Sanborn, and I were taken in together. Our blindfolds and bindings were removed.

When I looked up, all I could see was faces. At first, I wasn't conscious of the uniforms. Just faces. It seemed to me that the auditorium was filled with people. I don't know if there were a hundred there, or five hundred. But certainly, it was quite a crowd.

The room was unlike any courtroom I had ever seen before. Instead of a judge's bench and witness chair, as one would expect in an American court, a two-tiered platform or dais ran the full width of one side of the room, upon which two rows of Japanese officers were seated behind long tables covered with a linen cloth. If it weren't for the Japanese flag in the background, the scene would have reminded me of Leonardo da Vinci's painting *The Last Supper*.

On the top level were the high ranking officers. Many of them must have been generals. I didn't know all of the insignias, but certainly they were of high rank. And there were colonels, and majors, and captains. All had on their dress uniforms replete with insignias, ornaments, medals, and ribbons—all displayed prominently, with pomp and ceremony.

Behind us, the auditorium seating area was filled with Japanese civilian and military personnel who came to view the scene.

There we stood, the three of us in our ragged clothes—clothes we had escaped in, clothes we had been captured in. We had nothing to show that we were officers. In fact, we didn't even have insignia showing that we were in the United States Navy. We had on plain khaki fatigues, which consisted of trousers and a shirt.

I tried to size up the situation as quickly as I could. I needed to know what we were up against. Before coming in here, I didn't have any knowledge of whom we were dealing with, of what their mores or values might be. As an attorney in an American court, I would have tried to find out ahead of time all I could about the judge—his preferences and prejudices, and how he tends to act and react in various situations. And of course, I would have participated in selecting the jury. Here, however, we had none of these niceties going for us. It was like stepping off into a great abyss.

And as if all that were not intimidating enough, the platform was positioned at such a high elevation that, even though we prisoners were standing and the officers were seated, we had to look up to them. To the right of the panel (on our left) stood the interpreter.

Part of our overall strategy was to show respect but not fear. Knowing, as we did, that the Japanese place great stock in ceremony and formality, we dutifully made a polite bow to the panel as we took our positions. In Japanese tradition, a bow is viewed simply as good manners and does not necessarily connote obsequiousness; hence, we didn't feel we were groveling before our captors.

When we were led in, I managed to position myself in the

center of the group, with Tirk standing on my left and Sanborn on my right. I wanted to be directly opposite the senior Japanese officer—my hope being that the brunt of the questioning would be directed toward me, the lawyer. I assumed the role of spokesman since I was the only one who had any experience as a prosecuting attorney. I felt that I would probably have a better feel for the kinds of questions that the prosecuting panel might ask of us, and accordingly, I might be better able to frame the appropriate responses. Also, the Japanese knew that I had been a lawyer in civilian life.

There was a long, intimidating period of silence as the officers of the court-martial board stared down at us intently. It seemed as though they were trying to peer into our very souls. I had no idea whether they were trying to rattle us or what, but I found that silence to be discomforting. I wished I was able to discern what was going on in their minds. The suspense grew so terrible that I felt my left knee—the one that was badly damaged when we were recaptured—begin to quiver, and I became desperately afraid that it would betray some element of fear or weakness on my part. Fortunately, however, I managed to keep the quivering under control, and I don't think the Japanese noticed.

Obviously, I had never faced a situation like this, where I was fighting to save my own life. As we stood there through that long silence, the thought sped through my mind of how much easier it is to defend another person in a court of law than it is to defend oneself. When defending another person, the worst that can happen to the lawyer is that he loses a case; it's the client who pays the penalty. Here, on the other hand, if we lose the case, it's we who pay the penalty: we lose our lives. I found myself making a silent prayer that I would be able to think clearly and not let myself be rattled.

Of course, we didn't have the benefit of a defense attorney. That made our situation doubly difficult. You see, in an American court-martial the accused is provided competent legal counsel; here we would have to rely completely on our own wits. What's even worse, we had absolutely no knowledge about the rules, procedures, or protocols of Japanese courts-martial. Nor did we have even the faintest inkling of Japanese common law.

At length, the presiding officer stood up; and as if on cue, the other members of the panel rose with him. He said something in Japanese, the panel members all bowed deeply, and then they all sat down again.

"The Japanese Imperial Army is now in session in a court-martial proceeding," intoned the interpreter. He signaled that we were expected to bow. We bowed in unison toward the court.

"Please state your identities," we were instructed.

"William Berry, ensign, U.S. Navy," I said, leading off.

"Dick Tirk, ensign, U.S. Navy."

"Phil Sanborn, ensign, U.S. Navy."

The charges were read to us. We were accused of escaping from a Japanese prison camp. They didn't charge us with anything else, because we hadn't done anything else in violation of their rules. But we all knew that escape was the one vital, serious crime as far as the Japanese were concerned. And we knew that the punishment was death.

"Do you understand that that is a very serious crime?"

"No, Sir," I stated firmly. The panel seemed caught by surprise at this answer, and there were a couple of raised eyebrows. But that answer was planned to be the very heart of our defense. What we were counting on was an assumption that Japanese law would be similar to the American system of law with regard to what is known as "criminal intent." That is to say, in order for an American court to find somebody guilty of something, you have to prove that the person *willfully, knowingly, and intentionally* did something wrong. I felt certain that the Japanese would be going after criminal intent, and I was bound and determined not to give it to them. (Also, in my memory I could still hear the voice of Professor Wright at law school telling the class, "Never admit anything, even if you're defending a client who you know is guilty.")

"Why did you *not* know that it was a serious crime?" they asked.

"No one told us it was a serious crime," I replied.

"Had you not read the regulations concerning the conduct of prisoners?"

"No, Sir."

"Did you not know that the penalty for escape, attempted or actual, is death by shooting?"

"Sir, we didn't learn about those regulations until after we returned. We never saw those rules before we left — we couldn't have seen them, because they were never posted. As a matter of fact, it is my understanding that those regulations weren't even written until some time after we left Camp Cabanatuan." (Whenever possible, I tried to avoid using the word "escape," as that might tend to connote a tacit admission of guilt.)

Members of the court continued to hammer away on this point. One after another, we were questioned. Questioned together. Questioned separately. Questioned at length. But I steadfastly refused to yield any ground that would substantiate criminal intent.

Even though at this point I felt reasonably confident about my own line of defense, I could never be sure about where I stood with the court. Military courts-martial operate differently than do civilian courts of law. In a court-martial proceeding, the panel serves as judge, jury, and prosecutor — all three rolled into one. Each member of the court is a military officer but not necessarily an attorney. Standard rules of evidence do not apply. For example, hearsay and other forms of unsubstantiated testimony may be accepted. In our case, the court didn't produce any witnesses, any testimony, so they just hammered away at us.

Then they wanted to know *why* we had escaped, what had been going on in our minds.

I took the tack, "We were just trying to hide out. Men were dying all around us. We were fearful of staying in our camp, fearful that we'd contract disease or otherwise perish. We thought that if we were able to get out into the wilds or in the jungle we'd have a better chance of surviving."

They wanted to know where we were going. I told them, "We

didn't have any place in particular in mind. We weren't familiar with the area. We didn't speak the language. We were just trying to hide out in the woods until the war was over."

"Who helped you?"

"No one."

"What other Americans knew about your escape?"

"No one."

"Who provided you aid and service?"

"No one."

"You were gone for three months. Where did you stay?"

"We didn't know where we were," I replied. "We just wanted to hide out. We had had enough of fighting."

"Then you were afraid of being punished? Is that correct?"

Again, they were trying to trip us up on some acknowledgment of wrongdoing, that we knew we were doing something bad.

At that point a thought flashed through my mind: These men were creditable warriors. Resplendent in their dress uniforms and medals, they lived by the code of Bushido—"the way of the warrior." The thought of fear was foreign to their ostensible nature. Their dedication to duty was total. So I thought they might recognize that quality in someone else.

I measured my response carefully. "No. We were not afraid," I said. "If we were afraid, it would have been easier for us to stay in prison. It's easier to live in prison and have someone feed you and look after you than it is to live out in the jungle and have to fend for yourself. All three of us fought bravely all the way through the battle for Corregidor. And we did not show fear in the face of battle. Rather, we did not want to become prisoners. That is why we left Camp Cabanatuan—not because we were afraid, but because we did not want to be prisoners."

They seemed to understand and accept that response. Then they asked, "Did any Filipinos help you?"

"None of the Filipinos helped us," I said. "We didn't want to approach them because we thought they would be loyal to the Japanese. So we hid in the jungle. We had a Filipino soldier who would go into the villages and buy food for us. We didn't dare show ourselves." (We had resolved that we weren't going to implicate any of our Filipino friends, either.)

"What was this Filipino soldier's name?"

"We didn't know his name. He called himself Macario, but I don't think that was his real name. That was the name he gave us."

"Why don't you think that was his real name?

"Because, we didn't speak Filipino, and that was just the way his name sounded to us."

"Where is Macario now?"

"I don't know. He left us in the jungle."

"Please explain how he left you in the jungle."

"Well, one morning we woke up, and he was gone. He wasn't there. He just disappeared. We never saw or heard anything from him again."

In a way, it was a godsend to us—but I'm sure it was a frustration to the court—that all questions and answers had to go through the laborious process of interpretation from Japanese into English and back again. That delay muted the rapid-fire question-and-answer exchange we so often see in American courts, and it also served to blunt the cutting edge of their questions. In any event, I was firmly resolved that no matter what they asked, they were not going to get any admission of criminal intent out of me.

"Did you join a guerrilla group while you were gone?"

"No, we did not."

"Did you see or meet any guerrilla groups while you were gone?"

"No, we did not." (That, of course, was a bald lie, for we had in fact met Ferdinand Marcos, and we had stayed for two nights in a guerrilla camp. But we had already resolved that we weren't going to let the Japanese know about that.)

From the tone of the questioning, it became clear that the court didn't have any independent evidence or sources of information about us other than the statements we ourselves had given the Japanese in previous interrogations. Their main line of attack centered on trying to find any little inconsistencies in our statements, what we had said before, and between what each of us had said. They went over the same material over and over and over again.

Time and again, they would came back to the question of our knowing whether we had done something wrong. They seemed particularly interested in me because I was a lawyer in the United States.

"Surely, as a lawyer, you knew that it is a wrong thing to escape?"

I answered, "Well, as a matter of fact, even though I was a lawyer in civilian life I had never studied international law and really had no reason to be familiar with it." The presiding officer frowned and made a note on his paper. That seemed to stop the questioning along that line.

Finally, when the panel saw they weren't going to get any admission of guilt out of me, they focused their attention on Dick Tirk.

"Didn't you know it was wrong to escape?"

"No, Sir."

"What did you think would happen to you when you were recaptured?"

"I don't know."

But they persisted: "Surely, you must have given some thought as to what might happen when you were caught?"

Finally, after a particularly hard line of questioning, Dick blurted out, "We thought you might shoot us."

A faint smile of satisfaction flickered across the presiding officer's face. "Ah so," he murmured and wrote something on his pad. That seemed to be the answer they were waiting to hear.

I held my breath. I couldn't tell whether Dick's answer would be construed as incriminating or not. In my mind we still had not confessed to any wrongdoing or even that we thought there might be anything wrong with escaping. The only thing Dick had admitted to them was our fear that we would be punished if they caught us.

About that time, Phil interrupted the questioning and said, "Under the Geneva Conventions it is not considered a crime for prisoners of war to try to escape. We aren't supposed to be punished physically but merely put on a diet of bread and water for thirty days."

When Phil's answer was interpreted into Japanese, the whole panel broke out in a chorus of laughter. They thought it was ridiculous.

"Didn't you know that the Japanese government did not sign the Geneva Concords? Did you not know that they refused to sign that part of the Geneva Convention, the articles pertaining to prisoners of war?" asked the presiding officer coldly. "So it is ridiculous of you to think that we are bound to them!"

When I heard him say that, my heart sank. I didn't know what to expect next. It had never occurred to us that the Japanese government hadn't signed those particular articles.

Nevertheless, several things began to fit together in my mind and make sense. Japanese soldiers are not supposed to surrender. Surrender is a heinous crime against their god and their country. Japanese soldiers were told that by surrendering to our forces, they would be ostracized and ridiculed and cut off from their families. In their eyes, it was better to die gloriously in battle than to live the rest of their lives in shame. And now that I understood that attitude, it helped to explain why the Japanese treated American prisoners as such despicable creatures.

Now the officer in charge changed his line of attack, "Which one of you thought up the idea of escaping? Which one had the thought?"

I needed to be careful what I said here, because this was one of the points we had been interrogated on back at Cabanatuan. I didn't want to come out and point my finger at Dick Tirk, even though it was originally his idea and he was the one who more or less ramrodded it. But we all wanted to escape too, so it wasn't Dick by himself; we were all in it together.

So I said, "Well, we were all out at the latrine, and somebody else was talking about escaping—what they ought to do to get out of there, and so forth. And with that, we all looked at each other, kind of nodded, went back, and at that point we knew we were going to escape."

"Who was it that gave you the idea?"

"It was someone else's idea," I said, "but I don't know who it was. It was dark, and we couldn't see who it was, and I didn't know him anyway."

"What did you think you were going to do when you escaped?"

"We didn't know. We hadn't made any plans. All we knew was that we wanted to get as far away from that place as we could. We thought we could hide in the jungle until the war was over."

They tried to needle us with sarcasm: "You are all officers in the United States Navy. Surely you don't expect us to believe you were that naive and stupid?"

"Sir," I explained, "we were all civilians until the emergency came along, and we had very little training. In my own particular case, I was practicing law back in Stillwater, Oklahoma, when I was ordered to report, and I was sent to Manila without any military training at all."

Of course, it pleased them to hear that America was just jerking people out of their civilian jobs, putting them into uniform, and expecting them to be good soldiers.

Gradually it sunk into me that these were military officers, not attorneys, and they really hadn't been trained in the art of asking questions. It became progressively easier to anticipate what questions they might ask and thus deflect our answers away from incriminating information and toward something that might satisfy a military mind. As we sensed what answers they were looking for we would say something that might make them feel superior, even if those answers were totally false and would cast the three of us in a ridiculous light.

I don't think they ever caught on to the games we were playing with them. Of course, we didn't look at it as playing games; we were fighting for our very lives.

After a while the presiding officer perceived that the questions were going around in circles and the panel members had no new questions to ask. I guess they decided that they weren't going to pry any incriminating evidence out of us that they didn't already have. So they just gave up on us and sent us out of the room.

We waited outside in the hallway while they called in other prisoners for trial. The others with us had all escaped or tried to escape.

We could only wait and wonder. Had our strategy been successful? Or had we outsmarted ourselves? Many times in the past I had seen attorneys put on what they truly believed was a brilliant defense, only to see their clients convicted anyway. Out of this experience, I came to have a lot more sympathy for the ordinary criminal who is waiting anxiously for the jury to render its verdict.

"What do you think?" Phil asked anxiously.

"I don't know," I replied. "It all depends on whether they felt that we knew we were doing something wrong. If we managed to convince them that we were merely a bunch of jerks who didn't know what we were doing, we may come out OK. But if they think that we were out there in the jungle trying to join up with resistance forces, then we're sunk. It's all over."

The minutes ticked by, maddeningly slow, while the panel deliberated.

We made various attempts to try to cheer each other up, but our feeble attempts at gallows humor seemed to fall flat. I would have given anything for a cigarette at that moment. We didn't have any—not even a Japanese smoke.

After what seemed like hours—we had no sense of time, no way to tell time—the three of us were led back into the courtroom and made to stand before the bench. The presiding officer, through the interpreter, pronounced our sentences. They gave Dick, Phil, and me each the same sentence.

"You will be sentenced to three years as special prisoners under the control and under the authority of the Japanese military police and in their custody."

I felt giddy. All the blood rushed out of my brain. I couldn't believe it. We were going to live!

The reading of the sentence went on: "This sentence is subject to the will of the Japanese army, and it can be changed at any time according to its will."

Now, that second proviso was the sword of Damocles hanging over our heads by a slender thread, and it would constantly prey on our minds that at any time the cell door might open and we could be taken out and shot.

With the reading of the sentence, I could feel my entire body totter and sway. I was thrilled that we weren't going to be executed. Hope burned brightly in my whole being. I don't think I had really realized how much tension had built up over recent weeks. And now that terrible tension was lifted. I guess I felt dizzy because so much weight had been taken from my shoulders.

A Japanese officer on the panel became concerned about my tottering. Through the interpreter he called me by name and asked, "Are you all right? Are you physically all right? Are you ill?"

I thanked him for his concern, and I said, "My stomach is upset. I've had trouble with my stomach." I couldn't think of anything else to say under the circumstances. I couldn't tell him that I was giddy with joy over not being executed.

In a strange way, that episode gave me a positive feeling. I now knew that the Japanese — some of them, anyway — were capable of having a little tenderness in their hearts. I didn't see that tenderness often. Not directed toward me, anyway.

I don't know what motivated them to give us a prison term. To the best of my knowledge, we were the first lot of escapees to avoid execution.

With most juries, one never knows why they reach the verdicts that they do.

CHAPTER TEN

DAYS OF DESPERATION

SHU-JIN—"special prisoner"—was a classification given by the Japanese to those who had escaped or attempted to escape from one of their prison camps. People who had previously escaped were considered to be both a disruptive element within the prison population and a high risk with regard to trying again if an another opportunity should present itself. Therefore, in order to make their task of managing prisoners easier, the Japanese segregated all "troublemakers" into a separate section of Bilibid known as the Military Police Prison and guarded by the dreaded Kempei Tai, the Japanese Military Police, not ordinary soldiers. In this section were incarcerated the Japanese military prisoners and several Americans who had escaped or been captured with guerrillas and who were awaiting trial and execution.

Within the MP section, Tirk, Sanborn, and I were placed in a tiny cell measuring about ten feet by ten feet. The floor of our new cell was at an elevation about knee-height above the level of the corridor, so that to enter the cell one had to step up into it. Making it more awkward, the doorway was only about three feet high, which meant that we had to step up and stoop down at the same time.

Each time we entered the cell we were made to line up and count off. Now, that applied not merely to those of us who occupied this particular cell but to every prisoner in the entire cell block, Filipinos and Americans alike. (Japanese prisoners were handled separately from us.)

Further, the counting off had to be in Japanese: *ichi, ni, san, shi, go, roku, shichi, hachi, ku, juu, juu ichi, juu ni, juu san, juu shi, juu go, juu roku, juu shichi, juu hachi, ni juu.* Those are the numbers one through twenty. To get past ten, you take the ten, which is *juu*, and then add the number: *juu ichi* is eleven, *juu ni* is twelve, and so on. When you get to twenty, you take the two, which is *ni*, and the ten, which is *juu*, and then add the number. For example, *ni juu ichi* is twenty-one.

Under the circumstances, it didn't take long to learn the system. If we couldn't come up with the right number, the guards would beat us over the head until we got it right.

Dick, our master of languages, had already picked up a fair amount of Japanese. The first time we counted off coming down the column, Dick had counted ahead and told us our numbers. He told me that I would be *ni juu san*, twenty-three, and Phil would be *ni juu shi*, twenty four.

We were also given home-made emblems and told we had to pin them on our jackets and to wear them whenever we were out of the cell. The emblems were patches of red cloth about four inches square with a Japanese character written on them with a marking pen. The character looked like a box with a man in it. Dick figured out that the character was *shu-jin*, "special prisoner." As matters turned out, however, we rarely wore the tags when we were under the kempies, the American nickname for the Kempei Tai, because they kept us closely guarded at all times; it was only on those occasions when we were on the "other side," so to speak—in the hospital ward, standing trial, and so on—that we wore them.

Three walls of our cell were made of solid concrete, and the fourth was made of vertical four-by-four wooden beams spaced about an inch apart. At times there were as many as thirteen of us special prisoners confined there. In addition to the small door that we had to stoop to pass through, the front wall had a viewing slot through which the patrolling Japanese guards could look in on us and a foot-square opening at floor level just big enough to push food through. In the opposite corner of the cell a wooden trap door covered the rectangular hole in the hardwood floor that

Special prisoners' cell. Contemporaneous drawing by prisoner Don T. Schloat. Inmates sit facing the wall all day, not allowed to talk or move around. At night they slept where they had been sitting. A bare light bulb in the ceiling shone twenty-four hours a day. Only five prisoners are shown here, but the cell often held as many as thirteen. Those confined with Schloat were Ballard, Berry, Barnbrook, Cameron, Hanson, Klett, Sanborn, Thompson, Tirk, and Toups. (The poor quality of reproduction is due to the tinted blue-green paper, which is all the artist had to work with, on which the original drawing was made.) Courtesy of Don T. Schloat.

served as a latrine. It emptied outside the building. The ceiling was about fourteen feet high, in the center of which was a bare electric light bulb that burned twenty-four hours a day. Our only ventilation came through the small slits in the wall.

No one was allowed to talk or move around in any fashion. Any violations were immediately punished. If the patrolling guards caught us talking to each other, they would jab us painfully through the viewing slot with a hardwood pole that they always carried, or whenever they felt like it, they would drag us outside to be beaten. In either event, it was an effective way to keep down the talking.

Our clothing and everything we owned was taken away from us and we were issued receipts for them. In their place we were issued a G-string, a denim Filipino army jacket, a Filipino issue army blanket, a small rag for a towel, and a pint-size pillow. We had no shoes or sandals.

All day every day, we were required to sit in an immobile position facing the wall, half of us facing one wall and the other half facing the opposite wall. Furthermore, the sitting position was rigidly prescribed. We were required to sit on the bare hardwood floor, legs drawn up tightly in front of us and backs held straight. At all times we had to keep our hands and arms close to our bodies—that is, we couldn't use our hands and arms to prop up our weight or relieve the pressure on our backs.

As I mentioned, we were not allowed to talk, not even a whisper. We had no reading material. The only thing we had to do was just sit there, stare at the blank wall, and contemplate the gravity of the crimes we supposedly had committed.

At night we slept on the same spot where we had been sitting all day. We would stretch out on the floor and wrap ourselves in our blankets as much as we could. The blanket served mainly to keep the mosquitoes from us, because temperature was not ordinarily a problem. Usually we would wear our denim jackets to sleep in; I'm not sure why, because we seldom wore the jackets during the day. I guess they provided a psychological comfort. In addition to the little pillow under my head, I would roll up my towel and put it under the small of my back to ease some of the pain. Because of the injury to my back when I fell off the bridge (it later turned out that I had ruptured a disk), it was extremely painful for me to stretch out on the hard floor.

Food, such as it was, came twice a day through the little trap door and passed around among the prisoners. All meals were exactly the same. They consisted of about four ounces of rice gruel dabbed onto an oblong aluminum mess bowl roughly eight inches across and fairly shallow. The rice was of the lowest quality, and almost never did the rice have any meat or animal protein in it. Accompanying the rice was a cup of clear soup with some green vegetable tops floating in it called "whistle weed." The whistle weed had no nutritional value whatever, but it did add a bit of flavor.

Under this regimen, the days were boring. As I sat there, I would try to keep my mind occupied: I would think about happier days and things more pleasant than the grim setting that surrounded us. I would watch ants make their way across the wall. That was pretty much the sum and substance of my amusement. Sometimes I would put myself into a trancelike state by imagining myself to be a statue of a stoic philosopher situated in a Roman garden. Other times I would imagine myself to be an old Indian chief looking off into the distance. Then pretty soon the prison walls would just melt away and I would be all by myself in my own imaginary world.

Of course, we did develop other little outlets. We learned ways to whisper and talk without the guards detecting us. Our ears became highly attuned to the sound of their footsteps as they paced up and down the corridor outside our cell. From time to time, however, one of them would sneak up softly and peek into the cell. And if the guard happened catch one of us talking or being out of position, woe to that offender. He would be severely punished for his infraction.

I recall one incident when I happened to glance up at the viewing slot and saw a guard peeping in at us. I stared right back. I don't know what in the world possessed me to do it, but I

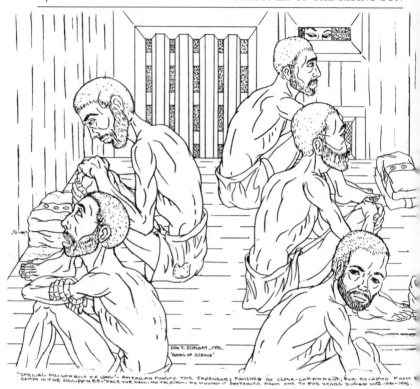

Special prisoners of war. Drawing made from memory by Don T. Schloat in 1992. Schloat is the prisoner on the left showing how thin they were by encircling his arm with his fingers. The man looking at us is the author. Courtesy of Don T. Schloat.

thought to myself, "Well, he's looking at me so I'll just stare him down." We stared at each other that way for several minutes. I was almost defiant in my manner. Presently, he called for the interpreter, who came down and opened the cell door. Through the interpreter, he ordered me to take a position on my knees, upright and facing him, while he struck me over the head with his club. The club was made of mahogany, about two and a half inches in diameter and three feet long. Each time he struck me, I would fall over; then he would make me get into an upright position again while he repeated the process. I may have exaggerated the effect of the blows a bit in hopes that he'd quit; nonetheless, blow after blow they came. I counted ten times that I was knocked down. After the count of ten, he stopped and ordered me back into my regular sitting position. It didn't take long until I could feel knots as large as goose eggs rising on my head. And from that time onward, I was never able to look a Japanese in the eye again. Instinctively, I turned away.

The special prisoners in our cell were a mixed lot. Our cultural backgrounds and ethics were very different. Tirk, Sanborn, and myself were the only officers.

Christian D. Klett was probably the most interesting. He came from Pittsburgh. Before the war, Klett had been with the merchant marine, so technically he was a civilian who just happened to be in the wrong place at the wrong time. Klett had never been to college, had no interest in going to college, yet he had the amazing ability to sing all the operas—he knew them forward and backward. He also could relate almost any story from classic literature. According to him, his favorite pastime was to go out and get himself a fifth of gin and a good classic, then stretch out and read the book and drink the gin. Klett told us that he was salutatorian of his high school class; considering that he graduated from a rather large high school in Pittsburgh, I took that to be a fairly significant accomplishment.

Physically, however, Klett was a funny-looking creature: potbellied—at least until landing in here—not very tall, about thirty years of age, snaggletoothed. His beard grew long and his hair was kept short. At times he could be very amusing, and at other times totally obnoxious. I had the impression that Klett had something of a persecution complex—always feeling that people were picking on him. And he was probably right, for Klett was one of those kinds of fellows who just naturally seemed to invite being picked on.

Ballard and Toups were the odd couple. These two were

together everywhere. Ballard's first name was James, but I never did learn Toups's first name. Ballard was tall, while Toups was short, and they made a kind of Mutt-and-Jeff combination. Ballard was lanky, with red hair, and had a good education. Toups, on the other hand, was a little Cajun from Louisiana who said that at one time he wanted to be a jockey. I was not sure if he could read and write, and it was my impression that he never finished grade school.

Edward A. Beyuka was a Zuni Indian from Arizona. He said that until joining the army, he had never lived outside his native village. Beyuka was a loner who had little to say to other persons. He caused no trouble. He looked so much like a Filipino that I don't think the Japanese ever would have caught him if his conscience hadn't begun to bother him. (As a matter of fact, there had been another situation up at Cabanatuan where an American Indian had escaped and was later found working as a Filipino mess boy in a Japanese army camp.) Beyuka became remorseful, worrying about his blood group being shot because of his escape, so he turned himself in.

Hanson was from somewhere up in the Northwest—Washington or Montana, I think. Like most people I met in the military, I never learned his first name. Hanson was a likable little fellow, and very sensitive to other people's words, but there were times when he would do things that were quite irritating. Sometimes he talked about having been to military school, but other than that he never told us anything about his background; we couldn't tell whether his family had been wealthy or not, although he seemed to give that impression.

A fellow named Russell (not the Bob Russell I had been with on Corregidor) was in there because he had killed somebody. We didn't get many of the details, whether the killing had been in self-defense, premeditated, accidental, or what. From what little I was able to piece together, he had killed a fellow American prisoner, and it was the Americans who delivered him over to the Japanese for punishment. We pretty much steered clear of him. Whether it was because the rest of us were fearful of our own well-being or whether he was basically noncommunicative, I don't know, but by and large he ignored us and by the same token we left him alone.

Don Schloat had escaped from a work camp on Palawan. He told us that originally he had planned to escape from Cabanatuan, but when the blood groups were formed after our escape he had put aside those plans until a later date.

A couple of other guys who passed through were named Cameron and Thompson. Again, I never learned their first names. Another was Fred Stamper, from Locust Grove, Oklahoma, who had been caught with a guerrilla group. The Japanese shot him.

As time went on, certain frictions developed among us. The fact that Dick and Phil and I were officers tended to set us apart whether we wanted it to or not. Even though rank meant nothing in there, still there was an undertone of hostility. But then, we all had some little quirks or idiosyncrasies that got on other people's nerves. It wasn't easy living twenty-four hours a day with six to twelve other men in a cramped cell and with nothing to do. But for the most part, we learned to adjust to each other and to overlook our petty dissatisfactions. We learned not to criticize each other or to talk down to one another. Nerves were on edge, people's egos were sensitive, and we learned to subjugate our feelings.

Much of the time we were filled with anxiety and fear. We never knew what the next minute, the next day, or the next week would have in store for us. Even though the court had sentenced us to three years, that wasn't the final word. We labored under the burden of knowing that our sentences could be changed at any time at the will of the Japanese army. This uncertainty had a worrisome effect on us: at any minute we could be yanked out from our tiny cell, marched out, and executed. We couldn't be sure of anything.

Just to give an example, once or twice a week—but never at regular intervals—the guards would take us out of our cells and let us try to get some exercise, which they called *tiso*. It was still painful for me to walk because of my lingering leg injury. Each time they marched us out of there, I couldn't help feeling cold, icy fingers clasp themselves around my heart, chilled by the fear that perhaps this time we might be marching to our death. Always it was a relief to find out that we were merely going for exercise; too many times in the past had I seen prisoners taken out, never to be seen or heard from again. Those Japanese guards had absolutely no regard for human life.

Our exercise periods followed a regular ritual. The guards would first make us line up, count off in Japanese, and then march us outside into the courtyard for *tiso*. They would have us do some light calisthenics, like throw our hands above our heads or march in place, or something like that. Thank heavens they didn't make us run or do anything strenuous, because we weren't strong enough for that. Then after a couple of minutes of *tiso*, they'd let us take a bath.

I say "bath" — actually, it consisted of little more than splashing water on ourselves from out of a horse trough. A pipe came up in the middle of the large rectangular trough, maybe ten feet long and four feet wide, and gushed a steady stream of water. We would splash our hands in this stream and throw a little water on our bodies and faces, and that was our bath. It was over in about ten seconds. Then we would line up again, count off, and march back to our cell. Outside our cell, we would count off again, get back into our cell, and be locked up for another week or so.

We had no way of keeping time, or even of knowing what day of the week it was. Phil Sanborn ingeniously devised a way that wouldn't be detected by the Japanese of scratching a little notch on the wall for each passing day. That rudimentary calendar helped us keep track of how long we had been in there.

No news from the outside world ever worked its way in to us. It was almost as if we were suspended in space and time. Our world was almost entirely limited to what went on within the four walls of our little prison cell. Occasionally we might be out in the exercise area and pick up a rumor from some Filipino who had recently been tossed in there; but even then the news was vague, generally about some naval battle taking place somewhere. Even this communication was under strict surveillance.

Despite all of these discomforts, we usually managed to sleep fairly well at night. Probably, this was owing to our total lack of energy. Sleep offered a blessed escape from the constant anxiety and worry of the day. I know that in my case I had some of the most fantastic dreams that I have ever experienced in my life. These dreams always seemed to have lots of light; there would be a beautiful room filled with lots of people—many of them my friends from college—and there always seemed to be a party or a dance of some kind going on. I looked forward to these dreams.

Sometimes I would wake up during the night, and when I did, there would usually be a "floor show" going on. This was what I came to call the "Dance of the Cockroaches." When everyone was quiet and still, everyone sleeping in the same position, the cockroaches would come out from their various holes and hiding places and form a line—always a line—to walk across the room. They would march up to the toes of someone whose feet happened to be sticking out from under the blanket, and they would start feeding on the sweaty grime that collected around the toenails. It was almost like a ritual dance the way they would strut and seem to show off. The moment that someone stirred, however, the party was over; the cockroaches would scatter and disappear like magic back into their hiding places.

About two feet below the hole in the cell floor that served as a latrine was a rectangular metal tray to catch our excrement. To use the latrine, one would lift the lid, squat astraddle the hole, and relieve himself. When finished, one would close the lid and go back to his regular position. We had no toilet tissue of any type. We were not prevented from using the latrine any time we needed to, so some of us developed the habit of using it "whether we needed to or not," as we used to say. That is, some of us went to the latrine more often than necessary for the sole purpose of being able to shift out of our sitting position on the floor.

Shortly after we were placed in the cell, the guards asked for volunteers to go out and empty the tray from underneath. Beyuka and I were the first volunteers. I figured that if we were going to have to take turns for this unpleasant task, I wanted to get my turn over with early. A guard went with us and kept us moving at a rapid pace. Beyuka and I pulled the tray out from its place and emptied it into a manhole. The stench and the untidiness was a bit bothersome, but at the same time I found it relaxing to get out into the fresh air and to stretch my muscles a little. The guard even gave us an opportunity to wash ourselves afterward at the water trough.

This practice was discontinued almost immediately, however, and that turned out to be the one and only time that any of us special prisoners were allowed to empty the latrine. After this one time, the tray was always emptied by someone else. The reason, I think, was not that we were such a privileged class, but rather that the Japanese were apprehensive that we might use the chore as an opportunity to try to escape.

One night there was an escape attempt in the cell next to us. Two of the Filipino prisoners decided they were getting out of there. Somehow, they managed to get up through the ceiling, which was about fourteen feet high and boarded over, and get into the crawl space. We could hear them from our cell above, moving back and forth, trying to find some way out of the building. They were caught and brought before all of the inmates of the cell. Their cellmates were interrogated as to why they didn't sound off when the escape attempt took place. I think they said that the two escapees had threatened them with death if they made any sounds. But that answer was not satisfactory to the prison guards, so they lined them all up against the wall, gouged their faces with the brush end of brooms, and beat them with clubs. The two escapees were taken out and executed.

From time to time a new person would be put into the cell with us. Always these were individuals who were awaiting execution. To the extent that we could, we would try to talk with them and to comfort them in their last hours. But they were heavily guarded, and little conversation was possible.

I remember one particularly sad case of a chap who was thrown in with us. The guards offered him a couple of cigarettes (something none of us had), but he just turned and gave them back to the guard, saying, "Here, you keep these." Now, these were the people who were soon going to execute him, and he just turned and gave his last cigarette back to his captors. That situation reminded me of a dog who is being beaten by his master yet keeps licking his master's hand.

The thing I observed about each of the condemned prisoners who passed through our cell on their way to the firing squad — I lost count of how many — was that they all seemed to have a hope inside that something was going to come along and spare them. I think they probably clung to this hope clear up to the moment the trigger was pulled.

Our troubles were not over. One heart-stopping day, the guards notified Tirk, Sanborn, and me that we were going back before the court-martial board the following day. We got little sleep that night, wondering what was in store for us. We couldn't think of any reason why the Japanese army would haul us back before the tribunal unless they had now decided to execute us. Certainly, we had already seen enough prisoners pass through our cell on the way to the firing squad to be fully aware that our fates hung by a slender thread.

The next day at midmorning we were taken down to the military headquarters in Manila. Again we were interrogated by the courtmartial board. I'm not sure that all of the officers were the same, but I do know that some of them were. As a matter of fact, I don't know when I've ever seen so many Japanese high brass in one place. At the end, we were given precisely the same sentence we had before.

After the trial was over and we were waiting to be taken back to our cell, the interpreter (who, incidentally, I felt was on our side) chatted with us and explained some of the reasons for our new trial. Tokyo had issued new rules governing the conduct of courts-martial, and it became necessary for us to be sentenced under the new Japanese law, not the old military law. He said that Tokyo was secretly negotiating with the United States for a stand-off agreement whereby Japan would retain control over all of the islands in the Pacific west of Hawaii. According to him, the Japanese Supreme Command had become concerned that if it became known how many prisoners were dying, that knowledge would reflect badly on Japan, cause the United States to seek revenge, and thus dash any hopes for a negotiated settlement.

The interpreter also told us that we were lucky that our first court-martial didn't take place three weeks earlier than it did—that is, before these negotiations got underway. Otherwise, he said, we would have all been executed without any hesitation whatsoever.

Whether any part of what he said was true or not, I had no way of knowing. All I know is that it was a tremendous relief for us to learn that we were not going to be executed on the spot. However, we still feared that any moment our sentence could be changed to execution.

Back in our cell again, it was the same old routine. Sit immobile all day; sleep stretched out in the same spot all night. The minutes passed, minutes turned into hours, hours into days, days into weeks, and weeks into months. The same old sameness.

One night I awoke to someone screaming, "Get them off of me!" It was a scene right out of a nightmare. Termites were swarming, and they had invaded our cell. Thousands upon thousands flew in, attracted to our light. The termites had black bodies about an inch long with white wings. We fought them off, tried to beat them down, but still they continued to fly in and surround us. The cell was absolutely filled with flying, buzzing insects. Finally, the interpreter came in to see what the commotion was about, and he ordered the guard to turn off the light. Even with the light out, it took more than an hour to get the last of the critters out. The next morning, the floor was covered with the bodies of termites that we had killed.

Klett came to the breaking point. He couldn't take it anymore. He had to get out of there at all costs. Deciding to self-inflict an injury that would get him into the prison hospital, he tried to break his arm. He couldn't do it himself. He tried many ways. Finally, he put his arm across the open toilet hole and tried to get one of us to jump on it and break it, but no one would.

Next, he tried to kill himself. But he didn't know how to go about the job. Lacking any utensils in the cell that could possibly do bodily harm, and having a ceiling too high to hang oneself from, Klett nevertheless came up with an ingenious solution. One day while out at *tiso*, he managed to acquire some dysentery medication from another prisoner. Now, there are two kinds of dysentery: the quick-acting, bacterial kind that causes a person to die in a matter of days, and the slow-acting amebic kind that lingers for months and usually ends up being fatal. Klett had the longer-lasting kind but already was showing blood in his stool. Since he figured the outcome was inevitable, Klett wanted to get it over with quickly. He asked how many pills he should take. The answer was one every four hours, and never more than two. Klett asked what would happen if he took them all. He was told that taking them all at once would probably kill a man. That night Klett took them all. Instead of dying as he had hoped, however, he merely got horribly sick—sick enough that he wished more than ever that he were dead. The ironic thing is that the pills did cure his dysentery.

Another time Klett got it into his head that the Japanese had a special regard for crazy people, so he decided to fake insanity. In the middle of the cell one night, he took off all of his clothes, jumped up and down, and screamed, "Spider! Spider! Spider," all the while waving his arms up and down as if he were trying to brush something off his arms and legs. Naturally, the guard came rushing in with the interpreter, wanting to know what in the world was going on. They dragged poor Klett down to the end of the hall and put him in the shower. All the while the interpreter kept saying, "See, no spiders. No spiders."

Finally when Klett had calmed down they put him into a cell by himself. Then they came back to our cell and asked if someone would volunteer to take Klett's clothes down there and dress him.

I volunteered. The moment I entered his cell, Klett winked at me, knowing full well that I knew what he was up to. After I got him dressed and bedded down on the floor with his blanket and pillow, he reached up and whispered to me, "I'll bet that's the first time any American got the Japs up in the middle of the night to give him a shower." I whispered the story to the guys in my cell and they all loved it.

As time went on, we all began to come apart physically from lack of nutrition. I noticed one day that as I was watching the parade of ants marching across the cell, the ant that was in the center of my field of view would fade out of vision. I held my eye on one spot steadily, and sure enough, as an ant crossed my center of focus it would seem to go out of vision, come into vision, go out of vision, and come into vision again. I didn't know at the time what caused it, but later I learned that beriberi, a lack of vitamin B1, had caused my optic nerve to deteriorate.

April 29, the emperor's birthday, was the occasion for magnanimity on the part of the prison officials. Apparently they thought this was a time for great rejoicing and thanksgiving, even among the prisoners. So about midday they brought around some tasty little rice flour cupcakes and passed them through the hole in our wall so we could help them celebrate. After we had finished eating the emperor's cupcakes, the guards came back around and, in another magnanimous gesture, announced that we would be allowed to pray in any position that we desired. Well, you won't believe what nonsense erupted around that place: Little Toups stood on his head. Someone else stood up and stretched his arms skyward. Another person leaned against the wall. Every kind of contortion imaginable took place.

"What in the world are you doing?" I asked.

"They said we could pray in any position we wanted, and this is the position we're praying in" was the answer.

Praying? Nonsense! What they were actually doing was taking advantage of the opportunity to move around and stretch their weary muscles without the Japanese guards hitting down on them. That was the way we helped the emperor celebrate his birthday.

Speaking of prayer, I might mention that I had a strong and vital religious upbringing that never left me, although I must admit that there were several times when my faith was sorely tested. Early on, I prayed silently and to myself almost every night. I prayed for what most prisoners prayed for, and that was to survive and for my family at home to be all right. Then one night as I was praying for strength of faith, I got to wondering to myself if this was worth it. Did I need to? And so I had stopped praying. The next morning I noticed that everything was still the same, that nothing seemed to change because I had stopped praying. So for the most part, I ceased my daily prayers after that incident.

We came into possession of a small GI New Testament in our cell. One day a guard gave it to us. Just one. We were told we could read it. So we worked out a schedule among ourselves: each person would have it for three days, then he had to pass it on to the next man. It went around the cell that way. I think my turn came up three times. That's how many times I read the New Testament while I was in there. Even though I had stopped praying on a regular basis, I remained convinced that my faith in God helped me through the whole time. I have no doubts about that, and I am fully convinced that my mother's prayers while I was in prison are one of the big reasons that I survived.

Most of the Japanese guards had short fuses. Some of them were downright mean and never passed up an opportunity to hit somebody. The bad ones would sneak up on us, made even more stealthy by wearing tennis shoes, and try to catch us in some kind of violation that they could punish us for. Some, however, showed a little more understanding, and everyone knew who they were.

One guard in particular, named Hachigama, had a soft spot in his heart. He would come into our cell and talk with us. He spoke a little English but not enough to carry on a sustained conversation, so he would bring the interpreter along. He'd sit there and talk with us about our families, where we were from, and all kinds of things. When he was on patrol, we always knew we could relax. Once in a while he would throw a lighted cigarette into our cell, which we would pass around and smoke.

But just because he was gentle didn't mean he couldn't be tough. One of the new members of our cell found that out the hard way. Lester Barnbrook had been tossed in our cell one night after he had tried to escape from the regular part of Bilibid Prison and got hung up in the barbed wire. Barnbrook was larger than any of the rest of us, a bully with a mean-looking scar across his forehead. One night Barnbrook had the lack of wisdom to make a sarcastic, impudent, out-of-place remark to this guard. Infuriated by his impudence, the guard screamed for the interpreter and ordered Barnbrook out of the cell. Barnbrook cowered as he went out. He didn't want to leave at all. The rest of us practically had to shove him out of there. For some reason they didn't shut the door after him, which was unusual to say the least. When Barnbrook got out there, the guard brought up his club to strike Barnbrook over the head. Barnbrook cowered, crouched down, and held up his arm to shield the blow. That made the guard even more angry, and he started banging Barnbrook on the head, on the shoulders, across the back, and any other place he could strike him. When Barnbrook fell, he kicked him several times and in general just beat the hell out of him.

Then the guard called for someone else to step outside the cell. No one else seemed to want to, so I stepped outside. When this guard came up to me, I stood at complete attention as he raised the club as if to strike me. I didn't flinch, didn't let on that I was scared, didn't even let my eyes blink. He raised the club three or four times but didn't strike me. I never moved. Then the interpreter told me to lean over, and he swatted me across the buttocks four or five times. The swats were not terribly painful, but nevertheless I gave out with a grunt each time a blow struck so as to give him some measure of satisfaction. Then he proceeded to administer the same punishment to each member of the cell. I advised the others to stand at complete attention as I did.

A couple of nights later this same guard came back to the cell and leaned in to ask how we were doing. I told him that we all wanted to apologize, that we thought more of him than of all of the other guards, and that we were sorry we had stepped out of line and needed reprimanding. I think I saw him blush. He said, "Sometimes I lose my head and I don't mean to become infuriated like that." That was the end of the matter.

Along about this time, another amusing incident happened. A high-ranking general came through on an inspection tour of the the special prisoners. When he came to our cell, he asked a series of questions: how we were, how we were being treated, and so forth. We perceived that the general just didn't know how bad off we were. So Phil proceeded to tell him. "We are being treated like pigs," he said. "We don't have anything to eat with, so we have to eat with our hands. And we have never eaten with our hands in our entire lives!" The general covered his nose, the smell was too much for him.

Every one of us held his breath, fearing instant retaliation. But nothing untoward happened, and the general went on with his inspection. About three hours later, however, a detail of guards came and took us out of our cell and beat us rather severely. Then as they put us back in the cell, they gave each of us a spoon.

Some things happened that were hard to figure out. One day a Japanese guard handed a pencil and a penknife to me through the viewing slot and asked me to sharpen it. I whittled away on the pencil, bringing it to a point the way we did back in Oklahoma. But when I handed it back to him, the interpreter said, "You Americans do everything backward." He laughed crazily as if he had said something funny.

We learned that if we were caught talking, we could usually avoid punishment by saying, "I was just taking care of so-and-so, who is sick and in agony." That was another little way of putting something over on the Japanese.

By the time we entered our fifth and sixth months of confinement, our health began to deteriorate rapidly as our physical condition progressively weakened. Phil Sanborn's legs started swelling so that he could hardly walk. Barnbrook's mouth cracked open and he got to the point where he couldn't sit up.

And I had severe beriberi. Most of it was due to a lack of key nutrients in our diet.

We were all down to skin and bones now and looked like walking cadavers. I guess my weight was down to about 110 pounds or less, which doesn't allow for much meat on a six-foot frame. Our rice ration was only a few ounces a day, and only rarely did we get any animal protein. As a consequence, our caloric intake wasn't nearly enough to maintain our body weight. As a matter of fact, we weren't even getting enough calories to generate body heat, and as a consequence we felt chilled much of the time even though we were living in a tropical climate.

The one thing we had plenty of was water. We drank lots of water. Probably too much. But with no food to fill our bellies, the water helped to stretch our stomachs and give us a feeling of fullness. I'm not sure what drinking all that water did to our bodies, but I imagine that it leached a lot of the necessary chemicals right out of our systems.

Phil's legs swelled up to the point where one of them burst open. When the doctor would come around—which was only about once a week—Phil would complain of it, but the only thing the doctor would do is paint it with a little iodine.

My scrotum swelled up to the size of both of my fists and scabbed over. The swelling was caused by a lack of vitamins. I complained regularly to the doctor about the swelling, but for a long time nothing happened. Then one night some of the guards got me out of the cell and took me to a room down the hall, where they stretched me out on my back and took some red solution and painted my scrotum. That was excruciatingly painful. Tears came to my eyes, it hurt so intensely. The guards thought it was funny. They just stood around and laughed. Back in my cell, I folded my towel to use as a little pad to rest my testicles on.

Barnbrook may have been an overbearing bully, but he got to be in such bad shape that I began to feel sorry for him. All I was able to do, really, was bring him some water and try to ease his pain by bathing him with a wet towel. No one else wanted to get near him. He'd been flat on his back for about two weeks, passing blood profusely from his stool. He hadn't eaten anything at all in over two weeks—didn't even try to eat. Others were eating his food. And here I was, getting in worse shape all the time myself, yet I was trying to do what I could to ease Barnbrook's pain.

Then one day some U.S. Navy corpsmen came in from the prison hospital, put Barnbrook on a stretcher, and marched him out of there.

I got to thinking, *This is the way to get out of here.* So I stopped eating. That was not terribly difficult to do, considering how awful the food tasted. For eight days and nights I stretched out on the floor flat on my back without eating a morsel. I thought I was dying. On the eighth day of my fast, I thought I would not wake up after sleeping that night. Strangely, I did not seem to mind the prospect of my pending death because in my weakened condition and state of mind I really was thinking that death would be a peaceful solution to my problems.

In the fog and haze of my mind, I could hear the doctor ask me if I had blood in my stool. I told him yes. Then through the fog I could see the corpsmen—the same ones who had come for Barnbrook the week before—and they were coming for me. I didn't know whether I was dreaming or dying.

But here were the stretcher-bearers to carry me out of there. The stretcher itself was comfortable, much more comfortable than the hardwood floor. I must have drifted off to sleep as they carried me, because when I woke up I was already in the isolation ward of the hospital in a bed with a mattress on it and mosquito bars around it. It felt sinfully comfortable and warm.

Soon the corpsmen brought me a cup of the most delicious liquid that I think I have ever tasted. It was a kind of milkshake, or protein cocktail, made out of canned milk with an egg and some sugar whipped in. Almost immediately I could feel the energy flowing back into my body. I was also given some bismuth and paregoric to control my dysentery.

When the doctors came in to examine me, I asked them what happened to Barnbrook. They told me that he had died the day

Berry, W.A. Ensign U.S.NR.   age 26   White
Nativity- Ripley, Oklahoma
Next of Kin:
    Mother: Mrs. Thomas N. Berry   Religion: Mormon
            Stillwater, Oklahoma

Admitted from Japanese Prison Camp

History:
    Patient had fever and chills while in the mountains but does not
know if it was malaria or not. Had no Quinine therapy.
Patient had diarrhoea at Cabanatuan, about a month ago. Received
sulfathiazole and improved.
Last attack started on the 11-20-42. Had 27 movements in 24 hours.
Had no blood but a little mucous.

11/22 Stool exam-Negative. E. histolytica. Few WBC noted. Emetine started
11/22 Paregoric 8 cc tid- Emetine course started.
11/23-5x Blood noted for the first time
11/24- 6x   1/12-1x-
11/25- 6x   1/13-5x- 24 two cent.
11/26 - 6x   1/14-1x-
11/27- 6x   1/15-2x-
11/28- 5x   1/16-1x-
11/29- 6x   1/18-2x- Sulfathiazole gm i q 6° x5 starting 10:00
11/30- 3x   1/19-1x - Stool spec. neg. Few WBC
12/1- 3x   1/20-2x - Stool Spec
12/2- 4x   1/21-2x-
12/3-4x   1/22-1x- Sulfaguanidine gm 3.5 g 8 two x21
12/4- 4x   1/23- 2x-
12/5-3x   1/25- 2x
12/7-2x Emetine Disc.   1/26-2x- 1/27-3x - Discharged to custody of Japanese
12/9- 2x   military Authorities
12/10- 3x
12/11- 2x -Stool for ova P-Negative
12/12-1x 2% Tannic acid enemas x4
12/14- 3x "   "   "
12/15- 3x   8/5/43 Readmitted
12/19-3x   Malnutrition + Diarrhea
12/21-6x
12/22- 4x
12/23- 2x
12/24- 2x
12/28- 3x
12/29- 3x Kaolin 1 T, tid   4- B.P.- 140/70-
12/30 - 4x
1/31 - 3x
1/4- 3x - GLD. & O.D.
1/5-3x - 1 blood.
1/6-4x - Kaolin 2½ t.id.   7/1 - B.P. 104/80
1/7- 2x   9/13-
1/8-3x
1/9-3x
1/10-1x £ Blad

The author's original medical record at Bilibid Prison. Courtesy of Dr. Paul
Ashton.

after he got there. Big tears welled up in my eyes and I began to cry. The doctors were stern with me and gave me no sympathy for that. They told me that Barnbrook had caused a great deal of problems. He had been in some kind of trouble with other POWs, and it had come to the point where he thought he must try to escape. That is how he ended up in our group.

Knowing Barnbrook as I did, I could see how that would happen. Not that he was mean, but he just stirred up trouble. Trouble seemed to follow him wherever he went. But in the close quarters of the cell, I did get to the point where I liked him and tried to minister to him during his last illness. Nevertheless, the doctors didn't want me to be feeling sorry for myself or having pity on someone else. They wanted me to get well.

At the time, I resented the way they seemed to treat me — so cool to the death of another person. But in time, I came to appreciate their attitude: it was the only attitude that they could have and survive, themselves, in that hellish environment.

It was Dr. Paul Ashton who was principally responsible for my survival, along with another doctor whose name I think was Brokenshire. Both men were American POWs. They didn't have much to work with, but what medicine they had worked many wonders.

The doctors came to see me at least twice a day. In addition to high-protein food, they immediately put me on a high dosage of vitamins, particularly vitamin B1, which I lacked in the prison cell. Twice-a-day doses of vitamin C were prescribed for my scurvy and other deficiencies caused by lack of this vitamin. I was also instructed to take nicotinic acid (niacin) for pellagra, as well as several other supplements.

The extra therapy, the vitamins, and the nourishing food worked wonders, and within a few days I began to relax. My mind was at peace.

I had managed to survive seven months of living hell.

CHAPTER ELEVEN

HARBORED BY THE HEALERS

LITTLE by little, as my strength returned, I became able to walk around a bit—first just around my cell and then up and down the ward. I had been assigned to the isolation unit, where they segregated the prisoners who had communicable diseases. It was not a hospital ward in the usual sense of that term.

This unit had not originally been built to function as a hospital. Rather, it was a barracks that the Japanese had pressed into service as a hospital unit in order to handle the growing number of diseased and dying prisoners. This section of Bilibid Prison, known as the "back compound," was separated from the main part of the prison by a twelve-foot wall and had but a single entrance.

The communicable diseases (CD) unit in which I was hospitalized—also known as the "isolation ward"—was a low masonry building that comprised eight cells in a row. The front and back walls of each cell consisted only of iron bars and were open to the weather, while the walls between the cells were made of solid concrete. The roof was covered with corrugated iron that extended out for several feet on each side to ward off the sun and rain.

About a hundred or so feet away and separated from the other buildings by a fence was an identical cell block that housed the insane. Beyond that was another ward that housed the amputees. On the rare occasion that I was able to visit them, it seemed to me that the amputees were the most bitter people in the camp.

Usually we had a guard standing outside the cell block. But here was not the rigidly controlled situation we had suffered through back in the special prisoner unit. By and large, as long as we stayed in our cells and didn't bother anyone, we were pretty much left alone.

I took up reading. Actually, without much strength to do anything but lie in my cot all day, I had little else to do. Five or more hours a day, I would lose myself in books. We had a modest library of some two hundred or more books down at the other end of the ward in the end cell. This library comprised books that had been gathered up by the doctors from the various prisoners who had passed through here. There was no particular order or design to the collection. But considering the catch-as-catch-can manner in which the books were collected, there turned out to be some remarkably good reading material there.

This gave me an opportunity, for example, to read Margeret Mitchell's *Gone with the Wind* and H. G. Wells's lengthy *Outline of History*. Another book of relatively little consequence but that I nevertheless found enlightening was William L. Riordon's *Plunkett of Tammany Hall*. It was about a councilman in turn-of-the-century New York who had come over as an Irish immigrant, learned down-to-earth politics, and rose to become a man of great influence in that city.

A couple of weeks after I got there, in comes Dick Tirk being carried on a stretcher. Boy was I surprised to see him.

As soon as the corpsman finished attending to him, I asked, "Dick, what in the world happened to you?"

"Well, no one ever accused Dick Tirk of being a dummy," he replied. "I saw what worked for Bill Berry, so I decided it ought to work for Dick Tirk as well."

The big difference was that Tirk, our Phi Beta Kappa from Cornell, went about the task a lot more scientifically than I did. He explained, "I'm not really as sick as I made out to be. But I remembered that it took Barnbrook nearly ten days after he quit eating before they took him out of the cell. And it was over a week before they hauled you out. So almost as soon as I quit eating, I notified the doctor that there was blood in my stool. And lo and behold, it wasn't two days before they had me out of there."

Dysentery ward. Contemporaneous drawing by prisoner Don T. Schloat. Toups is on the bunk, Gilbert is grating coconuts, and Cameron is facing him. Outside the barred front wall are a wash table and eating gear drying in the sun. This is cell no. 1. The author and other special prisoners were in cell no. 2 at the time this picture was drawn. (The poor quality of reproduction is due to the tinted blue-green paper, which is all the artist had to work with, on which the original drawing was made.) Courtesy of Don T. Schloat.

Within another few days, all of the guys from the other side were brought in—Sanborn, Toups, Ballard, Beyuka, Klett, they were all here. I guess that seeing what was happening to the special prisoners—Barnbrook dead, Berry near to death, and now Tirk—the doctors persuaded the Japanese officials that they better do something about the situation before everyone died.

The others were all in better shape than I was when I came over because they hadn't gone nearly as long without eating. As a result, they were up on their feet in a short time.

Activities picked up a little now that we had a few kindred souls in the cell. There were few restrictions on our talking or moving around in the cell, so we improvised various games that would help us while away the hours. One of the games was chess. I honestly can't say who first came up with the idea, but I know that at the time, it struck me as being a little odd that we should decide on something none of us really knew how to play. To complicate matters even more, we didn't have a chessboard either; but as necessity is the mother of invention, one of the guys came up with some cardboard, which he cut into both a board and the playing pieces. I had played a few games of chess back when I was a youngster, but that was a long time ago and the rules were all but forgotten by now. I think the others were pretty much in the same boat as I was. But somehow or other, we managed to cobble together some rules for the game that we all could live with.

Tensions had eased. The guards still manned their post outside our unit, but I don't think their hearts were in it. Generally they didn't bother us and we didn't bother them. For the most part, the guards simply stood there, immobile, helmets on, staring off into the sky as if they were wishing they were somewhere else.

As might be expected now that we had so many people in the cell, we began to have our little differences—not Tirk, Sanborn, and I, however, because we stayed pretty much to ourselves and tried not to get any more involved in the affairs of the other men than we had to. But again, we had to contend with the fact that we were officers and the others were not. That showed up in the subtle, underlying resentment that enlisted men naturally tend to exhibit toward commissioned officers. It also was keyed to our being better educated and having different cultural tastes and backgrounds.

People's nerves were easily rubbed raw. Because of that extreme sensitivity, we had to watch closely what we said and what we did. The slightest innuendo could be taken the wrong way and cause friction, and friction was one thing we didn't need in this situation.

For example, one day Hanson burst out singing a cowboy song. As I was listening to him, I got to thinking about what a marvelous voice he had and how he ought to turn professional after the war. Apparently, however, Hanson interpreted the smile on my face as a sneer. I tried to explain to him how much I was enjoying and appreciating his music. But nope, he took it as an insult, and I couldn't convince him otherwise.

We all knew that sooner or later we were going to have to leave the hospital ward and go back to that dreadful cell we had come from. Constantly in the back of our minds were the questions, When are they coming to take us out of here? What's next for us?

One day we were hurriedly tipped off by one of the corpsmen that the Japanese doctor from the MP section was on his way over to visit us. We knew that was a bad sign. Our immediate thought was that they were probably coming to take us back.

Dick Tirk said, "Well, I know what I'm going to do. I'm going to stretch out in my bunk, cover my face with a cloth, and pretend that I'm miserable and sick." So he hurriedly piled into his bunk. Everyone except Klett and me did the same.

I said, "That's silly. The guard out there knows you just crawled in bed." So I stood at attention and waited for them to enter.

When the doctor came into the cell with his entourage, Klett was standing beside me with his head bowed down and his hands clasped behind his back, looking dejected and depressed. Then all of a sudden he let out a blood-curdling yell, jumped for the bars, and started climbing the wall of the cell. I rushed over and grabbed him, pulled his hands off the bars, and said, "For heaven's sake, Klett, come down off there." I made him stand beside his bunk again and assured everyone that everything was all right.

As soon as I got Klett suitably quieted down, the doctor went about his business and examined everyone. Then he left, and we all breathed a sigh of nervous relief.

A few minutes later, however, the guards came back into the cell and marched everyone out—everyone except Klett and me, that is. The two of us were told to remain in the cell. At the time, I couldn't imagine what they had in mind for us. I wondered if they were going to take us out and administer some kind of punishment. But they never came back.

The others never came back either. I learned from a corpsman that Tirk, Sanborn, and the others were put back in the special prisoners' cell where we had spent such a hellish seven months. For the time being, that left just Klett and me there in the cell by ourselves.

We were never told why some were taken and others were passed over. But as I tried to piece things together in my own mind, it seemed to me that the Japanese doctor must have concluded that Klett was crazy and the others were malingering; and since I was the one who had tried to help poor Klett by pulling him off the wall and getting him to calm down, he probably decided it would be best for me to stay behind and take care of Klett. As I'd witnessed before, the Japanese seemed to have a special place close to their heart for crazy people. Anyhow, as I was mulling over these possibilities, I happened to glance over at Klett: there he was, lying on his bunk with his feet stretched out, his arms crossed behind his head to form a pillow, and whistling a tune from some opera. Sometimes I wondered which of us was the crazy one.

From time to time other prisoners were brought in and put with us for a few days. Usually these were men awaiting court-martial and sentencing. One such transitory cellmate was a civilian, Jim Needham. Before the war, Needham had been working as a mining engineer here in the Philippines, where his job primarily was to search for gold deposits. His work carried him to a sparsely inhabited province, and being unmarried, he was quite happy living with the Filipinos there. When the war came along, he remained behind. Eventually Needham got hooked up with a guerrilla band and ended up making explosives for them—something he was quite good at, incidentally, owing largely to his engineering background.

Needham was a nice-looking, tall, slender individual, a graduate of the Colorado School of Mines. I considered him to be a brave and honorable man. He was executed.

A fellow named Goldsborough was another individual who spent a few days with us in the cell. He, too, was a civilian. Unfortunately, Goldsborough had found himself working as a geologist in the Philippines at the time of the Japanese invasion and was interned in one of the civilian internment camps. Previously he had spent considerable time in the interior of China, and he told us many stories about the Chinese people and his experiences there. Goldsborough had the extreme misfortune of being caught after having tried to escape the internment camp, was brought in here, and was awaiting court-martial. He, too, was executed.

If ever I thought I could relax my vigilance, a sad incident that happened one afternoon forcibly brought home the reality of our situation to me. One of the prisoners from down at the other end of our row of cells, Sergeant Griffin—a tank commander on Bataan, a Chicago policeman, and one of the finest people I had ever known—was innocently walking down the row of cells when he came upon a Japanese guard. For no apparent reason, the guard called him to attention, pointed a rifle at his chest, held him in that position for a while, then pulled the trigger and shot him dead.

Our doctor, Captain Ashton, witnessed the event; and in a moment of uncontrollable fury he tried to wrestle the rifle away from the guard. In the ensuing struggle for the weapon, the muzzle of the rifle came up under the guard's chin and went off. I heard the shots in my cell and came rushing out. There lying on the ground was the Japanese guard with his entire chin blown off, screaming like a dying animal. He wasn't dead yet, but his tongue was sticking out and wagging as if he were trying to say something, and his blood was spurting all over the place. Ashton was covered with blood. Griffin was dead, arms and legs grotesquely askew.

Other guards rushed up and took the rifle away from Dr. Ashton and waved him back to his cell. I don't think at the time they realized that he was the one who shot the guard; they probably assumed that Griffin and the guard had gotten into some kind of shoot-out, and that Dr. Ashton had merely rushed out to render first aid and somehow had picked up or wrestled away the rifle.

The next day, however, Ashton was informed that he would stand trial for killing a guard. It didn't make any difference, of course, that Griffin had been killed by the guard's capricious act. No, the only thing that mattered was that a Japanese guard had been killed. Ashton's trial was a farce. Every Monday for the next several weeks, they would take him outside the main gate and conduct a kind of hearing, with each week being largely a rehash of the week before. Eventually, things just died out from lack of interest, and a verdict was never announced. Ashton was allowed to remain in charge of the CD ward, with the only noticeable difference being that he was now classified as a "special prisoner" and, accordingly, was placed in a cell just like the rest of us.

About six months later—I'm not sure of the exact time because the days, weeks, and months all blended into each other to form a seamless monotony—Tirk, Sanborn, and the other special prisoners came back. They were pretty well beaten down again and were in sorry condition. No reason was ever given as to why the Japanese decided to send them back over here to the CD ward, and we didn't really want to question their motives. The important thing from our standpoint was that our little group was back together again.

Care packages began to arrive from the United States contain-

ing canned meat, canned milk, dried soup, margarine, chocolate, and various other foodstuffs. The Care Packages were
shipped by the International Red Cross on ships from neutral
countries, such as Switzerland. Much of the stuff was pilfered by
the Japanese and sold on the black market, and only a small
amount ever trickled through to the prisoners.

Even with that, special prisoners were prohibited from receiving these packages. Nevertheless, the medical and kitchen personnel saw to it that we weren't completely left out. They would
often find some way to smuggle some items into us. For example,
we might find a little chunk of Spam stuffed inside the ball of rice
that we received at lunch. Or we might find our rice mixed with
condensed milk. And from time to time they might manage to
slip us a cookie or piece of chocolate. Some of the other sections
of the compound were allowed to have small cooking fires. Many
prisoners trapped rats, grub worms, and other critters, which
they would cook into their rice ration in order to add lifesaving
protein to their starvation diet.

We were not allowed to do any cooking in the back compound,
however. Everything we ate had to come through the kitchen.
Nevertheless, one day Dick Tirk somehow, in some manner that
he never explained, managed to get ahold of twenty American
dollars, which he used to buy a canteen cup full of dried black-
eyed peas. I don't know how we got away with lighting a fire, but
we cooked those blackeyes over an open flame. We had no seasoning, of course, but that didn't seem to matter. Mixed with our
rice, the blackeyes made quite a tasty banquet for Dick, Phil, and
me. For the first time in many months, my belly felt full.

My weight loss slowed to some extent, but little by little I kept
losing weight. Our weight loss was so gradual, so universal, that
often we weren't aware of how cadaverous we really looked until,
on rare occasion, we saw our reflections in a mirror. Then it was
as if a stranger was staring back at us.

I was able to get around better now; though I still walked with
the foot-dragging shuffle that is characteristic of a person suffering from the effects of beriberi. Also, my left knee, which had

been so badly damaged earlier, was now finally beginning to heal, and walking on it didn't cause me nearly as much pain as it formerly did. The doctors told me that I had fractured the kneecap in my fall and it was a wonder to them that I was able to walk on it at all during those critical days. My improvement notwithstanding, whenever I tried to trot or move too fast now, nearly a year later, the nerves were apt to tense up and immobilize the leg, causing me to stumble or fall.

From time to time I would have contact with one or another of my good friends from Manila or Corregidor as they passed through Bilibid on their way to some other prison camp, often to Japan: Jack Ferguson; Ensign Weiss, a fellow I had met at the BOQ in Manila; Ensign Metcalf, a Notre Dame graduate who came over with me on the *President Harrison*; and Jack Woodside; among others. Woodside, my roommate in Manila and my bunkmate at Cabanatuan the night I escaped, came into the prison hospital for an appendectomy. At the time I saw him, he was still in a weak, convalescent state, and I wasn't able to find out much from him about his experiences.

One day I was surprised by a visit from Lieutenant Henry and another navy lieutenant whose name, I think, was Golden. Henry was the person whom I had respected so much as a highly trained military officer. He was the one who back in Manila had ribbed me about carrying a .45-caliber automatic strapped to my hip without a cartridge clip in it. He had done me the favor of showing me how to load the gun.

Lieutenant Henry expressed his admiration for the three of us who had escaped. He said, "You guys had the courage to do that which is the duty of every good navy man to do. You tried to escape from a prisoner-of-war camp to carry on the fight against the Japanese." Henry and Golden thought it was highly improper for our senior officers to have forced us to turn ourselves in, and for them to have humiliated and belittled us for having done what our government expected us to do.

Henry said, "I promise you that if I survive this war, I am going to do what I can to call the attention of the Navy Department to this

kind of shameful activity on the part of our superior officers."
(Unfortunately, Lieutenant Henry did not live to fulfill his promise.
Word filtered back to us that later he was sent out to a Japanese work
camp and was himself killed while trying to escape.)

About the highest level of excitement we could expect was on
those occasions when a squirrel or cat would run across the high-
tension line that ran atop the prison wall. When that happened,
alarm bells would go off and we would all be rousted out of our
cells, made to line up, and be counted off. One night, however, it
wasn't a squirrel or cat that triggered the alarm: it was a Japanese
guard who peed out the window of his barracks onto the 1,200-
volt line. I guess he went to his maker thinking that that was the
biggest thrill he ever had in his life. This, too, could have been
merely a rumor, but it was told around the prison often enough
that people thought it was true.

As the months rolled by and we found ourselves well into the
year 1944, there arose an air of expectancy that something was
about to happen. We couldn't quite put our fingers on it, but it
seemed to me that the Japanese guards tended to ease off a bit in
their belligerence, and the tensions among the prisoners began to
subside.

From time to time rumors filtered in about the American
progress in the war. We lived for those rumors. We thrived on
them. The Japanese used a couple of navy warrant officers over
in the main prison to repair their radios, and whenever they got a
chance those officers would steal a part or two and smuggle it
back to their cell. Over time, they collected enough parts to put
together a radio that worked well enough to pick up the Japanese-
controlled Manila station.

Our best source of information was the men who were sent
down from Cabanatuan for one reason or another. Up at Camp
No. 1, the prisoners had jury-rigged together a clandestine radio
that was tuned in to San Francisco radio station KGEI, and they
always seemed to know what was going on. Of course, we
couldn't be sure how accurate the stories were by the time they
had been filtered in to us, or how much they had been embel-

lished in the retelling. Nevertheless, those stories gave us encouragement that the Japanese forces were being driven back across the Pacific. We heard about the great American naval victories at Midway and in the Coral Sea. Names like Guadalcanal, Tarawa, Kwajalein, Tinian, Saipan, and Guam were to become familiar words to us. We heard about the "Great Marianas Turkey Shoot," in which hundreds of Japanese planes were shot down. As I say, we didn't know how much of this was really true; but even if only a small fraction of it were, that was enough to give us hope and encouragement that soon the war would be over and we would be out of this horrible place.

We also heard stories about the Japanese annihilation of prisoners in some of the other camps. When the Japanese were ready to leave a camp and didn't know what to do with the POWs that were still alive, so the stories went, they would just wipe them out in a massacre. That's what happened with Ens. Bob Russell's work group that had been building an airstrip at Palawan. He told me that about half of the three hundred POWs, himself included, were shipped here to Bilibid in transit to Japan, while the remainder was massacred at Palawan. He said that the Japanese had sounded a false air raid alarm, and when everyone had gotten into the trenches, the Japanese poured gasoline over them, set them ablaze, and machine-gunned them down. Only nine men managed to survive the holocaust by jumping over a bluff and hiding in the bushes.

For all we knew, the same thing might happen to us someday. Occasionally, magazines would find their way into the cell. I didn't know where they came from, but they added a couple of ingredients that heretofore had been omitted from our Spartan existence: girls and food. We'd cut out the pictures of the girls to use as pinups. And we'd cut out recipes and try to imagine what the food would taste like. I distinctly remember cutting out a picture of something called "heavenly pie." It was some kind of fruit custard with a thick layer of whipped cream on top. Man, I would go to sleep dreaming about that pie.

Quite unexpectedly, one day I received a package from my

mother in Stillwater, Oklahoma. I don't know how the package managed to get through to me, because the Japanese usually intercepted them. But here it was, addressed in her own hand-writing and chock full of vitamins and all kinds of good things to eat. She and her friend who ran a drugstore in Stillwater had packed it with every conceivable thing they thought I might need. Unbeknownst to me, my mother had been sending me a similar package every week that I was in captivity, but this was the first one that got through to me. Later on, I was to receive a second package from her. But that was the extent of it. I guess that since the Japanese claimed that they weren't signatories to the Geneva Conventions, they didn't feel that they had any obligation whatsoever toward the humane treatment of their prisoners of war.

Along about October 1944 we got the feeling that the war must be going badly for Japan. One clue was that the Japanese guards were not quite as hostile toward us as they had been before. The difference was subtle, but there did seem to be a different tone in our relationships.

Another clue that the war may have been going badly for them could be seen in their decision to transport all able-bodied prisoners of war to Japan to be used as slave labor. Every week or two, beginning about the middle of October, fifteen hundred or so prisoners were rounded up from various prison camps and sent to Manila, where they were shuffled through Bilibid's gates for embarkation to Japan.

The tragic thing for many of these prisoners is that they were led to believe that they were going to be exchanged for Japanese prisoners being held by the American forces. They thought they were going home. As a result, many of them arrived here at Bilibid with high hopes—hopes that were soon to be dashed.

Others of them, however, seemed to have a premonition that something awful was about to happen. One of these guys, a Lieu-tenant Gordon, came over to see me and asked if I would carry a letter out with me to give to his mother. I told him that I would, but said, "I think you've got a better chance to get back than I do."

The ships that carried the prisoners to Japan came to be known as "Hell Ships" because of the unspeakable horrors that happened on them. The story that unfolded was one of large-scale suffering, torture, agony, horror, bloodshed, murder, and death. Men were packed into the holds of ships so tightly that dozens of them suffocated from the heat and lack of oxygen. Their only food was tubs of rice let down to them on ropes, but since they had no bowls or utensils to eat it with much of it got spilled on the floor. Most of the men had dysentery, and since there were no sanitation facilities, the floor was slippery with human urine, vomit, and bloody excrement. Human corpses were stacked up like cordwood until they could be removed and thrown over the side. Compounding the misery, none of the ships were marked as POW vessels, and many of them were strafed, bombed, or torpedoed by American planes and submarines. In some instances, prisoners would survive the sinking of one ship and be placed aboard a second ship, only to have that ship sunk too. The mortality rate on these Hell Ships ran to over 70 percent.

I was out at the washstand one day washing what little clothes I had, when the first American bombing raid came over Manila. The bombs seemed to take the Japanese as much by surprise as they did us. When I first saw the carrier-based planes overhead, I didn't realize that they were ours until they started diving and bombing. That was exciting. The guards shooed us all back inside our cells, however, so I was not able to see where the bombs landed; nevertheless, I understand that the planes destroyed most of the shipping in the harbor.

Thereafter the bombing continued intermittently, and we figured it wouldn't be long before we all would be rescued. I dreamed of the sky opening up and the Americans coming down to liberate us. But the Japanese were of a different mind; they seemed hell-bent on getting rid of all the prisoners in the Philippines, one way or another.

On December 13 they made a final sweep through the Bilibid and rounded up every remaining able-bodied man to be placed on a ship for Japan. By this time, they were scraping pretty hard at the bottom of the barrel. They went through each cell block, one by one, man by man, and picked out the ones they were going to ship out—including those who could barely hobble. A total of 1,619 prisoners had been rounded up, and the test of whether or not a man was able-bodied seems to have been, "Can he walk?" Some of these prisoners had to be helped along by their comrades, and some of them collapsed beyond the help of their comrades and had to be picked up by trucks—but that did not affect their status as able "bodies."

Jack Ferguson went out in this group, as did "Moon" Mullins, Bob Russell, Hanson, and Lowe. Even Jack Woodside, who was still recovering from his appendectomy and could barely walk, was taken from the ward and put in this group.

When they came to our cell in the isolation ward, the doctor told them *bahcum*, which means "crazy," so they passed over us. When they got to the wards housing the amputees and people who really were mentally ill, they passed over these too.

The prisoners they selected were placed aboard the worst of the Hell Ships, the freighter *Oryoku Maru*. The prisoners were herded up the gangplank of the Hell Ship and jammed into three holds with all the pandemonium of cattle being herded into the holding pens of a Chicago slaughterhouse. Their tragic odyssey lasted forty-five days, during which they were subjected to suffocation, starvation, dehydration, disease, bombing, shooting, and beheading. Of the 1,619 prisoners they gathered up on that fateful day and jammed into the hold of the freighter *Oryoku Maru*, less than 300 survived their terrible ordeal. Among my friends, only Mullins and Russell made it.

I am convinced that if it hadn't been for the courageous protection of the doctors, I too would have been on that starcrossed ship. As it is, it struck me as ironic to think that Lieutenant Commander Lowe, whose actions had sent me to the execution chamber and precipitated so much of my misery, should in the end have been the unwitting cause of my being passed over for the final voyage of the *Oryoku Maru*.

Once again, I survived the vagaries and vicissitudes of fortune.

CHAPTER TWELVE

RESCUED BY THE REGULARS

CHRISTMAS 1944 was right at our doorstep. It would be the first Christmas we had been able to celebrate in four years. In our cell, we decided we would draw names and each one of us would give someone else a gift. I'm ashamed to say that for the life of me I cannot recall whose name I drew, or what it was that I gave him, but I do know that it would have to have been something personal, something that I made. Dick Tirk drew my name and he made me a pipe, very small, very nicely carved, very appropriate under the circumstances. He knew that ever since Corregidor, I was smoking every chance I got. Certainly all of the gifts were appreciated. I don't think we sang any songs.

The war was coming ever nearer. Almost daily, American planes flew over Manila on bombing raids. They were all carrier-based planes from off the east coast of Luzon somewhere. As a rule, the raids didn't last long—mostly harassment raids, really—but they lasted long enough and were frequent enough to give a tremendous boost to our morale. The Japanese threw up a tremendous amount of antiaircraft fire whenever the American planes flew over, but there was more smoke and noise than deadliness. In fact, I don't think they scored more than half a dozen hits on our planes during the almost three months that the raids had been going on.

Two of the big antiaircraft batteries were positioned just outside Bilibid Prison. When those guns started firing, they shook the whole prison compound. Every time that happened, that heightened our awareness that American forces were in the area and drawing closer.

The battle for Leyte—one of the southern islands—was now over two months old. Our troops had landed there during the last week in October. Now, after two months of hard fighting, the battle was winding down. What was particularly fascinating to us, however, was the way in which the battle was reported in the Japanese-controlled Manila newspaper. According to the newspaper's description, the Japanese had intentionally let the Americans make a beachhead on Leyte and then allowed them to move inland so that the Japanese could form a circle around the Americans and crush them in the "lion's mouth." We found this account amusing because by this time we knew that our guys were on the verge of wrapping things up down there.

During the earlier stages of the battle for Leyte, we had been able to observe a few Japanese planes flying south over Manila, headed toward Leyte. Now, however, the Japanese planes weren't flying over anymore. We surmised that the Americans had knocked out the Japanese air force and had established complete mastery of the air. Nowadays whenever we heard a plane fly over, we knew without looking that it was one of ours. Accordingly, the roar of a plane's engine became a comforting sound for us.

One day as I was out at the straddle trench attending to nature's call, some American planes flew over and started dive-bombing the port area. Right away, the Japanese started firing back with their antiaircraft weapons, including the two batteries that were near us. I heard a whining, whirling, whistling sound, and suddenly I felt a burning sensation on my left knee. The rotating band off one of the Japanese artillery shells had hit me in such a manner that I was jarred off the straddle trench and ended up with a big gash on my knee. It was pretty obvious what had happened, but I finally got up and in the excitement I forgot all about the pain. There was no medication available, and eventually the knee got infected and left quite a large scar. It seemed ironic to me that with all the experiences I had been through the last three and a half years—the beatings, the injuries, the deprivations, being kicked and cuffed innumerable times—it should take this incident of relieving myself at the straddle trench to qualify me for a Purple Heart.

The prison population was down to just a few hundred men now since the last shipment of men had departed for Japan on the Hell Ships, and all but a few dozen of these remaining were so incapacitated that they could not be moved. Bilibid's population had constantly fluctuated because it was, among other things, used as a transient center, but during peak periods it had housed as many as four thousand prisoners.

Dick, Phil, and I, as well as the other special prisoners, were moved out of our cell on the isolation ward and relocated in the main compound in a building that was larger and had better accommodations. At the same time we were given pretty much the run of the whole back compound during daytime hours. At night we were still locked up. We weren't allowed to cross over into the main prison, however, but that wasn't a concern to us, because we found enough to do just exploring our own little part of the world.

I can't begin to tell you what a change our newfound freedom of movement meant to us. After two and a half years of close confinement, of being isolated within our own little unit, of being harassed or punished every time we stepped out of line, we now found ourselves free to roam out into the central gathering places and recreational areas of the prison. I drank in as much conversation and newly established friendships as I possibly could.

Just to give one example, during our long incarceration in the isolation ward we hadn't had much contact at all with the people over on the amputee ward. Now, however, I met several of those fellows. The one person in particular with whom I developed a friendship was an Ensign Chandler, a member of Lt. John Bulkeley's PT boat squadron. Chandler had been the executive officer on the PT boat that disabled that Japanese cruiser in Subic Bay back in January 1942. Two days later the squadron had intercepted an armed Japanese landing barge trying to get ashore on Bataan behind the American lines, and in the ensuing battle

Chandler had taken a bullet through both of his ankles, crippling him badly. If it hadn't been for that injury, undoubtedly he would have been shipped out on one of the Hell Ships along with so many others.

I also ran into some British soldiers imprisoned here as well. Previously, I had heard that some Britishers were incarcerated here, but I had never had the opportunity to meet any of them. One chap that I formed a friendship with was an officer from Leeds. When he saw how poorly I was dressed, he gave me a pair of his English tropical shorts. These shorts were of an unusual design; they had several straps that went around my waist and fastened like a belt. They were much more comfortable than the G-string I had been wearing previously.

When the news came that the Americans had landed on the island of Luzon on January 9, 1945, that was certainly the occasion for a great deal of joyfulness—for us, that is, but not for the Japanese. More and more, the guards became edgy and apprehensive, and it didn't take much to antagonize them. They didn't know what might happen to them. I'm sure that many of them feared reprisal for some of their past actions toward prisoners. And I'm sure that some of them maintained extra vigilance for that very reason, fearing that some event might trigger an uprising among the prisoners. So we learned to steer clear of the guards as much as we could.

One thing that tempered our joy and weighed heavily on our minds was the knowledge of the horrible things the Japanese had done in some of the other prison camps when they were ready to leave. There were rumors—whether they were true or not, I don't know, but they were very real to us—rumors to the effect that the Japanese had stored hundreds of barrels of naphtha and kerosene up in the overhead space of all of the buildings, and that they were going to set the buildings ablaze one night before the Americans arrived and cremate all of the prisoners before they could be liberated. We were never without the fear that this might happen, and the closer the Americans got to the city the more our anxieties heightened. It would be so ironic, so tragic, so cruel, to have made it through these many years and to have gotten this close to freedom only to have life snuffed out in the last days.

By the end of January, the American forces had gotten close enough to Manila that the booming of their artillery was clearly audible in the distance, working its way ever closer to the city of Manila itself. Then on the second day of February, we heard a great commotion just outside the prison walls. We could hear the rumble and clatter of armored vehicles in the street and the tremendous roar of their guns as they fired. We seemed to be encircled by them. We couldn't tell if they were Japanese or American. We could only sit and wait. But when dawn came, they were gone. Whoever they were, they had moved out during the night.

On the third of February, Dick came over and said to me, "Bill, our names are being paged over in the main prison, on the other side of the wall. They're calling for you and Phil and me by name."

I asked, "What does it mean?"

He said, "I think it means that they're looking for us in order to execute us before the Americans get here."

"Well, let's just lie low," I said, "and try to stay out of harm's way. Let's hope they don't find us."*

That night we heard some more shooting on the other side of the wall.

The next day at noon, the Japanese were gone. They just disappeared. They all changed out of their uniforms and put on blue denim jackets and trousers like those worn by Filipino soldiers, and they just marched out of there and tried to melt into the streets of Manila. Unfortunately for them, so we were told, they died in a hail of gunfire as they ran into a contingent of American troops.

Before the Japanese commandant, Lieutenant Hogi, left, he wrote a note for the American camp commander announcing that

*During the subsequent war trials, documents were introduced that showed that the Japanese had indeed planned to execute all of us special prisoners before we could be liberated.

the Japanese government was voluntarily releasing us as prisoners of war. The note further stated that if we remained within the prison compound we would not be harmed, but if we went outside we would be summarily shot.

Now, although we doubted very much that any guards were hanging around outside the gate waiting to shoot us, there really was something much more important on our minds: food. So the first thing we did was raid the food lockers, where we managed to find some brown sugar and some yeast. The cooks outdid themselves: they boiled up a tremendous amount of rice and mixed in the brown sugar and yeast to give it some sweetness and flavor. We ate it, and we all thought it was delicious. I even filled my mess kit with leftovers to eat later.

Along about midafternoon I was standing out by the wash rack with another prisoner, whose name was Bandoni. He was a sergeant from New Mexico. Over by the back wall, we heard a pounding noise and the sound of wood splintering. We looked up just in time to see a board being knocked off from the other side; through the opening came the muzzle of a rifle. Bandoni saw it first: the rifle was pointing straight at him, the sights were aimed right at his heart. Bandoni, of course, was wearing only his prison denims, a jacket and shorts, and since he had a rather dark complection there was nothing to signify that he was an American.

Bandoni let out a yell. "Who are you?" he shouted at the man pointing the gun.

"I'm a Yank," called out the voice on the other side. "Who the hell are you?"

"I'm an American prisoner of war! And we've been waiting for you for three years!"

With that, we were all thrilled beyond belief. We discovered that the Americans had bivouacked the night before right outside this wall of the prison, but they had no idea that right on the other side was a prison camp and a hospital.

When one considers the fact that up until that very moment the American soldiers had no idea that this fortresslike structure in the middle of Manila was actually a prison and a hospital, one has to believe in miracles to explain why we were never bombed or shelled during the entire episode. The Japanese had never put any Red Cross markings on the prison.

The battle for Manila was still raging around us. We could hear the artillery blasts in the distance. We could hear the shells whistling over our heads as they traveled toward their targets. And we could hear them hit. A tremendous amount of artillery fire was going on right over our heads. But to us it all sounded like music. It was like the Fourth of July. We were thrilled to be free.

An army lieutenant colonel found out I was from Oklahoma. He said he was from Oklahoma too, from the town of Marshall. He asked me if I needed anything, if there was anything he could do for me.

I told him, "Well, the only pressing need I have is for a pair of shoes."

The lieutenant colonel said, "Well, by God, I'll find you a pair of shoes." Sure enough, about two hours later here he came, toting a brand new pair of shoes that were exactly the right size.

A sergeant asked us about the kind of food we were eating. I pulled out my mess kit in which I had saved some of the leftover rice with yeast and sugar in it, and I offered him some. He looked at it, smelled it, and almost gagged.

"Take it away," he pleaded. "I can't stand it."

I looked closely at the rice and saw that indeed there were some bugs cooked in with it. By this time in our lives we never noticed such things. The rice tasted delicious to us, and we ate it bugs and all.

We spent that night in the prison. The "old city" section of Manila was burning and lit up the sky. But my sleep that night was the most relaxed that I had had in months—years, even.

The next morning, February 5, I wandered out to see some of the other parts of the prison. I visited the part of the compound where we had been held as special prisoners, thirteen people in a ten-by-ten foot cell. I looked on it with horror, and shuddered.

Outside, the Americans had brought in a bunch of Japanese

prisoners. Actually, I'm not sure they were all Japanese; I'm inclined to think that some of them may have been Taiwanese or Koreans who had been drafted into the Japanese army. Anyway, one of the American officers had a long club in his hand, and he offered it to me, saying, "Here, why don't you just go over there and hit these Japs over the head the way they hit you?"

I looked at him, looked at them. And I couldn't do it. I couldn't make myself go over there and retaliate for all those wrongs that had been done to me. Instead, I found myself feeling sorry for the poor bastards, because they were now where I had been then. And I thought, *Suppose I do hit them, how will that ease my situation?*

"Here, I can't do it," I said. And I handed the officer back his stick.

I went back over to the hospital side of the prison, and there were the photographers—newspaper photographers, magazine photographers, newsreel photographers. They were interested only in the most sensational, the most horrid, the most pitiable pictures. They picked out the most emaciated, the most crippled, the most diseased prisoners and paraded them out to take their pictures. I realize they were only doing their jobs in trying to get pictures that would tell the story, but somehow I couldn't escape the feeling that we, the prisoners, were somehow being exploited for the sake of what the American people would read.

We stayed at Bilibid for three or four more days while the fighting had moved farther away. When it was safe to leave, the army sent in trucks to take us out of there. Whatever personal possessions we had, which weren't many, we were allowed to take with us.

What happened next, I couldn't control. As the truck was driving out the gate, lots of Filipinos surrounded us, cheering us on. I don't know if it was the press of the crowd, the noise, or release from tension but I began screaming. I screamed and shouted at the top of my lungs. I couldn't stop myself.

We were driven three or four miles away from the battle area to an old shoe factory that had been pretty well bombed out. It still

Condition of the prisoners. This photograph was taken by a navy photographer of prisoners on the day of their release from Bilibid. From the left are Sid Roberts, a Scotsman, Whipps, a Londoner; Jim Ballard, a special prisoner; and Sgt. I. E. Raum, a TB patient. Courtesy of Dr. Paul Ashton.

had a roof and a semblance of walls. But the main thing it had was plenty of space. The army set up cots and blankets for us and served us food. The only food they had available was combat rations—corned beef, hash, Spam, and some other things like that. They apologized that they didn't have anything better to offer than K rations, but we didn't complain.

One detail of soldiers that came and looked in on us told us that we weren't far from the San Miguel brewery, and that although the brewery had been bombed there might still be some beer over there. Sure enough, some soldiers went over there and had their fill of beer. One fellow told me that he never knew warm beer could taste so wonderful.

The army moved us north to Lingayen Gulf, well away from the battle zone. MacArthur had set up a replacement center there—that is, a kind of depot through which both arriving and departing troops were processed. I asked if there was anyone around from Oklahoma and was told that there was a Bill Harrison. I didn't know who he was, but I made my way to the tent in which he had an office. It turned out that "Bill" Harrison was Walter Harrison, former editor of the *Oklahoma City Times*. He was very cordial to me, and near the end of our visit he asked. "By the way, would you like to go back early? I can get you a seat on a plane out of here tomorrow, and you can go as part of a POW troupe to tour the country and promote U.S. savings bonds."

Had I been able to comprehend the significance of Harrison's invitation, I might have taken him up on the deal. Instead, I told him, "No, I came over with this group I'm with, I was liberated with them, and I'm going to go back with them."

MacArthur had ordered double rations for us, which meant that we could have twice as much food at meals as the regular soldiers got. It seems like I was always ready to eat. Every time the chow bell rang, I would get in line, stack my mess kit with as much food as possible, then go back for seconds later.

Some guys asked, "How can you eat so much? Isn't your stomach all shriveled up from years of starvation?"

I told them that it doesn't work that way, that the human stomach has a tremendous capacity for expansion, and that I was out to prove it.

The "repo depo," as it was called, was several miles from the bay. Dick suggested that we go down there and see if we could find anyone we knew.

"How do we get there?" I asked.

Dick said, "Look, they have jeeps running back and forth all the time. We'll just go out by the road and hitchhike, and I bet someone will pick us up."

So we did. And someone did.

Down at the bay I ran into Phil Boyle, an old friend of mine from Oklahoma who was now stationed on a communications ship, the USS *Rocky Mount*, the flagship for Adm. Forrest B. Royal. By now Phil was already a lieutenant junior grade, while I was still a lowly ensign. I felt a twinge of envy: my commission had been earlier than his. Phil went down to his quarters and rummaged up a set of his old ensign bars so that I would have an insignia to wear. He told me that he had overheard one of the other officers remark of me, "Gosh, he must have a lot of money coming from all that accrued pay."

As Boyle was conducting me on a tour of his ship, the public relations officer asked us to step into his cabin. There on the wall was a big map of the United States. He got a photographer to take a picture of Boyle and me posed in front of this map and pointing at our state of Oklahoma. I had a big grin on my face as I pointed toward my home state. Unbeknownst to me, this picture was picked up by the news services and published in newspapers across the United States.

Finally in March the day arrived when we were scheduled to be transported back to the States. We'd been at the "repo depo" for about thirty days now, mostly resting, recuperating, reading our mail, and passing around rumors. Our ride home was aboard the USS *Pueblo*, a merchant marine ship now converted for use as a troop transport.

That was a long, slow trip. Even with a strong tailwind, the old bucket couldn't have cranked out more than twelve knots, and most of the time we plodded along much slower than that. One day, the engines stopped completely, leaving us bobbing up and

The author (right) with Lt. (jg) Phil Boyle. This photograph was taken aboard the USS *Rocky Mount* approximately three weeks following the author's release from Bilibid Prison. At the time the photo was taken, the author's weight was back up to about 120 pounds, still considerably less than the 185 pounds he weighed upon his original arrival in Manila. From author's collection.

down like a cork in the middle of the ocean for three days while repairs were being made. That worried us more than a little, because the *Pueblo* was traveling unarmed and without an escort. Never far from our minds was the possibility that some Japanese submarine or surface ship might still be lurking around the area. Obviously a ship drifting dead in the water would be a sitting duck.

It was my hope that we might stop at Honolulu for a few days on our way back. Honolulu held special memories for me because of my stay there on the way out to the Philippines. But we had no such luck. The ship passed right on by, some three hundred miles to the south, and just kept chugging its way toward the west coast of the United States.

When we finally got to San Francisco, that Golden Gate really

Homecoming

ON THIS DAY, PROBABLY THE GREATEST OF YOUR LIFE, WHEN YOU RETURN TO THE LOVED LAND FOR WHICH YOU SO GALLANTLY FOUGHT AND SUFFERED, WE OF THE TRANSPORTATION CORPS, PROUD TO HAVE SERVED YOU, EXTEND OUR HIGHEST PRAISES, BEST WISHES, AND WARMEST WELCOME HOME.

SAN FRANCISCO PORT OF EMBARKATION
TRANSPORTATION CORPS

A "Welcome Home" sign that greeted soldiers, sailors, and airmen returning from the Pacific war. Courtesy of Dr. Paul Ashton.

opened itself wide for us. Great throngs of people were gathered at the dock to greet our arrival. People had seen the pictures, watched the newsreels, and had read the stories about the survivors of Bataan and Corregidor, and now was their chance to see the real thing.

The navy put us up in the Mark Hopkins Hotel, which in anybody's book has to be characterized as one of the truly great luxury hotels in America.

My sister, Martha, had been lucky enough to get some transportation—as crowded as the trains were in those days—to come out to San Francisco to meet me. We were given several days together, which we spent touring the city and just getting reacquainted. There was a lot of family history to get caught up on.

On Martha's and my last day together, we visited at the home of one of her friends, a lady who had lost a brother in the South Pacific. Near the end of our visit, this friend looked over at me and shook her head in a resentful way. Martha asked, "What's wrong?"

The friend replied, "Why did he survive and my brother did not?"

William A. Berry, Chief Justice of the Supreme Court, State of Oklahoma. From author's collection.

EPILOGUE

BILL A. Berry separated from the service in November 1945 with the rank of lieutenant commander. He was awarded a bronze star for bravery. He entered the private practice of law in Stillwater, Oklahoma, in partnership with Robert Hert, who later became district judge.

A little over a year later, in February 1947, Berry married Carolyn Burwell of Oklahoma City.

In May 1947 Berry was appointed assistant U.S. attorney for the western district of Oklahoma, an office he held until 1950.

Berry ran for a seat in the U.S. Congress in 1950, but lost the nomination to John Jarman in a closely contested race. Again he returned to private practice. In 1953 Berry was appointed county judge in Oklahoma County in charge of the juvenile division.

Always a strong advocate for juvenile justice, Berry made over three hundred speeches in support of a successful bond issue to underwrite construction of a new juvenile detention center in Oklahoma City, the first such building in the Southwest specifically designed for that purpose. The new center was dedicated in 1958 and named The Berry House in his honor.

In 1958 Berry was nominated to the Supreme Court of the State of Oklahoma, where he was sworn into office in January 1959. He served a two-year term as chief justice during the years 1971 and 1972. He retired from the court in 1979.

Currently Berry resides in Oklahoma City with his wife, Carolyn. Their two children are Elizabeth Berry Payne, who owns a real estate business, and Nichols Burwell Berry, a prominent artist.

In the fifty years that have transpired since the events described in this book began, there have been three occasions when echoes of the past uniquely impressed themselves upon Berry's consciousness. The first occasion was in 1953, when Berry was elected national commander of the American Ex-Prisoners of War. The second occurred in 1960, when Oklahoma governor Johnson Murray asked Judge Berry to represent him at an event in Washington, D.C., commemorating the liberation of the Philippines. And the third was in 1990, when new surgical procedures allowed doctors to replace Berry's knees, which had been so badly damaged in prison camp, thus freeing him from the physical pain that had dogged him for more than forty years.

DICK TIRK

Following the war, Richard Tirk spent fifteen years in the advertising business. During that time he completed work on a master's degree at Columbia University. He began a teaching career in Ossining, New York and also taught in Machakos, Kenya, and Antigo, Wisconsin. Tirk never lost his interest in languages: in addition to the Tagalog and Japanese he learned in the Philippines and the French and Spanish he had learned previously, he learned Swahili in Kenya and German in Pattensen, a small town in Germany where he now lives six months out of every two years. The other eighteen months he and his wife, Marguerite, live in Neenah, Wisconsin. In 1970, on the way to an assignment in Kenya, Tirk stopped in the Philippines and visited the people in Magnak who had sheltered Berry, Sanborn, and him during their escape. In 1977, during a visit to Japan, he tried unsuccessfully to find Hachigama, the Japanese guard who had befriended them.

PHIL SANBORN

Phillip Sanborn returned to his native Rhode Island, where he worked as an art supply salesman before establishing his own firm, Allied Framing Products, in 1963. He never lost his sense of humor. Sanborn passed away April 15, 1980, at the age of sixty three. He was survived by his wife, Virginia, and a daughter, Marsha L. Montgomery.

PAUL ASHTON

Dr. Paul Ashton returned to California and built a medical practice in Santa Barbara, where he currently resides with his wife, Yvonne. He is the author of two books on the Philippine experience: *Bataan Diary* (1984), and *And Somebody Gives a Damn*, (1990).

JIM BALLARD

Jim Ballard continued his career with the U.S. Army, retiring in 1963 with the rank of warrant officer W-3, following which he joined the Riverside, California, civil service. He is now retired a second time and resides in Indio, California, with his wife, Shirley. The Ballards have four daughters.

EDWARD BEYUKA

Edward A. Beyuka returned to his Zuni tribe, where he pursued a career of making and selling Indian jewelry. From 1987 to 1990 he served his people as tribal councilman. Mr. Beyuka lives in Zuni, New Mexico, and, at age seventy one, still jogs, makes jewelry, and enjoys good health.

PHIL BOYLE

Immediately following the war, Phil Boyle became a petroleum geologist with Skelly Oil Company. Later, he came back to Oklahoma City as a geologist for Eason Oil Company. In 1956 he formed his own firm as an independent petroleum geologist, which he still heads. Phil resides in Oklahoma City with his wife, Delores, and is a regular golfing partner with Judge Berry.

JACK FERGUSON

Ens. Jack Ferguson died in December 1944 while enroute to Japan on one of the infamous Hell Ships. His death came as the result of an American bombing attack on the unmarked prison ship. His cousin Janelle Everest resides in Oklahoma City.

TOM HARRISON

Thomas R. Harrison returned to his native Salt Lake City, where he obtained his mining engineering degree from the University of Utah. After spending several years in mining and oil field operations, he joined Hercules Incorporated as superintendent of mechanical design. In 1989 Mr. Harrison published his own experiences in *Survivor: Memoir of Defeat and Captivity: Bataan, 1942*. Now retired, he continues to reside in Utah with his wife, Dorothy.

CHRISTIAN KLETT

Christian B. Klett returned to the United States but continued to suffer emotional problems resulting from his captivity. His current whereabouts are unknown.

GENERAL HOMMA

General Masaharu Homma was tried by a U.S. military commission soon after Japan surrendered. Homma was charged for failing in his responsibilities for Japanese atrocities at the beginning of the war. He was executed by firing squad in April, 1946.

TOM LOWE

Lt. Comdr. Tom Lowe (not his real name) shipped out on the ill-fated *Oryoku Maru*. He did not survive the war.

ENSIGN MULLINS

"Moon" Mullins was among the sixteen hundred prisoners shipped out to Japan on the *Oryoku Maru*. He survived the awful ordeal and finished the war in a Japanese labor camp. Following the war, Mullins came to visit Berry in Oklahoma; however, no further contact has been maintained.

BOB RUSSELL

Robert Enson Russell survived the terrible ordeal of the *Oryoku Maru* to return to the United States and pursue a successful accounting career with Pacific Northwest Bell Telephone Company in Portland, Oregon. In 1972 he created a special legacy for his children — a seventy-page handwritten document recounting his harrowing experiences on Corregidor and in Japanese imprisonment. An automobile accident claimed the lives of Bob and his wife, Jessie, on September 12, 1981, while enroute to Portland from their summer home in Lincoln City, Oregon. On June 20, 1982, the *Oregonian* published a special ten-page Sunday supplement on Russell's life and legacy.

DON SCHLOAT

Don T. Schloat has pursued a successful career as an artist. He attended art schools at the Art Student League in New York, Jepson's in Los Angeles, and the Universidad de Michoacam in Mexico, and later he worked for many years in animation for Walt Disney Studios and at Hanna-Barbara. Currently, Mr. Schloat owns his own company, Yellow Brick Road Company, in Valley Center, California, where he produces films and videos for science education in middle schools.

MEADE WILLIS

Meade Willis was among the group of prisoners shipped out in late 1942 to Japan, where he spent the war in forced labor camps. Liberated in September, 1945, he returned to Winston-Salem, North Carolina, where he married his sweetheart, Anne Haynes. According to Berry's recollection, Willis is the only officer from the intelligence office in Manila — other than himself — to have survived captivity. Currently, Willis is retired from Wachovia Bank and resides in Winston-Salem with his wife, Anne.

Severino Torres and family in 1959. The author's godson, Welfredo, is standing second from left. From author's collection.

EULOGIO SOLLEZA

For more than twenty five years following his release, the author maintained regular contact with and provided assistance to the Solleza and Torres families, who had sheltered him at the village of Magnak during the period of his escape.

JACK WOODSIDE

Jack Woodside shipped out on the *Oryoku Maru*. He did not survive the trip.

BILL LLOYD

Ensign Bill Lloyd, whose name author adopted during his escape, died May 6, 1942. At about 7:30 A.M., Ensign Lloyd, Lieutenant Bethol B.

Otter, and four enlisted men, launched an attack against a Japanese position. Lloyd and Otter jumped up and threw their hand grenades. They destroyed an enemy nest, but both men were killed by enemy fire.

APPENDIX

THE three young navy ensigns who escaped from Cabanatuan became legendary in their own time and served as a beacon of hope for other prisoners who fantasized about, even carefully planned, escapes such as they accomplished. Stories about their adventure have been chronicled in numerous books concerning that epoch in the American experience. These stories are not always completely accurate with regard to names and details — as rumors and legends seldom are. Nevertheless, the mere existence of such stories as the ones excerpted here serve as corroborating testimony to the veracity of Berry's gripping narrative. (EDITOR)

On Dec. 29, 1941, I came off duty at noon and went to my quarters to clean up before lunch. Bill Berry, a brand new ensign (who is now a justice of the Oklahoma Supreme Court) who had just arrived shortly before the war started, was with me. I had loaned our station wagon to another ensign to go to the post office. While we were waiting for him to return so we could go down to the tunnel for lunch the bombs started falling on Corregidor for the first time. We had seen many bombings from a distance, but it hadn't really prepared us for personal participation. The bombs made such a horrible shrieking sound as they were falling that they scared hell out of us before they even landed. We just laid on the floor in the house until the first wave passed, and then decided we'd be better off outside. At this point, more than 3 weeks after the war had started, we still didn't have any "fox holes" or other air raid shelters prepared. As we went out of the house, an army private ran up and said his buddy had been buried and he needed help. We ran over behind the theater where he was supposed to be, but all we found were his shoes. There was a drainage ditch nearby and we crawled in it and stayed until the 2nd wave had passed. We didn't like being all jammed in with a lot of other people so we decided to move to a hillside not far away. An air force major went with us and we stayed there for a couple of hours — until the bombing stopped. We walked up some steps in front of General Moore's quarters. Who should we run into but General MacArthur. He and a Filipino aide had been there all during the bombing. He was very calm and didn't seem to be particularly concerned. He apparently thought we had been in the tunnel during the bombing, and asked if you could hear the bombs falling from inside. Bill told him that he didn't know, but he surely would like to find out.

Robert Enson Russell, "A Kind of Personal History"
(unpublished ms., 1972), 19–21.

Escape was in the mind of nearly all the prisoners at Cabanatuan, particularly since we had before us the example of the three young Naval Reserve ensigns who had walked off into the jungle on our first night at the camp. The success of this effort, however, had made it more difficult for the rest of us. For, as a result, the Japs had formed us into the "shooting squads" of ten men each, with the threat to kill the other nine if any one man got away. It later developed, incidentally, that the three Naval Reserve officers were not as successful as we had thought. . . .

About once a week our chaplains arranged amateur theatricals or skits. The Japanese guards were usually the most appreciative spectators at these events, but all of us looked forward to them, despite what must be sadly admitted as a very low entertainment value. On an afternoon in late August, rumor quickly ran through the prison that the entertainment for that night had been canceled.

"Why?" I asked.

"Our three escapees are back," I was informed. "The Japanese are making them put on a show."

We did not know what turn this "show" would take, and we looked forward to it with foreboding. In this instance, however, our fears were worse than the facts. The three Naval Reserve ensigns, as I have said, simply walked out of the prison on our first night in the camp, and before the stockades had been put up. As we learned later, the three had hidden out in the jungle for three months. Food was plentiful, easily obtainable, and they could have stayed there indefinitely. However, they wanted to get out of the Philippines, so they made their way to the more thickly populated coast of the island of Luzon. The Japanese were in force on the coast, and the penalty for a Filipino harboring Americans was death. In fact, even a suspicion was enough to cause a Filipino to be executed. The three ensigns decided that without help escape would be hopeless, so they voluntarily turned themselves in.

That evening after our meal, and while it was still light, these three young officers were required to mount a platform in the center of the camp and read prepared statements about the hardships they had undergone while they were away from the camp. They told of weeks without food, of jungle water infested with snakes and ferocious wild beasts.

Actually, none of the Americans in the camp was fooled. The ensigns had been beaten up when they first gave themselves up, but beyond their bruises they looked better than any prisoner in the camp.

Melvyn H. McCoy, S. M. Mellnik, and Wellbourn Kelley,
Ten Escape from Tojo (New York: Farrar & Reinhart, 1944), 49, 61–63.

Editor's note: Six months later, Commander McCoy, Lieutenant Colonel Mellnik, and eight other Americans escaped from the Japanese prison farm at Davao and successfully made their way to Australia.

The same afternoon three young naval officers were brought in. They had escaped during the earliest days of Cabanatuan, before there was any organization, even before the barbed wire fence was put up. After a few months of roughing it they were recaptured. At the subsequent inquisition the Japanese asked one of the prodigals where he thought he was going when he ran away. He said he had intended to go to see his mother. The Japanese conferred among themselves on this phase of his crime. Then they asked him if he had a picture of his mother. He produced the picture. They examined it carefully. Apparently it met with their approval, for they did not shoot the three, as we felt certain they would, and the "defendants" still credit the mother's picture with saving their lives—probably correctly so, bless her heart.

Capt. Alan McCracken, U.S. Navy, *Very Soon Now, Joe*
(New York: Hobson Book Press, 1947), 30.

A short time after our arrival in Cabanatuan Prison Camp No. 1, three Navy officers, junior grade (Berry, Turk [*sic*] and Sanborn), escaped and were not apprehended until three or four months later when they voluntarily surrendered somewhere in the vicinity of Lucena or Mauban. They had been told that provisions had been effected for the repatriation of prisoners to the United States. At the time they turned themselves in, they were making their way south in an endeavor to contact a submarine or some means whereby they could be taken to Australia and back to our forces. They were returned to Cabanatuan, placed in solitary, and when I reached Bilibid in October, 1942, they were confined in the Military Police Prison in that compound.

Maj. Willard H. Waterous, MD, in Paul Ashton,
And Somebody Gives a Damn (Santa Barbara, Calif.: Privately printed,
1990), 268.

One morning, three American special prisoners were half-carried into the cell where I was confined. They were accompanied by a jap guard, a jap non-commissioned officer, an American naval doctor, and Warrant Officer Haase. The three men appeared more dead than alive. The were carefully examined by the doctor. The jap guard remained outside. Finally, the four of us were left alone in the cell and I learned the identity of the three men. Their last names were Turk [*sic*], Sanborn, and Berry. All three were naval ensigns and had been confined across the wall in the jap military police side of Bilibid Prison.

. . . They had escaped from Cabanatuan in early June, 1942, soon after their arrival there from Corregidor. After hiding out in the mountains for several months, they were captured by a group of Filipinos and turned over to the japs. The japs court martialed them. Afterwards, they were turned over to the Japanese military police, who transferred them to Bilibid, where they were placed in solitary confinement. They had been there since October, 1942.

For a few days, they were too weak to sit up. Finally, however, they were able to sit with their backs to a wall and talk to me. Turk was not very communicative. The other two, however, talked readily and I soon learned their backgrounds. Sanborn had graduated from Harvard University, and Berry from Yale University. As they regained their strength, they told me about their "life across the wall" as special prisoners. Altogether, there were 10 of them confined to a single cell that measured nine by nine feet. They had to sit in two rows, each facing a wall, and were not permitted to talk, stretch their legs, stand, or lie down. There was a single, bare, electric light bulb that burned constantly. A small latrine was in one corner, sunk into the floor. They had to ask permission to use it. Their food was the same as ours, but a lesser amount. Any infraction of the rules was punishable by having to kneel on a hard bamboo stick for hours or until they collapsed from the pain in their knees. This particular form of punishment (torture) was commonly meted out by the japs. Their wanton acts of cruelty and brutality was exceeded only by their callous indifference to pain inflicted on others. On alternate days, the special prisoners were permitted to shower and exercise briefly. On even the slightest pretense, they were beaten savagely by their jap guards. Only when near death from such inhumane treatment, were the special prisoners brought to our side of the prison compound to be "rehabilitated." When their health had been restored somewhat, they were returned to their cell in the Military Police Compound for further continued punishment. Thus, the American naval doctors delayed their ordeal by prolonging treatment. Turk had several such experiences, being more defiant of the jap guards.

I related to Berry more than the other two men. His name was William (Bill), and his uncle was Lieutenant Governor of Oklahoma for several terms of office. Bill grew up on a large farm just outside of Stillwater, Oklahoma, where Oklahoma State University (then called Oklahoma A&M) is located. As both of us were from rural areas in Oklahoma, Bill and I could reminisce about similar experiences. Bill and Sanborn often talked about their escapades in college. Sanborn apparently was more of a playboy in college, having belonged to a popular fraternity. Bill assured me that college life was more than fraternity parties, and encouraged me to get a college education when and if we survived captivity. I was intrigued by their stories of college life, and determined that one day I would be equally as well educated as they were.

Earl R. Oatman, *Bataan: Only the Beginning*
(Riverside, Calif.: Privately printed, 1991), 151–53.

Editor's note: Following the war, Mr. Oatman did indeed go to college under the GI Bill, ultimately earning a Ph.D. from the University of California. Currently he is a professor emeritus at the University of California, Riverside.

During the last of May 1942, the prisoners from Corregidor were herded into the new Camp #1 at Cabanatuan. . . . Among them were Ensigns Turk [*sic*], Sanborn, and Berry, who had a conference that evening. "Those boys from O'Donnel look as though they'd been through hell," Sanborn remarked, and soon there was agreement among the three friends, who became well known to me later in the Communicable Diseases section of Bilibid. They must escape or die. The next day they studied the setting of the camp. No stockade had been built as yet and it appeared easy enough to slip between the guards in the dark. The break was made the following night, June 3rd. Four weeks later, by easy stages, they had crossed the Sierra separating Cabanatuan from the east coast and came down from the hills near Dingalon after some adventures with friendly Filipinos.

The normally gregarious and imaginative farming and fishing people with whom they had been living gradually circulated the news of their presence, and fabricated tales that they were organizing a guerrilla band, and had a cache of arms! These were threatening tales, because if such gossip reached Japanese ears (and local bounty hunters would see that it did), the result would inevitably lead to reprisals upon those good people who had sheltered and fed them for months. This, in fact happened, and they were discovered and captured by a group of Filipinos early in September, near Padre Burgos, turned over to the Japanese garrisoned in the town of Calauag, and taken back to Cabanatuan. There they found that during their absence of several months about 2,000 men had already died from disease and starvation, although the situation was really becoming better!

The camp was now administered by U.S. Military personnel, though the Japanese imposed drastic penalties on any prisoner who escaped or even tried such a move. All POW's in the camps and working parties were divided into groups of ten. If any one tried to escape, or was successful, the other nine would be executed. While Turk's group was being tried in court martial, three other American officers made an unsuccessful attempt. They were beaten for hours, trussed up near the main camp gate for two days in full view of the entire camp, during which period unspeakable tortures were applied, such as "the water cure," as well as multiple fractures of their limbs. They were slowly kicked to death, and then shot.

Turk, Berry and Sanborn were tried and turned over to the Japanese military police, who transferred them on the 30th October, 1942, to the M.P. prison in Manila, which was a part of Bilibid. It comprised the part of the compound on the other side of the high wall that bisected the length of the prison. There they remained until the day of liberation, February 4th, 1945, except for the several periods that they became ill and were sent over to be treated by us in the Communicable Disease area of the main prison. . . .

Whenever the special prisoners became exhausted by the rigors of living in the Military Police side, they would be brought into us, usually more dead than alive. Their food was worse than ours, if that could be possible. The Military Police Prison as described by them, contained ten people who had also escaped and had likewise been recaptured. They were kept in a cell nine by nine feet and obliged to sit in two rows facing the wall. Forbidden to stand or lie down, they also could not stretch out their legs or use their arms to lean back and thus rest, and they were also not permitted conversation.

If any of them were caught talking, or committing any other small infraction of rules, the punishment would be to kneel on a hard bamboo stick for a day or more, a very painful and disabling inactivity! The unit consisted of three naval ensigns, Turk, Sanborn, and Berry; a marine called Thompson; Klett, a civil service employee; Barnbrook, an army non-com; and four army privates, Ballard, Cameron, Toups, "the Cajon," and Beyuka, a full-blooded Indian from New Mexico.

For small deviations, they were beaten, somewhat badly. When one of these men came to us, he was too weak to walk, his legs and belly swollen, and he was often badly bruised. His diarrhea and/or malaria were almost incidental. We spent much time trying to bring them back to some semblance of health, and then endeavoring to hide their improvement from the guards, who would insist on their return to the special prison as soon as possible.

> Paul Ashton, *Bataan Diary* (Santa Barbara, Calif.:
> Privately printed, 1984), 269, 243-44.

In spring the spring of 1945 I was a small cog in the Sixth Army's big machine mopping up the Jap on Luzon. General Krueger sent the Sixth Rangers deep into Jap held territory to rescue the Americans in the Cabanatuan prison camp. It was a complete surprise. The Rangers lost only one man.

We received the wretched skeletons of our own compatriots at Guimba. Some could walk. Some could stagger. Many were in a dopey daze. It was too much to believe that they had been saved. They came from Corregidor. They came from old Bilabid. They came from the brave little band that backed out of Manila down the peninsula before the invader. They stumbled back in the death march up Bataan.

I looked down to eyes as big as saucers in a tear-streaked, starved, thin death mask which called me by name. It was Bill Berry of Stillwater. Or the little left of him. He was just a bag of skin and bones. To this day I am not ashamed to say that I turned away and cried.

It's one thing to turn over a corpse in khaki and identify him through his dog tags. But it is something entirely different when there was a buddy in those boots. PW's are entitled to everything we can do for them when they are impersonal Americans. When you find one of your own among the rescued relics it does something to you. I resolved to do something for this Berry for so long as I should live.

The war department in Washington T W X'ed to us to hustle a C-54 load of these Americans back to the states as soon as they were able to travel. First prisoners of the Japs to be rescued. Good propaganda. I asked Bill Berry if he wanted to go. He thought it over and when I went back for the answer, he said he had come over with the navy and that is the way he would like to go back. And so he did.

Berry escaped from Jap concentration camps twice. Twice he was condemned to death. I saw the stone wall at Bilabid packed with lead litter breast high, where our men stood to be shot. In one death watch he was asked to write what he thought of his country. He wrote his tribulations in prison had made him realize what a great nation his country is. Our intelligence dug that letter out of the Jap files after the war and returned it to Berry. Why the Japs spared him no one will ever know.

Walter M. Harrison, *North Star* (Oklahoma City, Ok. Thursday, June 19, 1958).

INDEX

Note: Because references to William A. Berry, Phil Sanborn, and Dick Tirk occur throughout the book, they are not listed in the index.